BLACK LIFE IN CORPORATE AMERICA

L. A. Goffe

GEORGE DAVIS AND GLEGG WATSON

BLACK LIFE IN CORPORATE AMERICA

Swimming in the Mainstream

ANCHOR BOOKS
ANCHOR PRESS/DOUBLEDAY
GARDEN CITY, NEW YORK
1985

Black Life in Corporate America was originally published
in hardcover by Anchor Press/Doubleday in 1982.

Anchor Books Edition/1985

Reprinted, by permission of the publisher,
from *Career Strategies: Planning for Personal Achievement,*
by Andrew H. Souerwine, ©
1978 by AMACOM, a division of American Management Associations,
pp. 219–220.
All rights reserved.
From *Work in America* by Clark Kerr and Jerome Rosow.
Copyright © 1979 by Van Nostrand Reinhold Company
Reprinted by permission of Van Nostrand Reinhold Company.

Library of Congress Cataloging in Publication Data

Davis, George, 1939-
Black Life in Corporate America.

1. Afro-American executives. 2. Afro-Americans in business.
I. Watson, Glegg. II. Title.
HF5500.3.U54D38   658.4′09′08996073
AACR2
ISBN 0-385-14702-3

Library of Congress Catalog Number 81-22760
Copyright © 1982 by GEORGE DAVIS AND GLEGG WATSON
ALL RIGHTS RESERVED
PRINTED IN THE UNITED STATES OF AMERICA

IN MEMORIAL AND IN TRIBUTE TO OUR PARENTS.

ACKNOWLEDGMENTS

First and foremost we would like to express appreciation to the hundreds of people we interviewed, inside and out of major corporations, in order to make their experiences part of this mosaic of *Black Life in Corporate America.*

We would also like to express our appreciation to our editors: Marie Brown, who guided the book from its inception and continued with it even after she was no longer with Doubleday; and Loretta Barrett, who took over as editor and displayed the skill and patience needed to bring the project to its final form.

Thanks to many observers of the American scene whose formal and informal discussions with us sharpened the focus and enlarged the scope of the mosaic. In this regard thanks especially to Audreen Ballard, who helped us see much that we could not see.

And finally we acknowledge with gratitude the sacrifices made by family and friends during three years of researching and writing.

CONTENTS

BLACK LIFE IN CORPORATE AMERICA

I

INTO THE MAINSTREAM

ONE OF THE MOST UNDERREPORTED STORIES of the past three decades concerns the entry of black men and women into the managerial ranks of major American corporations. This book is our attempt to look at aspects of the mostly hidden effects on the personal lives of these men and women who in ever increasing numbers are trying to "make it" in the mainstream. It is also our attempt to give a view of the mainstream itself from the point of view of black managers as they attempt to swim ahead or simply to survive in these multibillion-dollar organizations—these uniquely modern ways of organizing a good percentage of the world's natural resources and technology, and a good percentage of the world's trained personnel into entities called Exxons and AT&Ts, IBMs, Sears, Fords and U.S. Steels.

This is our report on the human side of the story of men and women operating in foreign social space with unfamiliar protocol, with habits, manners, values and styles of thinking that until recently were very new to them.

By using interviews taken from more than 160 managers and experts, along with both scholarly and popular writing in the field, we have constructed a mirror into which black and white managers can look to see reflections on their work lives, not the entire lives but those portions where they interact across racial lines. We want to highlight some of the human issues that come into focus because of this interaction.

It has been said that the Negro (as we were once called) is America's metaphor. It certainly is true that what black people have experienced in American corporations is symbolic of what so many others experience.

Once we thought of making the epigraph for the book a para-phrase of a Rastafarian saying: "How can African man live in IBM without losing himself?" This saying, however, needlessly narrows the focus of the book because one of the biggest questions for all people and for corporations is, "How can any man or woman live productively and creatively in the modern corporation?" This later, larger concern is very implicit in the material of the book.

In certain sections we have been intentionally lighthearted and, we hope, amusing. For example the book is subtitled "Swimming in the Mainstream," which gives us the opportunity to describe some man-agers as "Waders," "Floaters," "Scuba Divers," "Splashers," "Back-strokers" and finally, "Swimmers."

The book is intentionally nonstatistical. No one can give an accu-rate statistical idea of how many blacks occupy significant manage-rial jobs in the mainstream of corporate America. No one knows.

The Equal Employment Opportunities Commission (EEOC) re-ported that in 1979, 7.2 percent of the managerial work force was minority. This means that perhaps 4 or 5 percent is black. We do know that the corporate black man or woman is fast becoming a significant actor in the drama of the nation. This presence in corpo-rations is bound to influence the flux that has forever characterized the modern corporation; and the presence is certainly affecting tradi-tional black American life, where formerly even "successful" blacks looked on work in terms of education, uplift and service rather than simple profit, where activities were viewed in terms of their human consequence rather than in terms of their abstract effectiveness and cold efficiency.

By viewing the process of the black manager's adaptation to the corporation, we can see some of the human problems that produce alienation in all workers, alienation that threatens American produc-tivity.

All along we were concerned that within corporations there was not a great deal of talk about race. It is mentioned only when it be-comes obvious that a racial problem must be dealt with. Subtle racial problems are ignored. Deep-seated ones are often treated as if they don't really exist.

On the surface blacks and whites get along quite well in most cor-porate settings. They don't seem to mind working with each other.

They laugh together and call each other "friend." However, blacks are often oppressed by this silence on race. Their careers and morale are affected by this thing that they cannot mention.

Even the "coon counter" (the Equal Employment Opportunity manager) is encouraged to stop complaining about racism and just count coons in a way that will make the company look as good as possible in the eyes of the federal compliance agencies. Many major companies have discouraged attempts by blacks to form caucuses to unify against obvious or systematic racial discrimination. We know of two companies that fired black employees for publishing black employees' newsletters.

A young attorney who is now in private practice after his corporate career started downward because he was elected spokesperson for a black caucus said: "We were trying to organize so we could present our grievances to senior management in a unified manner. We knew that when a person went in one at a time, management ended up treating the person as a malcontent or troublemaker rather than dealing with the issues being raised, so we went in as a group. I did the speaking and after that the word was out on me—I was a militant, I hated white people, you should have heard the rumors that were spread on me."

A prevailing attitude among whites is perhaps "They [blacks] ought to be happy to be here in the first place." The white manager then goes swimming along, looking after his own career, not wanting to talk about racial problems until a problem may affect him personally. This accounts for the wide disparity between white and black perceptions of how much racial discrimination still exists in this country. Polls indicate that whites feel most of it has disappeared. Many blacks, however, feel that though things have gotten better in some ways, many of the effects of discrimination have gotten worse.

This difference in the perception of discrimination as much as discrimination itself drives some black managers "crazy."

This book, then, is our effort to communicate some impressions of the issues which might not surface during polite chit-chat between the white men who run America and the black men and women who have recently come to work for them.

The larger point is that there are few instances in corporations where anyone is allowed to complain about the life in any significant way. Usually when managers have points of view that would improve the productivity of the unit, they have no way of making these points of view felt.

When a company has productivity problems it usually would rather call in expensive experts than let the employees generate change. Any employee who complains is, as we have said, branded as a malcontent or troublemaker. Top management's attitude seems to be: "You're getting well paid. Your job is to shove papers and not try to tell us how to run the company. Shut up and do your job."

The book is then about internal resistance and defensiveness, and nothing illustrates this more clearly than the way black managers are treated. The book is also a guided tour through the seldom verbalized feelings of the more than 160 black and white managers, corporate professionals, consultants and public officials we interviewed.

Late in the interviewing a friendly white senior vice-president said he was eager for us to finish the book so he could read it. "I'm looking forward," he said and chuckled. "I want to hear what you guys have to say. You know when we let you guys in we only told you half the story."

Well, some of us guys have seen much of the other half, and we've seen some things that our white friend has never seen—could not see, because he was too close, because of something we will describe later as cultural blindness since "seeing" is very much a function of the cultural conditioning of the eye and the mind.

Early in our interviewing we discovered that we were talking not simply about the racial integration of American corporate management, but about the adaptation of black culture to white culture and white culture to black. This adaptation could not be seen in the integration of schools because there we were not dealing with fully acculturated adults. It could not be seen in the racial integration of the armed forces, because the military has a culture of its own. It could not be well seen during the gradual partial integration of the blue collar work force, because in that there was little merging of cultures, little forced sustained social interaction, little mixing, melding or sharing of the subtle nuances of daily life.

The first place that it could be seen was in the integration of the managerial middle class of American society, where such mixing of nuances does occur. It can be more clearly seen in managerial integration because this is the aspiration level of America. Managerial life is the new American dream.

And so the book is not simply about the successes and failures of, say, affirmative action. Instead it argues for the necessary mutually respectful, multicultural formulation of the national life, and it describes America in microcosm since the 1954 school desegregation decision and the 1964 Civil Rights Act, those two great landmarks which sought to make one society out of the two that had grown up on the American continent. It is about the attempt to integrate the American dream during a period when women also want to change the power relationship between themselves and men.

Words from all of the people we talked to do not appear here, but we hope the spirit of the book reflects in fair proportion what we found during our three years of digging below the smooth surface of corporate life.

Most of the managers we interviewed preferred to speak anonymously. This is not surprising when you consider what happened to James Edwards, a Harvard M.B.A. who joined a large consumer products company and worked his way up to middle management. In an article in a national business magazine he spoke out on the loneliness and frustration of being a black manager in a mostly white corporation.

The negative reactions from superiors drove him to insomnia. His career was undermined. "They say that I am ungrateful for what the company has done for me," he wrote. They seemed not to understand that he was trying to break through the deafening silence concerning the sometimes phenomenal estrangement of corporate blacks from past and tradition of race and culture, to break through a kind of muting isolation from others whose voices might help the black manager understand and find a more comfortable place in the consuming life of the corporation.

"Whites are so consumed by the guilt over what has been done to blacks in this country that they think that every time a group of blacks gets together to talk about problems, the blacks are really plotting revenge," said one black manager we interviewed. "It makes them nervous for the three of us to be in here (his office) with the door closed." He implied, "Pretty soon one of them is going to look in to see what we're talking about."

Another black manager we interviewed wanted a written guarantee that his name would not be used. He said he made it a policy to "never put anything into the system that might be used against me." Another manager said, "They're just looking for something to hold against you, so you have to be very careful what you go public with. I don't even go to the same bathroom with my peers. I don't want them to smell my do-do and judge me on it. They've never seen me drink, smoke or shit. I don't want them judging me."

A female manager said, "I try to avoid saying anything personal. Whenever I'm around them I can tell they are keeping mental notes." The notes are not always mental, according to a funny scene in the contemporary film *9 to 5*. A female manager in that film hides in a stall in the women's bathroom. She draws her legs up so no one can see her feet and she takes written notes on what her coworkers say. She takes these notes to her boss.

"An innocent remark," said our female manager, "that is intentionally or unintentionally misunderstood could cause someone to say, 'You're not a good fit,' 'You're not a good corporate citizen,' 'You're not a team player.'" Even white managers dread that some such nebulous comment will retard their progress.

Such paranoia seems even more justified for black people, whose positions and promotions are tenuous at best anyway. The entire first chapter of Joseph Heller's comic novel *Something Happened* is about an office in which people

> do their best to minimize friction (we are encouraged to revolve around each other like self-lubricating ball bearings, careful not to jar or scrape) and to avoid quarreling with each other openly. It is considered much better form to wage our battles sneakily behind each other's back than to confront each other directly with any semblance of complaint. (The secret attack can be denied, lied about, or reduced in significance, but the open dispute is witnessed and has to be dealt with by someone who finds the whole situation deplorable.

If this is the picture for white managers, how much more deadly must it be for the black managers who roll around like self-lubricating ball bearings but are constantly ending up on the bottom and are nonetheless not expected to complain.

Heller goes on: "People in the company are almost never fired; if

they grow inadequate or obsolete ahead of schedule, they are encouraged to retire early or are eased aside into hollow, insignificant,
newly created positions with fake functions and no authority." As we
will note, these are the kinds of positions that many blacks are given
as a matter of course.

The kind of frankness we needed would not have been possible
had we not guaranteed that interviewees did not have to fear that
their real names would be used. For consistency, we decided not to
use the names of those managers and officials and experts who said
they didn't mind speaking without the cloak of anonymity. We were
more concerned about candor than the use of names and faces, and
so we put different faces with different statements and different corporate titles and workplace locations.

We were aware of the difficulties of speaking of so large a variety
of individuals' experiences in a collective way. This is why the style
of the book is impressionistic.

We went looking for a "truth"; it is not the only truth about black
life in corporate America, but we do not claim that it is. This is why
we take so much time to speak about our intent and our methodology, and why we will say so much about perspectives with regard to
methodology. Many black managers had not reflected deeply on their
corporate lives, or they had done so so long ago that the vivid images
of what their situation really was had faded in their consciousness.
We attempted to reawaken this by supplying them with material to
which to respond. We gave them material that they could use as mir-
rors in order to really see themselves and their situations. When our
information did not apply they were frank in saying so. When it did
highlight a half-hidden or suppressed aspect of their lives, they were
eager to enlarge on the information and give examples from their
personal experience. Which is what we wanted—the experience.

For about three years we conducted interviews. Like separate photographs for a collage, the book came together in the only way that
this kind of book can, not as a definitive statement but as a group of
impressions of what happened, what needs to happen and what is
happening to blacks in corporate America, and why.

"What happened," said a black manager sitting behind a kidney-
shaped desk in the middle of his large carpeted office, "is that a lot
of black people rushed in to where they had never been before. Of
course that blew a lot of people's minds. Let me close the door," he

said, even though the hallway outside was deserted because everyone, or nearly everyone, had gone home from corporate headquarters.

He was clean-shaven, trim, well dressed. "We could use your metaphor," he said. "Let's say they jumped in, or rather waded into the mainstream." The door closed like the door to an airtight compartment. He came back around his desk, smiled and looked out the window across the grassy slopes of the hill where corporate headquarters sat.

No ducks were on the pond, instead, they were probably where they had been earlier in the day, quacking along the road that circled up in front of the sprawling, modernistic office building.

He had mints in a bowl to offer the interviewer. His smile was constant and warm as he pushed the bowl of mints across a smooth, dark desk top.

Two weeks before, he had received the questions: "What is it like to be black in a place like this?" "How have you been received?" "What was the hardest thing for you to get used to?" "How do you feel about your chances of making it to the top?" "Do you still feel like a token?" "Of all your options, why did you choose the life of a corporate manager?" "Is life harder here for a black man or a black woman?" "Have you ever felt you wanted to quit? Why?" "Do you really feel you're in the midstream, or off in some special tributary set up by the company just to comply with EEO [Equal Employment Opportunity] directives?" "In what ways do you feel the white woman qualifies as a minority and in what ways does she not?"

"I'd rather you didn't use my name," he said. "Okay. Some people you talk to might feel different but I feel a little freer when I know I don't have to worry about any of this blowing back in my face.

"This is where the action is—in corporate America. This is where the money is, okay. This *is* America if . . ." he continued, voicing a sentiment often expressed during the three years of interviewing: "America is the corporate state. If any people hope to make it in America many of them will have to make it in the corporate world."

Only thirty years ago C. Wright Mills looked upon the world of the corporate manager as a powerful but not nearly dominant force in America. In *White Collar,* he granted that corporate types were "performing the major routine of twentieth-century society," but they were, as a class, split, fragmented, unsure of themselves, vague in their ideology and aspirations, without an internalized sense of purpose.

"The white collar man," he wrote, "is the hero as victim. The small creature who is acted upon but who does not act, who works along unnoticed in somebody's office or store, never talking loud, never talking back, never taking a stand." This book was praised for its accuracy at describing the life of the corporate man, at office and at home.

We blacks were not allowed into this world so we assumed that this is the way life was, back before corporate life became the mainstream of American life. Most blacks did not know we were facing so new, fragile and tentative a creature when the orders came down from the federal government in the late nineteen fifties and sixties that we had the right to be corporate managers too, especially if the corporation in question hoped to maintain its government contracts.

Even as unattractive as Mills's picture was, we, as blacks, would have wanted in. First, it was in so many ways better than the world we inhabited out in the swamps of the American economy—big fish in little ponds and little fish splashing about in the mud. Secondly, everyone, including C. Wright Mills, knew that corporate life was bound to get better. No one knew how much better. We didn't know how successful corporations would be at creating a whole new glamorous image of life for the corporate manager.

We didn't know that "bennies" (benefit packages) were going to become so sweet, that the "perks" (perquisites) would make the cup so damn full. We didn't know that the corporations would move their headquarters out of dingy downtown skyscrapers into plush, modernistic buildings out on the grassy slopes of corporate parks in the richest suburbs, or that managers themselves would become more self-confident and proud of what they do, and more aggressive in their imposition of management techniques and values to all areas of public and private life.

Make no mistake about it, anyone who works for any length of time in a major corporation will be changed. For even as new as they are, corporations have found ways that they want their people to be. If we are permitted to use a negative term for the process, management development is a sort of brain washing process. And the work itself demands that the manager develop in certain very particular ways. The work demands a different kind of attention from other work, a different kind of commitment. In deeper, more significant ways, the job has to become part of you. It necessitates adapting more of one's personal behavioral style to fit the demands of a system. It is abstract work that must fit into a larger picture in order for much of it to seem purposeful at all.

Industriousness and intelligence are *not* the primary qualities needed to do a good job. The primary qualities flow from a way of looking at work, at people—a way of looking at the human condition, human nature and human purpose. A method of viewing relationships and the emotional values that play in developing one's behavior, perceptions of self and perceptions of the way that others relate to self.

In order to fit in, one has to assume a new identity, negotiate a truce between the old and the required self. The corporation has its own pragmatic sense of how a person must be to get along, its own set of images that its citizens respond to, either positively or negatively, and its own vocabulary and way of speaking.

It has its own methods for resolving conflicts, its own motivational techniques, system of reward and punishments, and its own ways of looking at time and judging its use. Its fine points define permissible ways to be assertive without being too aggressive and of being aggressive without being hostile. It knows how to create conflict and manage that conflict in ways that are beneficial to itself. Over time it has learned this and reduced it to a way of life.

In order to do the work one has to know how to dress "properly," how to negotiate, how to role-play. One has to know how to control anxiety and stress, how to plan and forecast and how to minimize the personal effects of bad plans and forecasts, on the one hand, while calling attention to one's good work, on the other.

The jobs involve managing people and so people have to be looked upon as objects and as means of achieving bottom-line results—profitability. Thus, the manager has to know how to protect, promote and make use of the best people and, without too much remorse or fuss, "shaft" the ones who are not working out.

All managers have some problems in this area. But black managers have more difficulty with it because black life is further than white life from what might be called the corporate norm. Once black managers have undergone a process of "managerial development," there is greater estrangement between them and their families and communities, and yet often there is no correspondingly greater comfort level between them and the white managers they work with and for.

We, the authors of this book, were in college during the late nineteen fifties and early sixties, reading sociology and listening to professors who looked down their noses at the "organization men," the poor manipulated members of the "lonely crowd" in their uniformly baggy gray flannel suits.

Not precisely at the same time, but during the same era, one of us was at Colgate and the other at Howard—a good white school and a good black one—hearing about the mainstream from different points on the shore. As black men both of us remembered thinking then, as we listened to our professors, "What is the black man's place in all of this? How will this affect the people and the world that we grew up in?"

As undergraduates we watched the first small splashes. A few black men and women were permitted to wade quietly into the shallow water at the edge of the chilly mainstream of American corporate life.

In 1961 we both saw a hallelujah article in *Ebony* magazine announcing with pride: "Campbell Soups Corporation has hired a Negro; Burke Pierce, a Cornell graduate and incidentally son-in-law of Ralph Bunche, has been hired by General Foods Corporation. RCA has hired one in personnel, and so has the Metropolitan Life Insurance Co., as an assistant to the personnel director."

Hot zig-a-de-dog! This was like hearing that Jackie Robinson had hit another home run. This for a college student was like the barbershop crowd hearing that Sugar Ray Robinson had defeated Carmen Basilio.

Ebony continued: "Levi Jackson, former Yale football captain, is with Ford Motor Co. and Macy's in New York has Fred Wilkerson. This accumulation," *Ebony* concluded, "is a mere spit in the ocean compared to the employment potential."

Sometimes we sat in our dormitory rooms alternating between *Ebony* and *America As a Civilization,* in which Max Lerner said people in the mainstream

speak a language full of routine terms which constrict the range of their language within dishearteningly narrow limits. They dance to corny music and have corny parties. They spend the days of their years with monotonous regularity in factory, office and shop, performing routinized operations at regular intervals.

Every society has its routines and rituals, the primitive groups being sometimes more tyrannously restricted by convention than the industrial societies. The difference is that where the primitive is bound by rituals of tradition and group life, the American is bound by rituals of the machine, its products, and their distribution and consumption.

Later we found that Chester I. Barnard, in "The Functions of the Executive," spoke of large organizations in the driest of terms, as if they were things that human potential must be plugged into with little regard for human personality. Even the style of his prose spoke of the death of some vital part of the human spirit.

How then, we thought, would we, blacks, defenders of the stereotypic view that our lives were more spontaneous, emotionally expressive and human—how would we fit into all of this? Our liberal arts educations made us wonder, having led us to believe that the eternal war was between the individual's need for freedom and the system's need for conformity.

We allowed our eyes to drift back to the Speaking of People section that in those days always appeared on page 6 of *Ebony*. There smiled a picture of Floyd E. Pettit, Jr., thirty ". . . the first Negro so employed at General Foods . . . who was hired last June for the $6,000-a-year post," who said optimistically, "There's no limit to how far I can go in the company."

It seemed that every *Ebony* during that time contained a picture of a *first* Negro to hold some position or other. Like Darrell M. Clay, twenty-eight, "whose three-fold duties include setting estimates of production costs, analyzing cost reports to determine trends and setting up control curbs. . . ." From our vantage point this seemed like big stuff, and what about this other Negro at the bottom of the page who controlled a $500,000 budget—half a million dollars? Wow! We wondered how long it would be before people who were weaned as we were controlled a million-dollar budget, or a fifty-million-dollar budget.

We knew more than Max Lerner ever could about the deadening

poverty that faced blacks, in Jamaica in the West Indies, where one of us was born, and in West Virginia and rural Maryland, where the other came of age. We thought about the lives of our fathers and about what manhood was in the western world. "Could corporate life really be all that bad?" We wondered. "It couldn't be all that bad or else the college wouldn't invite so many corporate recruiters onto campus to tempt us."

In English class one of us pondered long over William Blake's statement, "I must Create a System, or be enslav'd by another man's." Applied to us this meant, "I must Join a System or be Enslaved by another man's."

"Mr. Davis, are you listening?" asked the tweed-coated professor, taking his pipe down from his thin lips.

"Yes, sir." I was listening.

After college we approached corporate life with a certain ambivalence, accepting it, on the one hand, as a necessary way of organizing work, and on the other, with some deep reservations about the way life might be inside the corporation.

This put one of us all the way into a corporation but holding out, and the other all the way out but hanging in—a good combination of vantage points to watch the stream and to make some observations on it, to see more and more black people becoming corporate "floaters," "waders," "splashers," "swimmers"; to see them "treading water," "going under," "coming up for air," "moving into midstream," "getting trapped in backwaters" or "drowning."

But before we get into a fuller discussion of black life in the mainstream, we will supply in the next three chapters a stream of impressions of the three-decade struggle of blacks and whites to racially integrate America's industrial life.

PART ONE

II

TOKENS: THE FIRST DECADE

"IT WAS VERY DIFFERENT when I came in," said the man who had been pointed out as a grand old black man of the corporate mainstream. "Back then [1947] you could go for days in one of these places without seeing anyone black, except the messengers and the janitors. The elevator starters were black and they would grin and say, 'Yes, sir, good morning, sir,' when you came in.

"I couldn't exactly say I was a manager because I didn't manage anything or anybody. I was a special assistant to the chairman. I did various things for the company," the grand old man said and laughed. He was a very pleasant, honey-colored man, with a forehead and chin that sloped gently away from the smile and the eyeglasses that dominated his face. We were charmed by him. We looked at him and wondered what did it feel like for the first group of blacks who waded into the chilly waters of managerial life. What kind of reception did he receive? What changes in life-style and values did he have to make in order to survive? What social forces, acts of conscience, executive orders, legislations and riots paved the way for him? What kind of job was he given? How did he fit into the formal and informal structure of the company? What was the nature of his relationship with peers, subordinates and superiors?

"You have no idea how different it was back then," he said. "You yourself representing the company on so many occasions that were outside your area of expertise—I'm an accountant by training. Whenever they needed a black face for a particular gathering, they would come in and get me. I'm sure this made it impossible for my supervisor to take me seriously as a member of his department," he said and laughed. "But being a token can work to your advantage too. If they need a black face at a certain level in the company, they'd put you on a fast track and promote you to that level. The disadvantage was they would never promote you above that level, or out of that particular area, never pull you back here." He held his clenched fist close to his chest, as a cog in the machine.

"But this promotion still caused resentment among the white guys in the department because I was being moved to a higher salary level faster than they. Some of this so-called backlash comes from this source. The guys in today's middle and top management remember how tokens were treated when they were working their way up. They are the guys who are yelling about reverse discrimination. You see the double bind you're in? There's no such thing as reverse discrimination if you're talking about a fast track to the executive suite in a significant job in the company. But I've been the affirmative action manager, the equal opportunity director and the vice-president of special markets—not the comptroller." He laughed. "That's the difference. This last job I had was a good one though, because when I came into the door we didn't do anything special to cultivate the black consumer. The entire special markets function I started back in nineteen sixty-eight–sixty-nine, and now it represents fifteen percent of total sales. I made power out of no power. Three hundred forty-seven million dollars," he said and laughed.

Once the term special markets was a euphemism for the black consumer, but in many companies there was so much success with marketing efforts targeted for blacks that companies began breaking the general market down into other special interest markets, and some of the approaches developed for black consumers by black special markets people have been adapted and have become the most creative elements in general marketing and advertising.

Weeks later in Chicago, down in the Loop at a fine, busy restaurant, the special markets vice-president told us: "Back then it wasn't that you had to be better than the white guy who worked next to you. You *were* better. They didn't pick that many Negroes for corporate positions and so they could choose the cream of the crop. In the East at least, which is what I know about. They would scout around the Ivy League schools or they would be up there recruiting white guys and if you were graduating, they might offer you a job."

This was the case with the men *Ebony* wrote about as the first corporate blacks, like Levi Jackson from Yale, Burke Pierce from Cornell and Fred Wilkerson from Harvard. These were men of the grand old man's generation. Back then it wasn't something that the federal government was forcing any company to do. There was some governmental pressure, but most of this came from states like Illinois and New York.

"Your pride in yourself made you work harder," the special markets veep said. "You worked harder because you were more visible. You knew you were being watched and so you tended to perform better.

"Perhaps some of it was racial pride. Sure, I guess so. You wanted to show these white guys that you were just as good as they were," he said and laughed far back in his throat. "Today there are a lot of black guys and gals coming in, but still in most cases they have to be a little better if they hope to make it." He looked around the room. "The company doesn't expect most of them to make it. That's why they aren't given significant jobs—jobs that are going to lead to the power positions in the company. That's why there are such a cluster of them in personnel departments and public affairs departments in these companies.

"Their careers have been put in holding patterns. They have not been permitted to land in corporate America. The companies want to see what the government is going to do, if the government is going to keep pushing, or if the government is going to back off. So they put them in noncritical jobs in case the government stops pushing, then all they have to do is cut back in those areas and they'll have things right back like they were—white only." He winked one tired playful eye. "I'm semiretired myself. I do a lot of traveling still for the company in the special markets area."

It had occurred to him that in some ways, his career too had been nothing but a holding pattern. He had never landed right in corporate America. He had been diverted several times to alternate airstrips. Special markets had been one of these, and he had made this the company's primary alternate. He was happy because he still traveled at company expense, to talk to other younger black managers. The fact that he was hired to do this proved something about the schizoid nature of this company's intentions. It wanted to help black managers as much as it could. It was a decent progressive company which had been a distant number two in market shares to the perennial industry leader. It was now making a surge toward number one and it was pulling all the stops.

His job was to help younger black managers make the maximum contribution to the marketing thrust, especially in the special markets area. The grand old man had convinced the chairman, whom he called by his first name and played golf with, that if the chairman would turn the black marketing people loose they could help the company establish an unbeatable position in Nigeria and all of Africa.

"I wish I was young enough to get back in the saddle. I would love to take [the perennial leader] on head to head in Africa. I would wipe the socks off of them. I'd get a few of these young black dudes and some hip young whites and some women and I'd set up in Lagos and by the time I was finished—oh, boy. Nigeria would belong to us. There are ninety million people over there . . ." He leaned across the table now speaking conspiratorially, as if the perennial leader might have the restaurant bugged. He laughed. He enjoyed dreaming the dreams that a lot of young black men and women shared. They waited, wishing their companies would get racial prejudice out of the way so they could make these dreams into realities.

"I've had a good career," he said as he ordered lunch in the executive dining room at corporate headquarters. Only employees above grade 25 were permitted to eat in this soft beige room which boasted table service, fine food, white tablecloths and yellow cut flowers in vases that matched the sculptured salt and pepper shakers.

The grand old man's experiences are very similar to the documented accounts in Steven M. Gelber's *Black Men and Businessmen*. Gelber wrote: "Employers sought and frequently found overqualified black applicants for managerial positions." According to him there was an unwritten mandate for companies to hire Negroes who were as "unnegro as the white recruiters."

"Hired for decorative rather than functional purposes, the token black managers could serve their purposes just as well in powerless junior positions as in senior positions where they might have real control over the company," wrote Gelber. The problem, however, was not so much that they were not promoted, but that they were not given jobs in the mainline of the company's business in the first place. They were, in most cases, the first residents of the "Velvet Ghetto."

During the fifties American industry began experiencing a manpower shortage—a shortage of trained people to manage the expanded industrial facilities of the nation. It was not a period characterized by deep moral fervor, but there were undoubtedly many whites who felt that it would be a decent gesture to hire more blacks. A white former corporate personnel director, who now works for the Service Corps of Retired Executives in New York, recalled, "Many of us felt it was the right thing to do. We knew that the resources were out there ready to be tapped."

Another older manager talked about his thirty-two-year career in a different light. "I was not in the business of turning fifty cents into a dollar. I never wanted to be in that business. We were out to save the world," he said and looked toward his wife, but he did not mean only her, although she too had been in corporate life for thirty years.

They were an extremely attractive couple, who gave each other space to speak. She tooted his horn although modestly, and he extolled her virtues. The people he referred to, who were out to save the world, were black and, like himself, lived in the New York area and had joined corporations during the first wave, not to turn fifty cents into a dollar, but to see if they could get some of those dollars flowing in humanistic directions. "We went through college during the thirties. *The New Republic* and publications like it were prescribed reading for us.

"We went to college at a time when business was looked down on. Anyone could turn fifty cents into a dollar," he said, and stared in a way that froze everything in front of him. "But what do you do with that dollar? Do you help or hurt someone? We were social worker types conditioned by our parents to racial service and responsibility and not to get out there and do everything we could to make a dollar."

They were members of the talented tenth, whose obligation was to help the other nine tenths of the race. "My job was to educate whites about black people. To show them, by example, that we weren't as biased as they thought. That's what I was supposed to do. I had no problem with that. That was the job I was there to do. I had meetings with the chairman, who was a very enlightened gentleman. I told him what books to read. I told him about organizations that the company should be making contributions to. I interpreted the black community to top management."

"You see at that time," said his wife, "white people only knew five Negroes—Ralph Bunche, Jackie Robinson, Roy Campanella, Joe Louis and one other." They both tried to remember who the other one was. They each came up with a different answer and laughed.

This man and his wife referred to black people as blacks, but they were of the generation that has used the term Negro. Their terminology had been changed by the revolution of the sixties, but they had been race-conscious long before that. He was, in W.E.B. Du Bois's term, "a Race Man," she, "a Race Woman."

His wife, sitting beside him in the backyard of their large suburban home in a stably integrated community, said, "It's important for younger black managers to know this history. They think they got there because they were good, and they may be good but they also got there because a lot of men like Bill made a lot of sacrifices. There had to be someone inside to open those doors." She too was modest, but there was a stronger urge in her to tell about the battles her husband had fought.

"Tell about the time you laid your job on the line," she said. In a matter-of-fact manner, he told about how he had insisted that the company hire black salesmen and allow them to sell to both blacks and whites, and how he got the company to change its discriminatory credit policies toward black accounts.

"Someone had to be a 'token,' as undesirable as that might have been," the wife said apologetically, but they painted a picture that seemed in some ways less harried and driven than situations in which many younger black corporate managers find themselves today.

"The Ives-Quinn Law of July 1945 set up a New York State commission which forced companies in New York to hire some of us, and so during the early fifties most of the big companies hired one or two. The law said that a company could not discriminate because of race, color or creed. Gender and age discrimination came much later," he said. "You have to remember that only a few years ago white people in the North did not think much about black people. I got the company to start using blacks in some of our company advertisements. Next I convinced them to develop integrated point-of-sales material. Maybe a white family and a black mailman or vice versa, and then I talked them into taking our ads in *Ebony* on a monthly basis," he said, and continuing to detail how his generation had made visible people out of invisible ones.

"Tell them about the black girl that they came to you about," said his wife. It took some conversation before he remembered which incident she was talking about. The incident occurred after the company began hiring more black clerical people. Most of them worked out very well, but there was one woman who was late twenty times in a short period, and her boss was afraid to fire her because of the commission.

The boss came to him and asked what should be done. "I told him the law doesn't say you have to keep incompetents. If your conscience is clear you don't have a thing to worry about."

"Bill was well known in the company," his wife said. "They came to him with various problems and if he couldn't solve the problem he would get on the phone and talk to a person in another company and get the needed information. They had a network. They met every first Tuesday of the month, calling themselves the Little Black Cabinet—you know, like the black cabinet that Roosevelt had."

She said she had been successful as a corporate woman, starting in 1952, because she has a very supportive husband. She had been hired by a company president who wanted to "make a statement" by hiring her and so he put her in a very visible position. They both talked about how supportive black people were to each other then, and they expressed sadness over the terrible isolation that many black managers experience today. "It's very sad," she said. "They've forgotten their roots."

As a senior trainer in the personnel department of her company, she came in contact with a lot of younger black female career women. "They are much tougher and bitchier. I ask them about their children and they seem very adamant that the baby-sitter or grandmother will take care of the children. They are very clear about not letting the children get in their way.

"There seems to be a lot of resentment in them. I guess the resentment comes from finally making it after so long. And these little guys —so bright and yet so insecure. They boycott meaningful relationships because they don't want anything to get in their way. They are so sad."

"Corporate life is very different now," said the husband. "It's very different for both black and white."

The corporation changed and people changed. Not that there are not younger couples like this older couple—both from stable families, both with a sense of place with relation to the other, both with careers, both with firm sexual role definitions.

They both grew out of what they described as very happy childhoods. They were brought up, they feel, in the manner that children should be brought up, with parental concern, affection, reasonable strictness, responsible freedom.

She had gone off to a private college in New England where she had studied liberal arts. During college, as before and afterward, she remained close to the church. She was an Episcopalian, not a Baptist and certainly not a member of a holiness faith.

Neither she nor her husband were "race ridden" people, but they belonged to both the Urban League and the NAACP and they expressed tremendous concern for the plight of poor black people. Success seems not to have dulled that concern. In fact they seemed proud of themselves for it.

We talked to several other older blacks whose lives in corporate America were not too different from the life of this couple. But we also talked to some whose lives dramatized some of the variety of that early experience.

For example, we talked to a vice-president for special projects who viewed his twenty-five-year career in a different light. "My experience is different," he said. "Sure you're going to have to adjust to any new situation, but I don't think I had any more difficulty adjusting than I would have if I were white." He saw himself as a businessman, pure and simple, "Yes, part of it could have to do with my background, but I don't recall any real problems in college, where I was one of the very few black students. There were only three in my graduating class. I had been used to operating in an integrated society when I came into the job market. Sure there might have been people here who didn't like me, for whatever reason, but you have to concentrate on getting the job done. That would be my advice to younger managers of both groups, guys and gals—concentrate on getting the job done and there shouldn't be any great problem, in most cases," he said. We handed him a list of terms that we had been using as a theoretical framework for some of our discussions. He read to himself:

Assimilation—the complete merging of an individual into a separate culture. *Culture Conflict*—mental conflict within an individual living between two cultures, both of which are partially accepted and which provide certain contradictory standards and opposing loyalties. *Overconformity*—excessive or compulsive insistence on conforming to a set of standards. *Culture Shock*—the often severe psychological and social maladjustment many individuals experience when they visit or live in a society different from their own. *Cultural Blindness*— a predisposition to not see things that people from other cultures see. *Culture, Explicit*—recognized standards or typical behavior standards of a group. *Implicit*—underlying assumptions, not usually verbalized, often not even recognized because they form for a group the "way things are done."

"I took a great deal of sociology as an undergraduate," he said as he handed the page back across his desk. "I don't think you're going to find much discussion of that sort of thing among senior people in a major corporation today unless you talk to people in human resources."

He sat waiting for the next question, which did not come quickly, without altering his gaze. "What is your background?" he asked. He smiled when we answered creative writing. Had he not consented to the interview he might have walked around his desk to escort the interviewer rapidly into the hallway, but he waited, curious to hear what others, including some senior whites in industry, had said. He listened: impeccably tailored, no facial hair, a light brown complexion that was lined rather than wrinkled. A lion's mane of bluish gray hair was impeccably combed back from his sunken face.

"Younger blacks must either take advantage of opportunities that are offered in all major fields or they have no one to blame but themselves. American business is fascinating. But you can't stay in it and continue to think in terms of black and white. Sure there are still problems, but if you've traveled in many other parts of the world as I have, you'd see that America still offers more opportunities even to the black individual than any other country. There are more opportunities here than anywhere in the world," he said, rocking in his chair and making a tent of thin, finely manicured fingers. "I tell all young people regardless of race to deal with the demands of corporate life or get out and go back to teaching school. If you want a career, learn how to be effective in a corporate context or forget it. To blacks especially, I say that every person who comes into a corporation is not going to make vice-president. Every white guy is not going to make vice-president. So the idea that an individual is not making vice-president or even director because of color is absurd.

"No, I'm not denying that racism is a factor in American life. I'm simply saying that everyone was not cut out for a career in business. The reality is that competition is stiff in corporate life. The higher you get the more fierce it becomes. We as a people had better start producing more young men and women who can cut that competition. We had better capture some of these slots. You don't do it for social reasons. You do it because you want to prove you can do the job, and accept the challenge of leadership. The results, however, have social significance. You can help the race without at the same time using race as a crutch. You help the race by being the best damn manager that you can be."

A corporate personnel director of a major oil company sat in a booth at Diamond J's, a wateringhole for the upperwardly mobile in White Plains, New York. "Of course," he said, "it makes a difference being black in corporate America. For one thing they react to you differently, and if you're talking about the situation when I first got a corporate job [1961], it is pretty much the same thing today. One example of this is that I could never get accurate performance feedback because they didn't think I was going to move up anyway. I was tolerated. My boss would say that I was doing fine when I knew I was really fucking up. He would keep on saying I was doing fine, and then when it came time for a promotion he would say I wasn't quite ready yet, or when it came time to put me in for a raise, he would put me in for three percent, the minimum allowed by the merit plan. It's hard for them to take you seriously. They know that the government forced you into the corporation and so they feel that the corporation doesn't take you seriously," he said. His face reflected the trouble inside him. He seemed too mellow for active bitterness but bitterness seemed to have made his personality more sober than it might have been.

"They had these preconceived notions: you're black so you really can't do much better than you're doing. I don't think these attitudes exist to the same extent now, but there is still some residue. Then I had another manager who was just the opposite. He thought that since you were black you should be better than anyone else. He got really pissed off when you goofed up, as if you weren't living up to your potential as a black man. He was a compassionate old civil libertarian who thought that all blacks were superstars. If you made a mistake he felt you were being ungrateful for the opportunity to be there. He almost never spoke of race directly, but he would say I had a wonderful opportunity to make some gains for my people, and I should not be making mistakes. This guy used race as a whip. He really did. 'Be a credit to your people. Don't take a coffee break. Don't take lunch. Don't get sick. Don't go on vacation—work.'

"I didn't know it at the time but he was frustrated because he had peaked out in the company. He was bitter because I was young, college educated and might get further than he got. He would make cracks like: 'The Kennedy brothers are sure treating you people good.'

"There was more overt racism back then, more open resentment and little respect for blacks. You had to bend over backward so that it wouldn't seem that you had a chip on your shoulder. One thing they wouldn't deal with is an angry black man, so you had to be very careful even about the tone of your voice.

"Because they hadn't been around too many black people they used to test you. For example, they would tell a racial joke to see if you would laugh. Then they would tell "nigger jokes" and substitute pollack for nigger." He laughed but his laughter crackled with the phlegm of bitterness.

"Nobody talks about race much anymore, but I remember another set of incidents. During the riots, when the brothers were burning the goddamn city down, whites would always want to know what I thought. I'd be out by the coffee wagon in the hallway in the morning, and it seemed they'd elected this little Irishman to ask, because when he asked me it seemed everyone in the hallway stopped to listen.

"It was like that E. F. Hutton commercial on television: 'What did your broker say?' 'Well, my broker is E. F. Hutton and my broker said . . .' and then there would be that dead silence on TV and everyone in the joint would lean close and a husky voice would come out of the sky saying: 'When E. F. Hutton speaks, people listen.' For months I thought I was E. F. Hutton," he said.

"It's funny," said another corporate manager of major accounts, who is coming up on twenty years in corporate life. "I know the company hired me because I was a star athlete in college, and so it's bothered me that if you're black you have to be something special, when if you're white all you have to be is white. But after I got hired my size and color began working against me. I had a manager, a small white guy, what else? He had given me my annual performance appraisal, and I wanted to discuss it with him. By company rules we are supposed to discuss it before I sign it, so I asked him to set up a meeting.

"He kept delaying and delaying until one day I saw his office door open, and I went in: 'Bill, could we discuss my PA now?' I closed the door and sat down.

"He fumbled in his desk and came out with his copy of the PA. He started talking nervously, telling me this and that, but nothing very much. He could barely speak and he wouldn't look up at me. I knew he was afraid of this big black dude facing him. I just tried to listen. Then all of a sudden, he exploded: 'I don't have to justify my actions to you or anyone else. I made my judgment and that's it. I've been in this job for seven years and I've been in the company twenty-three years, and I'm not going to let you people come in here and tell me how to do my job. We give you people a chance . . .'

"I was shocked. I said: 'But, Bill. I'm not trying to tell you how to run your job. Actually I thought you had rated me too high. I just wanted to talk to you about some areas in which I can improve, and I wanted to thank you for being a more than decent man.' I reached across the desk to shake his hand. He was already shaking with fear.

" 'Okay,' he said, 'let's settle down. There's no need to get excited.' He was red as a beet and the top of his bald head was sweating. He had to leave the room. I felt really sorry for him and so I eased out and told his secretary that I was going out to keep an appointment I really didn't have. I knew he needed time to regroup. I was embarrassed for him. It was very difficult for me to work for him after that."

Another black man who entered mainstream management in the very early sixties summarized his experience this way:

"I wasn't typical of the guys who came in at the time that I came in. A lot of them had gone to integrated elementary, junior and senior high schools and colleges with white kids. My background is fairly middle-class but I came out of a segregated situation, which doesn't mean that I was poor—far from it. My mother was a school-teacher—typical—and my father worked for the State of Virginia. He also owned a fleet of school buses that used to take black kids from all over the county to the one colored high school in the county—so when people talk about busing, they're being ignorant and hypocritical. Busing was always used to maintain segregation. White kids were bussed past the black school and black kids past the white school so they each could go to segregated schools. I lived right down the street from a white high school, but I was bussed seventeen miles.

"But anyway, I would agree that most blacks who came in were already accustomed to the values of white America. Among my black peers, few as they were, there weren't a great number of adjustment problems. I saw the way they wanted things done, and I learned to do them that way. I encountered very little overt racism. I mean every once in a while I'd meet someone who I knew didn't like me because I was black, and they didn't think I should be there, but I could usually ignore that person.

"Someone high in the company had personally chosen you and you were always placed with a manager who didn't mind having a black work for him. In some ways it was ideal. You automatically had a 'godfather,' a corporate mentor, someone who was going to look out for you.

"The funny thing is initially I didn't know what a godfather was. One of my managers told me early on, 'You know you've got someone looking out for you?' I didn't know what he was talking about. Nor did I think very much about it when the president of the company used to come down to our section to personally see how I was doing. I didn't know that was a signal to the men in my section not to fuck with me because I was the president's boy.

"See, you can have good race relations in a company. I think most of the old-timers will tell you that it was like that. You can have good relationships when all you have is a *few* token blacks. I was invited to the president's home. I used to play ball with his son. His son sort of worshiped me as an athlete.

"At social functions like formal dinners I always sat next to the president and his wife. She always made a point to dance at least one dance with me, even though she couldn't dance. She would sit next to me and all during dinner, she'd be whispering catty little things to me about all of the other wives of vice-presidents—which one had had a nervous breakdown, which one drank too much, which one dyed her hair—it was funny.

"I was too dumb to wonder why this lowly junior staff person, which is what I was, was getting invited to all these important social functions. I even drove his kid up to college, Dartmouth, because he wanted me to give him a little kick in the ass to make the kid work harder. I mean around his mother and father the kid acted like a spoiled brat, but he had this respect for me—being six foot five and black as the ace of spades. I think there was a little fear on his part, but respect too. I think the kid really respects me. The kid is a doctor now in Los Angeles, and I take a lot of personal pride in that, because a dozen times, it must have been, I kept the kid from dropping out of school. I talked to him like my father talked to me. I put it to him straight—'You can be a man or you can be a punk, and a rich punk is still a punk'—and we became good friends.

"One difference was that the president had been a millionaire ever since he was seventeen. His wife was a millionaire from the time her granddaddy was born—old Mayflower money, Boston Brahmin. These were people who weren't threatened by the progress of a black man. That's the difference. Back in those days the presidents and vice-presidents of most of these companies were people of wealth. They were from the American elite and so they were more secure.

"Nowadays you have a lot of average to poor whites who fought their way through the ranks to get to presidential or vice-presidential slots. They're very threatened by blacks," he said, without a great deal of intensity. "Especially if the blacks are more qualified than they."

Most of the older blacks we interviewed did not have strong racial feelings, proving perhaps that it is hard to exist in the mainstream if you do not suppress such feelings.

One of the few exceptions was an intense little man who lives on Long Island and went each day like a burly little time bomb to his corporate job in New York City. "By all rights, if I weren't black, I would be chairman of the board of this company right now. There's no way to get around it. I went to Stanford University. Isn't that one of the best in the country? I graduated summa. I starred in two sports, was captain of the team. Wherever there was an objective scale I beat them. The problem is that inside a corporation everything is subjective. The marketplace is not truly competitive. They don't promote the best talent, they promote their friends. The competition promotes its in group, and so you don't have the best rising to the top. You have the mediocre competing with the mediocre and patting themselves on the back as if they were the best in the world.

"That's why the Japanese and the Germans are kicking the hell out of them as far as productivity is concerned. It's like the Olympics," he said bitterly. "Every country used to kick the hell out of the U.S. as long as the U.S. wouldn't let black men compete." He gripped the steering wheel of his green Dodge tightly, whispering through his teeth as he honked his horn feverishly at someone who had not moved with the green light. "It's like the NBA and the NFL. Until you have the blacks in the competition, competing freely, you can't say that the men who run American industry are the best we have.

"You know what they know. They know there are some hungry, black, mean cats out there, coming up in some of these companies, and they don't want to give these dudes a fair chance. They're too lean and mean, too hungry. They don't want to have their children competing on equal footing with these brothers and sisters. I tell you. That's it. That's the root of the problem," he said, and honked his damned horn again.

The attitude of this little time bomb was not characteristic of the period of tokenism that existed throughout the nineteen fifties and early sixties. Although he was a harbinger of things to come, no one could have predicted that he was the exception that would come more and more to be the rule.

Most of the older managers we interviewed were genteel folk. Of course there were a few tough-minded business types, but most were not of this ilk. Most were more full of social concern than of fierce competitiveness. In fact we encountered more social concern among them than we did in any other place in the corporate world.

They were mostly modest and moderate people. Most were proud of their roles as door-openers. Many were somewhat apologetic about many of the ways that black people were not like white people; thus there was not a great deal of resentment among them over the way that "our people" are discriminated against.

They were much like the people described in an article by Aaron Antonovsky in *Phylon* called "A Study of Some Moderately Successful Negroes in New York City." The eighty-three men and women in this study were caught up in horizontal-vertical mobility, i.e. movement which was not only upward in income, occupation and education, but movement out of the circumscribed Negro economy into the larger American work system.

The respondents in the study were overwhelmingly from stable families. They were shielded from the harsh realities of discrimination. The collective impression was that they had "near-ideal childhood(s) . . . They were brought up, they feel in retrospect, as children should be brought up. Parental concern, affection, reasonable strictness, responsible freedom, sense of belonging—these were some of the terms which describe this image . . ." the authors of the study say.

"We were well-disciplined. We had all the things in our home. Mother loved supervised play. Father and mother were both liberal . . . (they) encouraged the children to confide in them . . . and it worked," said one respondent.

"With very few exceptions, [they were from] . . . good church-going families. Established churches, rather than sect groups, were the rule for them," the authors write. Many of the parents of these people were from the South, but they did not tell their children much about the "old country." They had come to New York to escape all that, and they attempted to snuff out all reminders of it for themselves and their children.

They sent their children to "good" schools, which meant white schools. They would never think of sending their children to the Caribbean or Africa. Most, however, could afford vacations to Europe, in order to absorb some "culture."

They did not have a great number of problems fitting into corporate life because they had programmed themselves to slip into the mainstream without making even the slightest ripple. The feeling that they were uplifting the race assuaged some of their loneliness.

III

TROUBLED WATERS: THE
TURBULENT NINETEEN SIXTIES

IN THE NINETEEN SIXTIES THINGS CHANGED because America changed. No one can say exactly why, but one of the biggest reasons was that black America made one of its periodic surges toward fuller participation in American life.

Such surges have occurred every twenty years since the turn of the century. In the first decade the surge was related to a vigorous concern for the social welfare of black people. Many black schools and institutions were born during this turmoil. The NAACP was founded.

During the twenties it centered in Harlem and gained for blacks greater recognition of their contribution to the cultural life of the nation. In the forties blacks fought for equal rights to produce goods and to go into combat to help fight the Second World War.

And finally in the sixties there was a revolution. The revolution can be called successful even though no one overthrew the dominion of white males over America and the world. We blacks, however, overthrew the rule of white men in our minds. We underwent a psychological revolution.

Before the sixties, only a few among us actively questioned the rightness of whiteness. The march of civilization was toward the white way of being. The idea behind the long battle to integrate public schools was to give black children an opportunity to mix with children of the ruling caste, and thereby join the march.

It seems that no one intended to alter all this, and certainly few people outside of psychological circles knew that such a revolution was needed. There was no psychological intent to the 1955 Montgomery bus boycott. Rosa Parks was simply too tired to get up and give a white man her seat on an Alabama bus.

At first Martin Luther King, Jr., intended nothing more psychologically profound than racial integration. The nine kids who were stoned and spat upon at Little Rock Central High School in 1957 could hardly have known the full psychological impact of their defiance of social custom.

The sit-ins began as simple efforts to win blacks the right to sit and drink coffee at the lunch counter of a dinky Woolworth's in Greensboro, North Carolina.

Blacks and whites confronted each other in Birmingham, Alabama, where whites used police dogs, cattle prods and fire hoses. Four young girls were killed in an Alabama church bombing. The bombers went free. Civil rights workers were mutilated and killed in several southern states. The nation watched on TV. Guilt swelled like a knot in white throats.

Gunnar Myrdal had said in *The American Dilemma* that racism kept a moral uneasiness simmering just below the surface of American life. TV brought it to the surface as never before since the Civil War.

Meanwhile anger swelled in black throats, especially in northern cities. Northerners seemed to know better than the blacks of Birmingham and Greensboro that the right to have coffee at a lunch counter or to sit on the front seats of buses was not going to end the nightmare.

A giant march on Washington was a huge success. Martin Luther King's speech took a stronger hold on the conscience of the nation. "I have a dream," he said, and both whites and blacks hungered for the adventure he promised—a chance to feel for and with others, to dare to be brave in pursuit of a better world. King seized the moral leadership of the nation.

John F. Kennedy had been elected president and blacks quickly pinned hopes on his intentions and his style. Liberalism deepened its commitment to head off bloody confrontation between the haves and the have-nots, between blacks and whites. At the same time, however, automobile bumper stickers began appearing around the country: "Get the Kennedy Boys." Not surprisingly President John Kennedy was soon gunned down.

In 1964 Cassius Clay, the new supersmart black man, defeated the menacing "bad nigger" Sonny Liston to become heavyweight champion of the world. Immediately he announced he was a Black

Muslim and his name was Muhammad Ali, and he would not go off to fight America's war on Vietnam. The Black Muslims preached that the white man was the devil, and not only should blacks avoid *jumping* into the mainstream, they should separate themselves entirely from it. Even though many of their exhortations were more rhetorical than real, their power grew tremendously.

The new President, Lyndon Johnson, signed into law massive amounts of civil rights legislation. "It is the glorious opportunity of this generation to end the one huge wrong of the American nation," Johnson said to a black audience at Howard University in June of 1965. ". . . The barriers [to freedom] are tumbling down. Freedom is the right to share, share fully and equally, in American society— to vote, to hold a job, to enter a public place, to go to school. It is the right to be treated in every part of our national life as a person equal in dignity and promise to all others."

The promise came too late for the bad dudes of the northern streets: they began burning things down. At first the incidents were small. In the summer of 1964 the first of a series of urban uprisings flared in Rochester, New York. It lasted two days and the National Guard was called in to put it down. In 1965 the bigger uprising in Los Angeles shocked the nation. Thirty-four people were killed. Thousands more were injured, and more than $35 million in property was burned, wrecked, looted or defiled.

The following year Newark burned. LBJ's promise came too late for that city's twenty thousand pupils who were on double sessions, for thousands of dropouts who composed about 33 percent of the city's high school–aged youth. (Of 13,600 blacks between sixteen and nineteen, more than 6000 were not in school.)

In 1960, over half of the adult population of Newark had less than an eighth-grade education. "The typical ghetto cycle of high unemployment, family breakup, and crime was present in all its elements. An estimated 40 percent of Negro children lived in broken homes," said the Kerner Commission report.

The riot was supposed to be "the big payback," but the result was that black Newark, instead of American society, paid. Damage occurred only in the neighborhoods where blacks lived. Only two whites—a city detective and a fireman—died, but twenty-one blacks did, including six women and two children.

In Detroit in 1967 black anger was ever more intense. Of the forty-three who died, ten were white. All told, parts of more than a hundred American cities burned during what came to be called the "long hot summers."

Slowly, however, the slogan changed from "Burn, baby, burn," to "Say it loud, I'm black and I'm proud." This, then, was the revolution—a simple joining of two words: black and beautiful. "Black is beautiful" became the marching song.

In 1968 Martin Luther King, Jr., was killed. Blacks in normally subdued Washington, D.C., raged to within ten blocks of the White House.

While running for president, Robert Kennedy was murdered. Along the edges, the privileged classes in America were beginning to show some disarray. Some young whites freaked out. They made their hair nappy and stuck flowers in rifle barrels of National Guardsmen defending the establishment's establishments.

In the early seventies media exploiters came out to bay at spotlights long enough to write heroic books about their siege on America, now that there was no chance that a siege could really work. The sincere and the extremely disaffected broke up into bands of urban guerrillas such as the Black Panthers and the Weather Underground. Opportunists and paid informers moved in to expose, mop up and exploit those whose fervor for the ideals of the revolution had not died.

On top of all this there was plenty of money in the streets. The War on Poverty had opened the smaller coffers of the Treasury to the common man, while spending for the War in Vietnam was enriching the well-connected. Corporations were hiring like crazy. Educated blacks were being drawn and pushed into the mainstream.

The Equal Employment Opportunity Commission gradually gained enough power to bring suit against corporations who did not open opportunities to minorities. AT&T had to pay $38 million to people it had discriminated against. Sears, General Motors and General Electric lost money and face. In such a setting it was not difficult for a smart young black dude to get himself a good job in a corporation. Such was the case with J. Carson Branford.

One of the authors of this book had known him in the Air Force when they were among a very few blacks in officers training school. Even then it was apparent that J. Carson Branford would make it in the corporate world, that he'd probably, before turning forty-five, be vice-president of a Fortune 500 company.

He was a smart and adaptable young man. During the early seventies things worked out well for him. He became a manager, then director of a company in the second 500, and then saw an opportunity to move up to a top 500 company in a better slot, as a director of personnel.

His office was large and plush. His bachelor's apartment cost $500 per month in 1973 dollars; he paid $100 per month to garage his car. He could have afforded more if he had had to. He could buy the many hundreds of things he liked. He could take frequent vacations and make payments on his Mercedes 450 SEL.

He was, in black economic terms, a successful swimmer in the mainstream. From the outside it looked as if he were making big decisions, motivating subordinates, impressing peers and superiors, dressing for success and talking corporate. How could we have known that director of personnel was not really a power slot in a corporation, that he did not control a budget center, that his job was soft-core.

The only thing we knew was that he seemed to be "doing it." It seemed that he had planned this assault on the corporate world even while he was in the Air Force. "America is the corporate state," he said; "you must learn to function in its environment." His voice was robust, intelligent, precise. He was from Georgia, but he worked hard not to sound like a Southerner. He rolled his Rs and said "ciao" rather than "good-bye" whenever he departed. His "phony" accent was almost laughable, but the wise knew that people are judged on superficial characteristics—methods of speech, mannerisms, dress. From the time he had first seen New York City on television, our friend had been acquiring the trappings of success.

When he introduced himself, he used first initial, middle name, last name—so the entire thing would roll off the tongue like the name of a successful business scion—K. Wentworth Dunn, H. Hamilton Bradstreet.

He knew that no disheveled, slow-talking black man named Willie Jones was ever going to be taken seriously in the corporate world. Some people laughed at him back then, but he was no buffoon out of E. Franklin Frazier's *Black Bourgeoisie*. Branford was a competent young man who had the instincts to know that certain situations demand certain kinds of preparation.

He knew how to pick the people who might be important to his advancement. He learned how to be friendly but abrupt with those who were not in a position to advance his ambitions. His credo seems to have been, If you want to be someone in life, imitate people who've already attained what you hope to attain. Surround yourself with the right people. Make the right connections. "That's true," he claimed, "no matter what your race."

Several other black managers we interviewed had a strange ambivalence toward the need to imitate their white corporate superiors. Their ambivalence was quite natural. During this time blacks outside the corporation were trying to establish a separate sense of identity. Some, in fact, were trying to separate themselves entirely from American life, which they felt to be spiritually sterile, overly mechanistic and "packaged."

"They want you to be like them," said one scientist-manager. "They want you to suppress certain aspects of your racial identity—your life-style, sense of humor, way of dressing—existential things that are part of your racial heritage. I can do it. I can 'behave.' 'Behave' means act the way they want you to. 'Behaving' is a problem for me because I'm from an entirely different background.

"I have doubts about my ability—no, I doubt my desire to 'behave' much longer. Soon I might just do something 'real,' like wear the 'wrong' clothes to work—a pair of patent leather shoes with three-inch heels just to mess with their minds. Something ridiculous like that."

Another scientist, with a master's degree in engineering and a Ph.D. in chemistry, was very happy with his new job. He was part of management but he didn't manage anyone but himself and three junior scientists who aided him on a special project. He loved the money he made—about $20,000 a year (in 1977)—but he was ambivalent about the subtle corporate demands on his taste and lifestyle. "For example," he said, "most people in the scientific community drive Volkswagens or Volvos to work. They question my scientific dedication when they see my Cadillac in the staff parking lot. They want me to accept their values. They probably feel that all a black wants is a Cadillac. They want me to give up my values and accept theirs before they can feel completely safe about me. They want me to wear Robert Hall suits and Hush Puppies before they can accept the fact that I'm a good physicist, an excellent one," he said.

It was certainly the black revolution of the sixties that created such disinclination to assimilate. It was the force of the Civil Rights Act of 1964 that brought so many "black" blacks into the mainstream. These were not members of the established black middle class, as most of the tokens were. This new black man or black woman might have come from a stable family background, but could just as easily have come from one of those broken homes that crowd the statistics on black life.

He or she was likely from a churchgoing family, but the church could easily have been one of the temple-of-fire gospel churches which taught that God's relationship to life on earth was immediate, judgmental, rewarding or punitive, as the situation demanded.

As likely as not, this new black manager came from a turbulent childhood full of extremes of agony and ecstasy, defeat and victory. Hunger and obsession may have affected him or her, but usually not in the extremes that would prevent the young man or woman from getting through Howard, Morgan State, Harvard or Michigan and into corporate management. The memories of childhood hungers and obsessions were usually strong enough to fill the manager with fear of ever having to return to that life, or of ever having to raise children in a similar climate.

To some degree many of these black men and women had experienced the system as victims. Some were ambivalent about any implications that by joining the system they had become victimizers. Some, as we will see, did everything they could to avoid identifying with the black masses from which they sprang, while others wanted to cling tenaciously to an identification with past and culture, sometimes in rebelliously immature ways. Many encountered a great deal of racist resistance, but sometimes what they interpreted as racism was not racism at all. Some of their problems stemmed from their own unfamiliarity with the way big impersonal organizations operate. For example, some blacks complained that it's dishonest to pretend to like someone you don't really like, as corporate life demands that you do. Wilbert Moore in *The Conduct of the Corporation* points out that this kind of "emotional dishonesty" is necessary. The single greatest advantage of the corporation "over other forms of human interaction is the capacity for inducing strangers and even potential enemies to cooperate in accomplishing the collective mission."

This aspect of corporate life was harder for blacks to adjust to because they had more potential enemies, who were more unreasonably hostile. Many young blacks felt that there was something wrong with "grinning in the face of someone you didn't like and who didn't like you." Their parents had had to do too much of that. Blacks had gotten used to "telling it like it is," "being for real" and "letting it all hang out."

Conformity was difficult, and even dress codes became a source of contention. J. Carson Branford felt that such protestations were immature, that all splashers were immature. He was a swimmer. "If you're in the Army, you wear the uniform. It's the same with a civilian dress code or behavioral style. And a corporation is not a place where you assert your identity. You're there to get a job done. To do that job, you have to provide the reassurance which your peers and superiors need before they can feel comfortable trusting you with certain responsibilities. You have to cultivate a certain image."

All jobs in corporations do not necessarily preclude spontaneity, honesty of feeling and integrity, but many of them do. "But if you want to play the game you've got to pay for a ticket," Branford said. "Getting used to this atmosphere is the price of the ticket."

Most black managers, even during the hot sixties and early seventies, tried very hard to conform, and usually, with greater effort than their white counterparts, they were able to do so.

Most admitted they were glad to be in corporate life, and they acknowledged that they were there because civil rights groups and the federal government pressured their companies into giving blacks a chance, but all felt fully qualified, often overqualified.

The patterns of their adjustment were similar in many ways to those of countless generations of European immigrants adjusting to America. But the visible racial difference and hundreds of years of systematic attempts to dehumanize black people made adjustment more difficult for them in many ways. And many of them seemed to be saying that there was some persistent blackness of their spirits that kept them from wanting to assimilate.

Among many blacks there was a great deal of *anomie,* a condition resulting from the breakdown of traditional values and norms of an individual who cannot or does not want to assimilate the values of a new, more complex and often inhospitable environment. *Anomie,* according to Don A. Martindale in *The Nature and Types of Sociological Theory,* often results in feelings of isolation and the loss of intimacy found in traditional cultures.

Several interviewees admitted that they may have had a touch of something like that, but one of them stubbornly refused to have it called by that name, as if to escape the name were also to escape the disease. Even J. Carson Branford admitted that he had to take strong measures against feeling isolated in a way that would sap his strength and initiative.

Anomie was only one of the many diseases that afflicted corporate blacks. Guilt was another. Some managers suffered because they were making so much money while many of the blacks they grew up with, even members of their own families, were still struggling to survive. Others felt guilty over allowing themselves to be regimented, their behavior and speech to be standardized. A young manager we interviewed recalled becoming increasingly annoyed at a black house party with another young man's conversation. "I hate those people," he recalls saying. "I bet that that guy over there talking is a goddamn IBMer. All of those bastards talk alike." He left the party despite the fact that he himself was an IBMer—or, more likely, because of that fact.

And there was another disease: many of the managers we interviewed confessed that a black manager might have to cultivate a high level of paranoia. J. Carson Branford agreed. "I'm a little paranoid for my own protection. You've got to watch yourself all the time."

"Sure," said a female manager at a giant electronics company, "there are a lot of people out to get you, more so because you're black. Some people might resent you because they don't think a black should have such a high position. Some might feel you got the job only because you're black. Some might not like black people in general."

A male manager for the same company agreed. "You've even got to watch out for your secretary. She might not give you the proper respect or loyalty. She might do little things because she doesn't like taking orders from you. But you must be careful how you move on any form of insubordination. You might not be able to attack it directly. Your secretary might be especially friendly with someone two levels above you, or she might be in their protection, especially if she's been around the company longer than you. You have to bide your time until you're sure she doesn't have a sponsor. Then you move in on her; but make sure you have documentation."

Getting used to the water of the mainstream was not easy. One problem was that there was no clear way to determine what was corporate behavior and what was racist corporate behavior. One manager expressed the view that black people are too sensitive in their dealings with whites. "You have to look at how white people treat each other," he said; "then you'll feel better about the disrespect and insubordination shown toward you. White secretaries hate white bosses sometimes, too; but white people know they don't have to like each other to get the job done. What black people want to do is have a personal relationship. What white people do is remain outwardly cordial while subtly cutting each other to ribbons, if necessary. We have to learn to work this way."

One senior director recalled an example of another sort: "I was on a trip to Chicago with the chairman of the board. In the morning, I was down in the hotel lobby and he said, 'Hey, Williams, go up to my room and get my luggage.' My first reaction was to say 'Get your own luggage. What do I look like, a redcap?' But I swallowed my pride and got his bags. My jaws were tight for a week. Then I began to notice how the white vice-presidents, senior vice-presidents, knocked each other down to take care of the chairman's luggage, get him checked out of hotels and see that his limo was waiting. 'Yes, sir. Yes, sir. Can I do anything else for you, sir?' See. I learned. You can be a so-called man and work in the mailroom for the rest of your life, or you can take some crap and make sixty-five thousand dollars per year. Everybody in a corporation takes crap, and the higher up you go, the more you have to take. They use it to test you." It is not surprising that during the sixties this problem kept coming up: How to be properly black and properly subordinate to all those white superiors.

And there was also, as we have stressed, a growing emotional distance between the black manager and his former community. Moreover, the kind of emotional closeness that many blacks had been used to did not even exist between one white manager and another. There was no hope that it would exist for blacks. This was an environment where contacts between people were utilitarian more than anything else.

White people regretted this also, but America as a whole was experiencing an accelerated breakdown in community as a result of something that Alvin Toffler called future shock.

In his book by that name Toffler described thousands of new inventions and new processes and ways of looking at things that, all of a sudden, modern people had to adjust to; and he described hundreds of ways that some of them adjusted, thereby creating hundreds of behavioral adaptations that others, in turn, have to adapt to.

America, and certainly corporate America, therefore, was experiencing the stress and disorientation that accompanies the efforts of individuals and organizations to adapt to new technology, new frontiers of knowledge, new sociological and economic status values, new psychological and moral orientations, new concepts of race, gender and class, new waves of perceptions creating overstimulation and information overload, and new advances in mass transportation and mass communication.

This all implied hundreds, if not thousands, of ways that old norms and values were changing, including corporate norms and values. "Organizations now change their internal shape with frequency—and sometimes a rashness—that makes the head swim," wrote the eclectic Toffler, who had been an editor with *Fortune,* a Washington correspondent, a free-lance writer, a professor of the "sociology of the future" at Cornell University and other places and an adviser to the Rockefeller Brothers Fund, The Institute for the Future and IBM.

He had certainly had wide experience in the world of which he spoke. "Titles change from week to week," he wrote. "Jobs are transformed. Responsibilities shift. Vast organizational structures are taken apart, bolted together again in new forms, then rearranged again. Departments and divisions spring up overnight only to vanish in another, and yet another, reorganization."

This is future shock. For many black managers future shock collided with culture shock. Culture shock is, in this case, the severe psychological and social maladjustment many individuals experience when they have to operate in a culture different from their own.

"For the individuals within organizations," Toffler wrote, "change creates a wholly new climate and a new set of problems. . . . With each change, he must reorient himself." With any new managers there were bound to be periods when they were adjusting to what used to be, times when they were tuning into what *was* rather than what was coming.

Expectedly, many black managers we interviewed seemed to think of a corporation in the same way that old-timers did. They were eager to be accepted and so they imitated those who had been there longest. They became slaves to the old rules. This made the "corporate nigger" even more estranged from his or her brothers in the street who had been so recently symbols for the national search for a new vision.

For if the revolution of the sixties was nothing else it was a search for a new vision. It was not simply a black revolution as we called it in the first pages of this chapter. We called it a black revolution because blacks fired the first shots, and all during the decade the image was the image of rebellion against the old order.

But the sixties was really characterized by a search on the part of many people, black and white, male and female, for alternatives to the old order. During this time the lines of demarcation between class, caste and gender began falling before the banner of egalitarianism. Too many people, black and white, male and female, had felt themselves abused under the old system of class and caste, and under the old divisions of gender. The Vietnam War, for example, dramatized to the newly awakened consciousness just how much the sons of the poor could be abused. This alliance against abuse forced the federal government to recognize the potential for insurrection. The ruling class had to yield, at least for a time, until it could marshal its defenses, until it could pick up defectors, until it could co-opt enough members of these "armies of the night" or until a truce could be worked out.

That the revolution in America was part of a world revolution is attested to by the fact that lines of demarcation between class, caste, gender and race began shifting in all parts of the world. There were, of course, the obvious battles for national liberation, but on a subtler level the revolution was carried on in the minds of people. In Toffler's terms, the media, especially television, spread the vision of new possibilities to the masses of the world in much the same way as the writings of Isaac Newton and John Locke, moral philosophers David Hume and Immanuel Kant, other writers of the Enlightenment like Rousseau and Voltaire and finally the American pragmatists Thomas Jefferson and Thomas Paine spread visions of new possibilities during the first Age of Revolution, which produced the first American Revolution and the French Revolution of 1789.

Like returning merchant ships during the Age of Discovery, television programs and television advertisements brought to the hungry masses a vision of new possibilities for sharing in the bounty of the earth. Television news showed people their degradation. They fought to end that degradation.

Even if American corporations had welcomed blacks with open arms, there would have to have been an unsettling period of adjustment, but from the first there was no really open-armed reception. From the first there was much hostility and much hypocrisy, and the hostility increased as blacks made more advances into those areas in which white males' sense of superiority rested.

Then in the middle and late nineteen seventies money got scarce. The Vietnam War was over, but few Americans were ready to admit that the war debt was one of the major reasons for scarcity. Most Americans were more comfortable believing that excessive government spending on social programs (the War on Poverty, the War on the Economic Caste System) was to blame, even though the home front war cost one one-hundredth the amount of the War on Vietnam.

In the mid nineteen seventies even many of the staunchest supporters of the home front war were willing to claim that it had failed. Even some of the blacks who got their chance to come into the mainstream during the nineteen sixties piously forgot that the War on Poverty did defeat a lot of black poverty. It put some money into some black pockets. And perhaps this is why it became so unpopular, as unpopular as the 1964 Civil Rights Act and the EEOC were becoming in the late seventies after they began to defeat some black underemployment.

Surely some whites were ready to argue that the federal government was giving the country away to niggers even though there was never a time when as much as 1 percent of the money the government gave away ended up with the 12 percent of the population that black America represented.

If one in a hundred workers in a plant was black, then more than a few of the ninety-nine remaining white workers would grumble that blacks were taking white people's jobs. Allan Bakke went to court against the University of California at Davis charging that the university was giving away sixteen slots in the freshman class of its medical school to black students; thus denying access to these slots to white people like himself. Bakke won, but not unconditionally.

A "meanness mania" swept across America. Meanness mania is what Gerald R. Gill called it in his book by that name. Meanness, Gill said, denotes selfishness, stinginess and malice which created "an increasing unwillingness and hostility upon the part of many citizens to share more equally the benefits of American society."

The meanness was intensified by international events. Arabs wanted more money for the oil beneath their deserts. Japanese began producing more, better and cheaper automobiles and electronic components. Unable to meet the competition, American industry began contracting by laying off workers and looking for scapegoats.

Because America is a new culture still searching for itself, it swings back and forth. In an older, more balanced culture like that of Japan there is a sense that a diversity of values can be respected, indeed must be respected, and have influence in the culture at the same time.

America is different. It swings back and forth in cycles of, as we have said, a little more than twenty years. For about ten years during the nineteen sixties America swung left to respect personal self-expression, compassion for others, idealism, spontaneity, creativity, change—values that produce political liberalism.

The swing toward these values caused too great a disregard for others, and so the pendulum swung back and the country began searching for a sense of structure. It became more authoritarian, materialistic. It generated an attitude that said, "If I can make it, then everyone ought to be able to, and shame on them if they can't, regardless of the barriers that are placed in their paths."

Some social commentators say that the periodic swings of the business cycle cause these periodic contractions of the national spirit; but we who approach history with a broader perspective see that an imbalance in the values of the culture causes the swings. If a greater range of values were respected simultaneously we would not have the swing back and forward searching for what we neglect to respect.

Starting in the late nineteen seventies conservative values began to pervade the entire society. They reached down into the colleges, which cut back on liberal arts courses because increasingly students wanted business courses or engineering courses.

It is shortsighted for diehards from the idealistic period to condemn the new products of the realistic period. The little black technocrats, one forty-year-old female manager called the young blacks in their twenties, fresh out of college, with no sense of the "debt to the past or to anyone for helping them get to where they are. They went to college for the sole purpose of 'making it.' The little snits planned their educations carefully so they could fit into the job market in just the right place, never mind what their aptitudes and interests were. Their interest was in making money.

"I talk to them all the time," this manager told us. "They make me very, very sad. Where is our historic commitment to someone other than ourselves? This is what blacks have kept alive in this country. This is why these little niggers make me so mad and sad," she said.

One of the kinds of people who make her mad and sad told us, "I don't see why we (blacks who have made it) have to keep reaching back to try to pull them (poor black people) forward." She had earned an M.B.A. and an engineering degree and she was looking forward to a salary of $35,000 annually in a few years.

During our interviewing we ran into a good number of black managers who did not express themselves candidly but were nonetheless stubbornly interested in their own careers and blithely resistant to any social concern. Many of them had gone to college with white members of the "me generation," and they were in full accord with their white classmates. In his book *New Rules: Searching for Self-fulfillment in a World Turned Upside Down,* pollster Daniel Yankelovich is kind to them. His polls could easily make the case that they are selfish rather than seekers after self-fulfillment.

The polls he cites are full of me-firstism, more-ism, unrestrained self-absorption, narcissism, protective shallowness and obsession with salary level. With only slight differences these conditions often apply to blacks as well as the whites who carved out good careers for themselves during the hazardous economic environment of the late seventies.

Yankelovich argues that the self-centeredness of these young, affluent professionals is related to some genuine search for personal creative expression, some bold commitments to self-analysis and some risky experiments in living. He supports his argument with polls in which affluent young professionals say they spend a great deal of time thinking about themselves, that satisfaction comes from shaping oneself rather than from home and family life.

They claim to have strong creative needs and strong needs for new experiences. When we look to see some of the new experiences we find that they like jogging, not simply for the exercise value but for the personal psychological lift; they like special diets, not to keep the weight down but to make the body a better machine; they prefer travel to spending more on possessions; they seek out new foods and tastes; they feel the need for more excitement and sensation.

Yankelovich calls them the "strong-form group." Robert McMurry, in an article in *U.S. News & World Report,* says they are part of our "new elite," who "for better or for worse . . . have fallen heir to all the benefits of the 1960s without having to fight for them. They know the goals they have set cannot be achieved without the system and so they are supporters of the system but they do not either believe in it or disbelieve. If the act of believing is essential to humans then they are in spiritual limbo."

Yankelovich and *U.S. News* find something grander in their lives than we do. What they say they want does not, to us, add up to a genuine search for personal creative expression or some risk-taking experiments in living. The economic uncertainty around them seems to have made them *more* cautious with regard to the important decisions of life, and more free and creative in their own self-indulgent leisure.

We think that Yankelovich and *U.S. News* are wrong about the new form group being more free and creative in their leisure. They are more conspicuous in their consumption of leisure. They are not more free. They are not more creative. They are just as uptight and structured in their play as they are in their work.

And unfortunately, since this is a racist society, blacks among the strong-form group face a dilemma: They are believers in self-reliance. They themselves are not overly altruistic. Yet in a racist society a lot of them might become victims of the lack of altruism on the part of their white counterparts. They, like their struggling brothers, might become victims of backlash.

IV

BACKLASH: THE NINETEEN SEVENTIES AND NINETEEN EIGHTIES

JAMES DOCKETT, A MAN with a wide, smooth dark face and wide light-rimmed glasses that made him look like an owl, sat at his desk in a windowed office on the floor his firm had rented as quarters for its midwestern operations. "We've known for a long time backlash was coming," he said as if he were speaking of a tidal wave or other natural disaster, "but there was nothing we could do but get tied down to wait it out."

We interviewed Jim Dockett in 1980. He said he had seen backlash rising for about five years—building, quietly growing. "It had to come. There were too many people who were angry, for various reasons, about the gains that were being made. No one wants to have to fight an equal fight for opportunities. Everyone wants an advantage and so if a white male has an advantage because of race and sex then there's no doubt that he wants to keep that advantage—if that's all he's got going for him," Jim Dockett said and raised an arm, held it close to his body, and pointed a finger like the outside feather on an owl's wing. He laughed.

Backlash is the word that came into vogue in the early seventies to describe the actions of the privileged to preserve their position from the inroads of the underprivileged.

There is no doubt that a great deal of backlash was based on open racism and sexism, but there is also no doubt that some of it comes from sources more complex.

James Dockett continued:

"I think there are some of us with good jobs in the mainstream who will hold on to those jobs. There will be some rollback, and some attrition due to the fact that when some blacks get fed up and drop out their places will be taken by nonblacks; but on the other hand I think that corporations will continue to hire young well-trained blacks for entry-level positions, and some of these will work their way up in the system. Yes, definitely, the door won't be open as wide, but it will remain open in many instances."

He closed his office door behind him and told a red-haired secretary that he was going out to lunch and that he would be back in about an hour. "I do think there're going to be a lot of careers put on hold. White people really believe in this reverse discrimination thing," he said.

White males began to accuse companies of reverse discrimination when a minority candidate or woman got a job that a white male "should have gotten."

"Let me say," said James Dockett, "some people believe in this reverse discrimination thing and it just depends on whether the ones who know that it's bullshit will stand up to the ones who want to use it as an excuse.

"I don't think there's going to be a complete turn around but I think that it's going to be rough for a while . . . it's going to be tough with Ronald Reagan's people in there."

James Dockett's voice was sad. He had explained that during the early seventies he had been speeding toward success and all of a sudden he had been hit by a tidal wave of backlash. He said he didn't fear getting fired. The system was not that unfair, and he was not going to give them any reason to fire him.

"Some blacks will stay on because there are senior white guys in these companies who know that blacks have made a contribution. It's been like so much else in America, blacks haven't gotten the credit for it, but white guys know that blacks've made a contribution and they want them to keep on making this contribution.

"For example, I remember the company I used to work for. They let a whole parcel of brothers in at the same time, in the Washington market. I was there and these brothers were breaking every sales record in the books. 'Rookie of the Year,' 'President's Club' or 'Hundred Percent Club' or whatever they called it. It was amazing.

"They were like Grambling brothers breaking into the National Football League—running backs, wide receivers—a whole parcel of niggers, making plays that nobody else could make.

"These niggers were jumping off of the moon catching passes. You wouldn't believe it. There was a legendary brother who could walk and talk with a huge typewriter balanced on the palm of one hand while he used the other hand to demonstrate the features of the machine. Amazing! Secretaries saw this brother and they wouldn't touch another kind of typewriter.

"There were brothers who would sell their annual quota before the end of May. I know, man. I know," James Dockett said. He was talking about a group of guys who were splashers. "They pushed for more territory. They stretched the rules, they balked at regimentation. In order to sell they had to be themselves and instead of the company negotiating a truce, it put the muscle on them. One by one they were broken or forced out. The company took it all racially and got rid of them, sent a couple of them to see psychiatrists."

It was apparent that the company preferred the dully efficient to the nonconformingly creative, the safe over the effective. James Dockett said, "They didn't like us because we were black, but they knew we were good, and so they'll always bring in some brothers like this and tap their creativity and then force them out."

Parenthetically, later, a white female manager disagreed. "They didn't dislike them because they were black, they disliked them because they were successful. This was very threatening to the other guys in the sales force. It was not their color that was threatening." The woman was referring to an odd kind of catch-22 situation that we encountered in other places in the corporate environment: The black manager was expected to do a better job. He expected this of himself and he knew that if he messed up as much as the white guy did, he would be out on his butt, but if he actually went ahead and did the better job, the white guys would consider him a threat and undermine him anyway.

James Dockett continued, "I usually hit my yearly quotas by July, and I remember this very hip white guy sidled up to me and whispered out the side of his mouth, 'You're hitting your targets, you're keeping your nose clean, Dockett. You're messing up. I'm warning you,' and then he laughed and went off. I still remember this guy. He quit the company and went off to teach college because he was tired of getting penalized for being conscientious.

"Then you'll get some of these little black mavens, I call them. By getting a better education than the white guy and working harder and keeping their noses clean, they'll advance just a little slower than the white guys next to them, and some of them will do very well because there's a whole crop of them coming out of the best white business schools.

"They've been educated from kindergarten with white kids and so there's not a great deal of difference between them and the white guy, the corporation will find a place for them. Most of them don't know and don't care much about black culture or any other kind of culture. They want to make that money. They talk that talk just like the white guys.

"They have no racial consciousness at all. They won't even speak to you in the hallway when they see you, but they'll speak to the white guy, and so they do have a negative racial consciousness," James Dockett said.

During the interviewing we encountered a number of the "new niggers" as James Dockett also called them. Incredibly well-focused, incredibly aware of what personal qualities had to be cultivated to "make it." There was no way to know what their fate would be. They had gone, in the words of writer Julian Mayfield, "into the mainstream and oblivion."

"And then there were the scientists. There's such a shortage of good scientists that the companies will hire scientists no matter what color they are.

"Then you've got some special markets people. They've done a tremendous job in some companies that sell to black consumers. White guys admit that they don't know how to tap this market, so they will always hire some black guys to do this. But you know what's the amazing thing about this is that these black guys develop some fantastic marketing psychology in the special markets area and the company turns around and uses this psychology in the general markets.

"Look at television advertising. The attitude, the psychological approach behind most of your popular television ad campaigns is black. You never thought of that, did you? Check it out.

"I mean with backlash coming, I don't think it's going to be a case of all of a sudden throwing blacks out. For one thing, all of these companies know they have to deal in a world that is increasingly multinational, and so they will want to have some blacks for this reason. But what I'm talking about are the top jobs, those jobs are reserved for their friends, even if their friends are incompetent. They will hire a super staff to support their incompetent friend, but the friend will get the job.

"And then the nondescript jobs, the jobs that anybody can do no matter what level the jobs are, they will save these jobs for white males who are absolutely too incompetent to do anything else: 'Oh, Bill, he's a great guy. Let's give him that job down in quality control. I don't think he can fuck up anything down there.' It's incredible. If you ask me what's wrong with American industry, I'd say that this is one of the major things. And it happens in the blue collar labor force too—unions and foremen protect their own.

"And there is not a white man out there who can deny this. If I'm lying ham ain't pork, grits ain't groceries, chickens have lips and Mona Lisa is a man," James Dockett said, showing some of the flair for language that had made him, in the words of someone who knew him, one of the best teenage "rappers" on the streets of Philadelphia during the nineteen fifties.

We, the authors, had noticed just what James Dockett had noticed. We were working on this material while watching a National Basketball Association game on TV. Three of the starting five players were white, and the white players were really playing fantastic basketball. They were fighting like crazy to win. They had egos like black ballplayers and they had refined their talents so they could play great basketball.

Two years before you would never have seen three white ballplayers starting on a winning team in the NBA, but what had obviously happened was that white ballplayers at all levels had seen black ballplayers taking their jobs and so they began working harder, honing their skills.

In American industry, we concluded, what we need is an NBA-effect. Allow minorities and women to compete for all the jobs, fairly. Give the job to the best person, the best not in terms of a preconceived notion of how the game ought to be played but in terms of who gets the ball in the hoop, or knocks the ball out of the park, or gets the ball across the goal line.

Do this and American industry will get better performances from its white male ballplayers. The NBA-effect was our answer to entrenched incompetence.

The white guys on the court were fantastic, but we knew that they would not have been if they had not had to compete with black guys, and if they had not, finally, borrowed some tricks from the black guys. This back and forth borrowing should be done openly by white guys. There is nothing for them to be ashamed of. This is not an admission of inferiority on their part. The black guy doesn't admit to inferiority when he admits that the entire game of basketball he borrowed from the white guy.

Many white males feel that there is something wrong with admitting that blacks and minorities have some things that they don't have. This is what makes America such a truncated culture, cut off from human fullness and ever tending toward sterility.

If these white males who are threatened by it are able to reverse affirmative action, to make the hysteria over reverse discrimination seem real, they will, to continue our basketball analogy, be pushing the game back toward the era of the set shot and the feet-flat-on-the-floor chest pass; and the run-and-gun Japanese will keep on keeping on.

This is one of the things that the conservativism of the 1980–81 period means. It is an attempt to slow the game down. Conversely, a good part of the rest of the world is speeding it up. This effort to slow the thing down is what got Ronald Reagan elected president in 1980. This is why so many Americans, including much of the former liberal establishment, are not openly critical of his game plan.

Out there in Iowa and down in Mississippi and up in Maine a great many people believe in the slow, deliberate game. They want to give this new coach a chance. In New York there seems to be some "Okay, wait and see. Maybe it will work."

Certainly Ronald Reagan was not elected president in 1980 in order to put an end to affirmative action programs. He was elected because he proposed a new approach to the nation's problems; an approach that was different than that of previous administrations, even the administration of Richard Nixon, who was of the same political party.

Reagan's style was different. He was friendly, cool and businesslike. He seemed almost corporate. He convinced many people that big government was responsible for many of the nation's troubles. Charmingly, he promised to "take the government off the backs of the American people." Plainly, to the enemies of affirmative action, this meant that he wanted to get the government out of the business of forcing companies to end racial and sexual discrimination. In fact, he said that he was philosophically opposed to affirmative action.

And so during the first year of his administration, the government began quietly putting this philosophy into practice: The Administration told corporations with a combined total of more than 7.5 million workers that they no longer had to draw up detailed plans for hiring and promoting women and minorities. It changed the rules under which female and minority workers could sue to collect back pay for jobs or promotions they didn't get. It forbade any employer with a government contract from hiring women and minorities over equally qualified white males even to atone for the effects of past discrimination.

These measures, the September 7, 1981, edition of *Time* argued, were trial balloons to see how politically wise it might be to take further anti-affirmative action steps. Being philosophically opposed to affirmative action the Administration was testing to see how wise it would be to be operationally opposed as well.

Of course there were other reasons for the ridiculous charge by white males that minorities and women were being favored over them. The economic infrastructure of the country was still overwhelmingly based on the white male wage earner. When inflation went into double digits and unemployment, in some sectors of the economy, surpassed the rate of inflation, a tightness of spirit set in and meanness came out. Competition grew more fierce and charity began to dissolve.

This played right into the hands of those who had been angry since the early seventies when the federal government first stepped up the drive to end employment discrimination.

As *Newsweek* pointed out in its June 17, 1974, issue, Richard Nixon had "never been regarded as a champion of civil rights, yet in a quiet and highly pragmatic way during the past two years, the Administration's civil rights strategists have been waging a tough fight—and a remarkably effective one—on behalf of minorities and women."

The fight was much more brutal than *Newsweek* implied. Many of the blacks interviewed for this book got their positions because of the effectiveness of that fight. For the first time, in 1972, the Equal Employment Opportunities Commission was given the right to go to court to enforce antidiscrimination measures. By 1974 the budget for EEOC had tripled to more than $44 million. EEOC was at war.

The EEOC attacked the largest companies in several industries, and hoped thereby to frighten the others into line. It took on AT&T, Sears, Exxon and General Motors. With hundreds of EEOC officials and attorneys working together, the war assumed the intensity of a holy crusade.

The Labor Department's Office of Federal Contract Compliance (OFCC) and the Justice Department were also in the fight. The OFCC had a weapon more powerful than the authority to go to court: it could declare a company ineligible to receive federal contracts if the company failed to design and implement an acceptable affirmative action plan. This threat was a nuclear warhead in the antidiscrimination arsenal.

The federal government attacked on a number of fronts, and even the heads of some federal enforcement agencies admitted that the effort had spawned a patchwork system of confusing and often contradictory regulations and decisions. The Defense Department, for example, monitored contract compliance in most basic manufacturing, the Treasury Department in banking, the Commerce Department in certain kinds of interstate commerce, the Labor Department monitored the unions, and Health, Education and Welfare kept an eye on colleges and universities. Thus monitoring power was anything but centralized.

Often corporations that intended to comply with the letter or spirit of the law found themselves in noncompliance simply because they did not know what to do. Those companies that did not want to comply found in all the confusion either a number of excuses or a number of smoke screens.

Media coverage suggested that the government was seeking vengeance against both the poor beleaguered billion-dollar multinational corporations and the white men for past sins. A cartoon appeared in newspapers depicting a puzzled, dark-haired white male standing in front of a bulletin board with a job-opening sign on it. The sign read: "Immediate openings, white males need not apply. High salary in highly specialized area, qualifications waived."

It was a simplistic cartoon, but it dramatized the feelings of some white males toward affirmative action. "What happened," said Tyler Wilson, a white man who worked in the congressional liaison office of a large chemical company, "is that these people had been kept *out* of the system for hundreds of years, everyone understands that, but what you have now is the federal government saying that you have to plug this black, or Negro, person or this woman into a system at a level, or you have to quickly promote them to a level, ahead of a white male who has been waiting in line for years to reach this particular level. You've corrected a social injustice but created individual injustices to the white man who has worked hard for this promotion." Tyler's face was red and earnest.

"Okay, it's true that the black man or the woman could not have been waiting in line because they were barred from the line, but can't you see that if you put that person in the middle of the line or you rush them forward in the line, then you've created problems with the white man who had been hoping and planning for a promotion to buy the things he needs for his family?"

Tyler knew all the standard arguments: He said he was against numerical quotas, but finally he admitted that there was absolutely no way to assure equality of opportunity unless you actually went in and counted the number of women and minorities who had been hired by a company and then later you went in to see how many had been promoted. He admitted that his company would not hire or promote minorities and women willingly despite any claims to the contrary and so you had to count bodies to substantiate the claims, and if the actuality did not conform to the claim you had to set mandatory targets—quotas. He laughed.

He argued that quotas destroyed the meritocracy by promoting not the best-qualified person but the kind of person needed to fill the quota.

He accepted easily, however, the fact that there has never been a true meritocracy in America, not even among white men, and how, he was asked, could there have been a true meritocracy when prior to the sixties 99 percent of all blacks and 99 percent of all women—two thirds of the population—were excluded from the competition regardless of their merit?

"But let's talk about now. It's the white men who have the experience," he said, "and until the minorities get it then you can't expect them to perform to the same high standards," he said.

He accepted the contention that they could not get the experience unless they were let in, making it absurd to say they shouldn't be let in until they have the experience. He laughed.

"Okay, I guess what you have to do is have special training programs and move the thing along gradually." He laughed again. "Yeah. I have to agree that a good percentage of the white males who run American industry are incompetent as hell. I'm sure there are women and minorities who could do a better job," he conceded.

As we interviewed other white males, it was hard for us to tell how much of the tidal wave of backlash was composed of men like Tyler, men who mean well but, deep in their hearts and against all reason, support and fuel backlash. At some point we learned that it is confusion, fear and different views of life, rather than hatred, that produce among so many white males this feeling that minorities and women are moving too fast.

We spoke to an older white man, a purchasing agent for a discount store chain. "I understand that these people have rights," he said in his New York buying office. He had once been a member of the Minority Purchasing Council, an organization which helped minority firms sell goods and services to major corporations, but he resigned because he had become disgusted with black efforts to become suppliers for the corporation he worked for. "Some of them are fine people who catch on to the business fast and have given us some good service, but then you get the rotten apples that spoil the barrel. They're late with shipments and they send the stuff out poorly packaged. If it is broken when it gets here, they want you to pay for it. I know it takes time and I know that any new company is bound to make this kind of mistake, but it's very touchy dealing with these Negro suppliers.

"I'm speaking solely from the point of view of this company. There's no way to deny that it ran better when you didn't have this influx of women and minorities.

"I'm not talking about skills *per se*. You're right: skills can be learned. I'm talking about the long period of disruption that we're in the middle of as we bring these people in and try to get them up to speed. Then you have to wonder if we're ever going to get women and minorities to fit in as smoothly as white males did in a system that contained only white males. I have to be frank. I'm talking about small things that make all the difference in the world. When you bring the racial and gender thing into the picture people are just not able to work with each other with the same kind of harmony they had when you were just dealing with one group—white males." He looked out the window.

He was speaking from the point of view of a man who had spent most of his working life in one of the tightest old-boy networks in America, the one that exists among purchasing agents and major suppliers to diversified retailers. Over long periods of time relationships are built up within this network between white men who are comfortable making deals among themselves by passing, perhaps, a little graft, a few favors, even if the favors are no larger than a free night out on the town chasing girls or tickets to the Super Bowl or a free color television set. This is all easier when the system contains nothing but good old boys.

"That's why the Japanese system works so well. Because you have one Jap talking to another Jap. There is a level of unity and understanding that makes the Japanese system cohesive," he said and turned back from the window. He did not seem, in any strict sense, a racist, nor did he seem to be a political Neanderthal. He said he was sure that a great many white males thought as he did.

His world was being invaded, from all sides. He said that frankly he didn't like having to buy so many of his lines from Japan, "But you can't get around it. They produce it better and they produce it cheaper. To stay in business that's what we have to buy—better and cheaper." He laughed.

He said he felt there was already enough affirmative action. He said that right now a minority or a woman had more rights than he had. "If I don't get promoted who can I complain to?"

This feeling that affirmative action programs created an avenue of redress for individual females and individual members of minority groups without creating such avenues for white males gave rise to outcries that the government was promoting discrimination in reverse.

One of the first books to advance this argument was Nathan Glazer's *Affirmative Discrimination*. Because of who he was—a distinguished author and editor, a Harvard sociology professor, an old-line liberal who had broken ranks and recanted his liberalism—because he was Nathan Glazer, *Affirmative Discrimination* was just about the largest intellectual salvo fired at affirmative action for black people.

Professor Glazer ignores the fact that affirmative action programs have been successful at getting corporations to reduce racial discrimination, which is, at the same time, illegal, immoral and counter to the best interest of the nation because in the long run it is not viable. He ignores the success in order to base his argument on the few instances when absurd confrontations between corporations and government enforcers produced lamentable results. He concentrates on the few instances, among the hundreds of thousands of hirings, firings and promotions that take place in corporate America, when a more senior or more qualified white candidate's plans were put on hold in order to advance a less experienced black candidate.

Arguing, as he did, that affirmative action programs should be scrapped because they do little to relieve the plight of the impoverished black masses was like arguing that aspirins should be scrapped because they do little to relieve brain cancer.

Arguing, as he did, that affirmative action destroyed the meritocracy was, again, to claim that a true meritocracy did exist back when two thirds of the American work force was barred from competing for most of the best jobs in America.

"Moreover," wrote William V. Shannon in a New York *Times* review of the book, "although in the long run merit must be the controlling consideration, everyone knows that there are many well-paid white collar jobs in our economy for which the criteria of competence are either so hard to define or so minimal that there are always enough white applicants whose hiring could be justified if the federal government did not intervene to make sure that blacks obtained their share of such jobs."

Honest white men admitted to us that even among white males there has never been a true meritocracy. One balding white vice-president of corporate affairs laughed at the idea of a meritocracy. "This is something that we've got people sold on. It's the myth that keeps the system going, but everyone knows that the person with the most merit is not the person who rises to the top. Are you kidding me?

"Listen," he said, speaking as an old boy to the new boys on the block. "I know a man right here in this company who has never been successful at a single goddamn assignment. He is ambitious and he knows how to kiss the right asses. He has bungled every assignment he's had.

"Right now he's in a vital position in the company, and they've given him a strong staff to support him, and his staff, I know, is happy when it can get things done effectively despite him. This is not an isolated example. This is just one glaring example of what I mean.

To a lesser or greater degree it operates all across the board. Everyone knows this.

"This meritocracy thing has always been a myth, but it is a necessary myth. It keeps the troops in line. It keeps them working as if their hard work will get them promoted. I'll tell you that one of the productivity problems in American industry today is caused by the fact that younger troops, white males, know that there's no such thing as a meritocracy."

He laughed. "I think they ought to let more minorities and women in because they work hard. They still believe in the meritocracy."

Another myth that was trotted out as soon as the mainstream began to show some diversity concerned the level of conformity and the nature of the conformity that is needed to produce the cohesiveness that a corporation says it needs.

Mary Cunningham, a white female who had been drummed out of a top-level corporate job because of claims that she was sleeping with the chairman of the board, said in an article in the Washington *Star* newspaper that one of the big problems of American industry is "the absence of a shared value system . . . A subsociety like a corporation is devoid of cohesion if it has no common values."

Instead of facing up to some of the complex reasons why American values themselves are in flux, and should be, many writers on corporate America claim that there are no cohesive corporate values because too many minorities and women have been forced in. As the purchasing agent said, "That's why the Japanese system [a cohesive value system] works so well. Because you have one Jap talking to another Jap."

This obsession for cohesion around a value system no matter what the content of the value system is creates the pressure on female and minority managers to become clones of white males, pressure on them to become "one Jap talking to another Jap."

In industry there seems to be a great urge to have this fabled national cohesion not so much to defeat the Russians in a possible war, but to defeat the Japanese in the fierce economic competition that is already underway.

As Richard Pascale and Anthony Athos say in their well-documented book *The Art of Japanese Management*:

A country the size of Montana, Japan has virtually no physical resources, yet it supports over 115 million people (half the population of the United States), exports $75 billion more goods than it imports, and has an investment rate as well as a GNP growth rate twice that of the United States. Japan has come to dominate one selected industry after another—eclipsing the British in motorcycles, surpassing the Germans and Americans in automobile production, wresting leadership from the Germans and Swiss in watches, cameras, and optical instruments, and overcoming the United States' historical dominance in businesses as diverse as steel, ship building, pianos, zippers and consumer electronics.

Few of us really want to face the truth that American industry has never been noted for efficiency—even when it was run totally by white males. Its great productive capacity was due to cheap, sometimes almost free labor and plentiful raw materials at home and cheap ones from abroad before underdeveloped countries who owned these raw materials became strong enough or sophisticated enough to start charging higher prices for them.

Furthermore, Pascale and Athos's book suggests that it is not the homogeneity so much as the content of the Japanese value system that makes Japanese industry so effective. This suggests that alterations in content, not a retreat to white male hegemony or management cloning, might be the key to the problem of inefficiency in American industry.

The inclusion of women and minorities in management, if handled properly, is our best chance of making the necessary changes in the content of our national work ethos and philosophy. The male emphasis on independence, dominance, egocentricism, rigidity, nonemotionalism, aggressiveness and self-reliance, coupled with the American drift toward "me-ism," short-term goals, personal career advancement above all else and self-promotion might form a set of values that can be homogeneously held, but these values cannot produce anything but an inefficient, spiritually empty work force whose internal pettiness and mutual antagonism, tough, subtle and controlled, is destructive of individual, group and national well-being.

America seems to need maturity of values rather than premature cohesion of clones. It needs to respect its female spirit and the spirits of its racial minorities.

Japanese companies are, for one thing, more nurturing, says *The Art of Japanese Management*. This gives the workers a sense of acceptance and security which makes them feel that they are working for *their* company, *their* nation. Western companies, built on the ideology of white males, are less nurturing. "Nurturing activities at work reveal that many male managers are uncomfortable and embarrassed at having to do what has traditionally been assigned to women in our culture." Male managers speak of nurturing activities in the most disparaging terms—"hand-holding," "breast-feeding," "wiping someone's nose."

Japanese managers and American women seem to have less trouble admitting that they don't know something. Several of the people we interviewed commented on how difficult humility is for the American male ego. Mistakes are often made simply because it is often impossible for the boss to admit in front of his charges that he doesn't know something as well as they might.

The emphasis in corporate life is on confidence, but nothing is more destructive than a fully confident blockhead—firm handshake, steady eye contact, square chin and empty head. "You can't be modest about yourself," said one young fresh-out-of-B-school manager we interviewed. Yet, in his case, as in many others, modesty could do him, and the company, a world of good. It could, for one thing, make it easier for him to learn.

"Even if you don't know, you've got to bluff it through or you'll lose control of your meeting," said a more senior manager who referred to himself as a tough son of a bitch who fought his way out of the stockroom into a middle-management job. American male toughness is often no more than a display of the most childish bravado. It was sad for us to hear a quaking female middle manager, who had the knowledge and charisma to exert leadership in other ways, refer to herself too as a tough little son of a bitch. It was sad that she had to assume this posture in order for her peers, superiors and subordinates to respect her. The unassuming Japanese style, or any unassuming female or black style, is likely to get lost in the mad scramble of egos that characterize the American corporate rat race. The authors of *The Art of Japanese Management* point out:

"Those who adopt a low profile are often better able to accomplish things than are their more markedly competitive colleagues. However, the Japanese value system which explicitly rewards this kind of behavior increases the likelihood of smooth internal organizational functioning."

Women in western society have a better history of keeping this kind of low profile when they are in supportive roles. One erroneous assumption that flows from *The Managerial Woman* is that women are not as good as team players because they did not play team sports as often as men in their formative years. The opposite argument can as easily be made. White women, at least, have been nothing other than good team players in their supportive roles as wives and mothers in middle-class white families. One of their most legitimate complaints seems to be that they have not always been given the respect they deserved for the roles they played on the teams.

"The managerial women often seek and achieve a higher development of interdependence than do their male colleagues," write Pascale and Athos. However, the authors go on to say, this is viewed so negatively by others in the corporation that these women (and minorities) often do not seek heightened relational satisfaction in the end. They often find corporate life most dissatisfying and many of them drop out of its cold sterility; those who remain suffer unduly trying to maintain themselves in a system that does not, on a human level, work well for anyone.

"Western companies," say the authors of *The Art of Japanese Management,* "tend to favor strategy, structure and systems. When an American manager wants to make changes, the odds are he'll reorganize *structure,* introduce a new *strategic* direction, impose a new control *system.*" The emphasis on these three S's "produces an arid world in which nothing is alive. An organization is often given its life through the soft S's: Staff, Skills (interpersonal skills included), Style (that produces smooth interpersonal relationships) and Superordinate Goals.

"The tremendous success of many Japanese companies," say the authors, is not due so much to a homogeneous racial population with a single-minded values system as to "Meticulous attention to the soft S's, which act as a lubricant in the organizational machine to keep the hard S's from grinding one another away."

More germane to our point, the authors go on to say:

> Perhaps it will occur to some readers, as it has to us, that the most important contribution many women might make to cor-

porate life would be to role-model the forms of interdependence that many men need to learn. That may be a troublesome pill for many executives to swallow, but research on the inclusion of other 'strangers' into companies suggests that those companies which include minorities are better managed in general than those which do not. It appears that the inclusion of different 'cultures' in a corporation widens its repertoire of behavior, which in turn makes it more effective generally (and not just in meeting affirmative action quotas).

PART TWO

V

WHY BOTHER?

WITH ALL THE TROUBLES that black managers referred to in the previous chapter, the question arises: "Why did so many of them fight so hard to be in managerial life, to suffer the alienation, the culture shock, the racism, the all-consuming work load, the psychological discomforts of the period of adjustment and the prospect that even after the period of adjustment a tremendously pressure-filled existence awaits those who expect to succeed or even to stay afloat?"

Unless one keeps in mind during the entire reading of the book some of the material of this present chapter, the above question begs another question: "Why don't they just quit, or why did they come in in the first place?"

The most obvious answer to the begged question is: "If they did quit where would they work? And what would it matter?" There is no other world large enough to hold them but the corporate world. They don't quit for the same reasons that whites cannot quit: Like it or not, corporations dominate modern life. For example, the way corporations develop their managers will dictate the value preferences of the entire middle class of the nation, and in a modern democracy middle-class values are national values.

Right now corporations can have the greatest possible impact on black underemployment and unemployment. Already a great number of blacks work for federal, state and local governments. A disproportionate number of them work in the military. Nothing is left but the private sector, where, for example, in 1980 the Fortune Top 1000 companies had $1.2 trillion in assets and employed 17.6 million people.

That blacks complain about corporate jobs is not surprising. Most Americans complain about their jobs.

That most Americans complain is made very clear in the book *Working* by Studs Terkel. Most of the interviewees featured are white. Most of them complain. Terkel quotes from William Faulkner to suggest one of the reasons: "You can't eat for eight hours a day nor drink for eight hours a day nor make love for eight hours a day— all you can do for eight hours is work. Which is the reason why man makes himself and everyone else so miserable and unhappy."

The last sentence, we feel, is something of an overstatement, but the entire passage underscores the point that work is the predominant experience of adult life, and if people complain about having to work eight hours, consider how many more complaints they might have if they had to work ten or twelve, if they had to take work home on weekends instead of leaving it on Friday evenings. This is what managers do.

But managers also do what might be considered "better" work than most of the people in Terkel's book. There are many factors involved. The most crucial factor is that we have no way of measuring happiness or unhappiness. When people are asked in a certain way, they say they are "satisfied" with their work. This is true of blacks and whites, and it is also true that when asked in another way most people will say they hate their work. An interesting survey is found in *Work in America,* edited by Clark Kerr and Jerome Rosow (see top of page 71).

Commenting on these surveys Amitai Etzioni, professor of sociology at Columbia University, concluded that satisfaction levels among blacks might be slightly different in relation to certain aspects of the job, but on the whole they appear to be not a great deal lower than among whites. The surveys suggest, then, that a relatively high number of black workers do find their jobs satisfying.

Of the one hundred black managers interviewed by Richard America and Bernard Anderson for their book *Moving Ahead,* about a fourth were described as satisfied, about the same number were dissatisfied and the remaining half were "cautiously optimistic." In 1979 the international management consulting and executive search firm Heidrick and Struggles mailed questionnaires to 638 men and women identified as black executives in newspapers, magazines and

PERCENTAGE OF "SATISFIED" WORKERS, 1958–1977

YEAR	SOURCE	PERCENT "SATISFIED"
1958	Survey Research Center*	81
1963	Gallup Poll*	89
1962	National Opinion Research Center	83
1964	Survey Research Center, University of California	91
1964	National Opinion Research Center*	92
1965	Gallup Poll*	87
1966	Gallup Poll*	92
1966	Gallup Poll*	89
1969	Survey Research Center	85
1969	Gallup Poll*	92
1971	Survey Research Center	91
1971	Gallup Poll*	88
1971	Gallup Poll*	86
1973	Gallup Poll*	88
1973	Survey Research Center	90
1974	National Opinion Research Center	85
1975	National Opinion Research Center	87
1976	National Opinion Research Center	86
1977	Survey Research Center	88

Males only; all others comprise both sexes.

directories. Fifty-nine percent returned the questionnaires. While keeping in mind the limitations inherent in such a survey method, the survey found even more positive results:

Black executives express an above average degree of satisfaction with their career progress. More than 71 percent rated their satisfaction as either high or very high, and only 6 percent described it as below average. Just one individual expresses very low satisfaction with his progress. The level of career satisfaction evidenced by blacks is comparable to that of women officers and is not significantly lower than that of senior corporate officers. However, possibly because of rising expectations, the average level of satisfaction among black executives declines with age.

Our book has a great deal more to say about the latter part of the Heidrick and Struggles statement, but otherwise the findings of the H&S survey are not very dissimilar to our impressionistic look at the work life of the black manager.

Although many of the people we interviewed said they liked their jobs, the way we asked our questions tended to bring out more discontent than would surface in a mailed questionnaire. We were *looking* for racial problems, in order to examine the kinds that still exist in corporate America, more than eighteen years after the passage of the Civil Rights Act.

We knew that our results were bound to be more negative than the results of the *Work in America* surveys or the survey by Heidrick and Struggles. We also knew we were going to find more discontent than Richard America and Bernard Anderson. We probed for areas of discontent in order that black managers could get a clear view of them and therefore be in better positions to root them out. We wanted corporations to have the fresh insights of these new managerial recruits so that corporations might see some of the conditions that only those new to the environment have the innocence to see.

By concentrating on problems we are not trying to suggest that black managers function with constant awareness of racial problems. If so they would not be doing, on the whole, so fine a job. That many blacks suppress awareness, that in fact the corporation demands that its managers suppress awareness, is evident in two cases that we came across during the interviewing. A cheerful, laughing black female manager in the governmental affairs office of a major company said she had absolutely no racial problems on her job.

About three days later she called back crying to tell us that she had been thinking about our question and she wanted to talk about how hard it was to function in a situation where suggestions were ignored. She said she would be in a meeting and no one would acknowledge her comments. They would simply listen to her and then continue the discussion among themselves.

Even when at a later date they would find out that her comments if heeded would have caused the group to arrive at a better decision than they arrived at, even then they would not acknowledge her because they wouldn't even remember she made a comment.

Sometimes she would go to meetings that concerned affairs in her area, and the white males would still talk around her. "After the decision had already been made, one of them would turn to me and ask me if I had any suggestions, as the others were scraping their chairs against the floor, pushing back from the table to leave."

Her delay could indicate one of several things: racial problems are so infrequent that it took her a long time to remember them; in order to function she represses a sense of these problems; compared to other kinds of problems in the corporation or compared to racial problems in the society in general, her corporate racial problems didn't amount to much.

On the other hand, there were managers who talked about the corporate environment as a living hell for the black manager. We heard repeatedly that when you reach a certain level your career is stopped dead by the unwillingness of white males to accept blacks into the decision-making positions at the top of the company, or to accept them in line management jobs that control profit-and-loss. "And," said a young Pittsburgh-based personnel manager speaking of his own job, "you're not really a power in the company unless your activity directly relates to profit-and-loss."

What happens when the black manager bumps his or her head against the relatively low ceilings? It's certain that this adds additional stress to an already stress-filled life. Since black people have been more accustomed to handling stress, many black managers do not speak up about their frustrations. They do not want to feel like complainers and they perceive that whites do not really want to hear their complaints. This is illustrated by a second story told to us by a middle level white manager in Denver about a black coworker.

"I had no idea that Ray was having serious problems. He was always joking and happy. I used to go out drinking with him and we used to talk about things, but I didn't think about them as deeply as he must have. I guess when it's not happening to you, you tend not to dwell on it, and I'm sure if he had dwelled on negative things I would not have wanted to keep going out drinking with him. That's why I was very surprised when he went home from work one Friday, pulled all the phones out of the wall and blew his brains out."

What had happened to Ray is that he had worked extremely hard for a promotion. He had already been passed over three times and so he was three steps behind many of his contemporaries. He was bright and everyone in the district thought that he was going to finally get his promotion. The Monday before he killed himself his boss had called him in and apologetically told him that the company had decided to promote someone else. The someone was a white male of less experience and far less education, a white male whom he had trained. This was the second time that this had happened. He freaked out.

An article in the June 1981 issue of *Psychology Today* asks: "Can Companies Kill?" We know of course they can, but we also know they can be very fine places to work.

"Most people are going to say that they like their jobs," said Bill Waters, a manager in the quality-control department of a major textile-manufacturing firm, "because they look at a job as a necessary evil, and it's impossible to spend so much time on a job if you ever start admitting to yourself that you don't really want to be there. You psych yourself up for it. You learn how to enjoy the benefits it offers and ignore the things you don't like.

"The main psych factor is the money, and the knowledge that if you were not working for the XYZ Corporation, where in the world would you be? Unemployed. This is the context in which you have to understand the comment 'I like my job.'

"This is why they hate these people on welfare who don't have to put up with the bullshit they have to put up with, and they really hate them too. They would rather money be wasted in almost any other way than spent on someone who doesn't have to put up with what they have to put up with. I think these satisfaction percentages are unreliable."

Evaluating the meaning of something as complex as job satisfaction is found to create some ambiguities. This mood is captured in the hyperbole that opens Studs Terkel's book:

> This book, being about work, is, by its very nature, about violence—to the spirit as well as to the body. It is about ulcers as well as accidents, about shouting matches as well as fist fights, about nervous breakdowns as well as kicking the dog around. It is, above all (or beneath all), about daily humiliations. To

survive the day is triumph enough for the walking wounded among the great many of us.

The scars, psychic as well as physical, brought home to the supper table and the TV set, may have touched malignantly, the soul of our society. More or less. ("More or less," that most ambiguous of phrases, pervades many of the conversations that comprise this book, reflecting, perhaps, an ambiguity of attitude toward The Job. Something more than Orwellian acceptance, something less than Luddite sabotage. Often the two impulses are fused in the same person.)

For the black manager the struggle can be even greater because, consciously or subconsciously, many of them are attempting to acquire a better grasp of the ethos of the managerial life while holding on to the rhythms of their own black lives. We mean "rhythms" in the broadest sense. We mean not simply the beat and pace of life but the entire spectrum of actions and reactions that seem to blacks more natural and therefore more human. This is the black conceit.

Contrary to popular stereotypes, black Americans, especially those who held it together well enough to make it into corporate management, are likely to be very tradition-oriented. In their own ways they are firm believers in the Protestant ethic and the strong morality that this implies, and, as we will see later, they have been taught that it is hard work, and nothing else, that will save them.

Despite the racial stereotype, they are among the strongest believers in delayed gratification. Few people in America can claim to be more long-suffering. "If there is one thing that I know how to do," said a branch manager of a major office equipment company, "it's sacrifice."

Yet these same managers might have received from their culture a love for style and grace. And they have as strong, if not stronger, needs for the things that those fat corporate salaries can buy.

"I like the money," said a brown-skinned woman with a flyaway hairdo who works as a manager in Training and Programs for a major electronics firm. "I have two children to raise by myself and I like the money."

Money is probably the most obvious of all reasons for undergoing "management development." In the past blacks who desired high incomes usually had to become doctors or undertakers. Some became small shop-keepers and businessmen, especially in real estate, and managed to become well-to-do. A few had the strength and capability to build million-dollar businesses and to get their picture in *Black Enterprise* magazine. Nearly all of these businesses catered to the needs of black people.

Some black lawyers were able to build lucrative practices, and ministers of large churches often did well. But now blacks by the thousands can earn high wages by simply, or not so simply, getting into, and hanging on to, the corporate life.

"I tell you the truth," said a female assistant production manager in a large food products firm, "I like knowing I can buy things that I used to only dream of. When I see a Jaguar on a sunny day it gives me great satisfaction to know that I could afford to buy one if I chose too. I like my Datsun 280Z. I have no intention of buying a Jaguar, but it makes me feel good to know that I can buy one if I want to, and to know that the person riding in the Jaguar is no better than I am. It makes you feel like you're part of the big world."

"I like being able to travel anywhere I want," said another female manager in Atlanta. "With money I can do that. I travel for my job, which is great, but I can also choose to go somewhere on my own without having to worry about the cost. On one week's salary I can take a vacation in the Caribbean. I know people who save all their lives and can't afford to take that kind of vacation. I can also fly to Washington for a Saturday-night party and be back in Atlanta for work on Monday. I like that kind of freedom."

"The money is important," said a retired Air Force major who now had a second career as a corporate affairs manager, "but it's really only an indication of how much they value you, which is related to how much you value yourself. Because if you're working for less than what you should be getting at your level and your experience then you've not set a high enough value on yourself. In America, money is the measure of your worth."

A tall light-skinned woman who after graduating from Howard University had earned an M.B.A. from the University of Indiana said she liked to keep tabs on what others were making for the exact purpose of knowing how much the company valued her presence, "and to know how hard to push when I'm looking for a raise, or if I'm looking to change companies." She pulled out a large accordionlike computer print-out which contained data on the entire managerial staff at corporate headquarters. "This material is confidential, but anyone who wants to buy it can get it."

The computer sheet showed that the chairman of the board earned $527,000 per year and that the assistant to the chairman, his private secretary, earned $32,000. The president earned $478,000 a year and his assistant earned $29,000. Various senior officers of the company earned amounts in the $200,000–$400,000 range. Scores of them earned more than $100,000 and other younger, fast-track managers were in the $80,000–$90,000 range. She seemed very proud of the computer sheets. The fact that sheets like this are secretly distributed inside her company suggested that the internal politics of the company were rough. She confirmed this opinion. "You ought to see some of the things that the white guys do to each other—it's rough."

She told about dirty rumor campaigns, and she told about times when projects were set up to fail in order to embarrass certain people and prevent them from getting promoted. She knew of situations where people were given false information to act on.

Some managers said that these myths were exaggerations, while others said that in some companies the politics are so bad that "you have to spend half your time covering your ass."

"This is the highest black guy in the company," the woman continued as she further unfolded the accordionlike computer print-out. "He gets a hundred and thirty-seven thousand per year. His title"—she ran her thin fingers across the page—"assistant general counsel. His age"—she let her fingers flow to the next line—"forty-one. Marital status: married. I got the data," she declared proudly. "This guy's also black," she said pointing to another entry on the sheet. "He's the director of community affairs—seventy-eight thousand dollars."

Her company seemed typical of many of the more progressive companies in the Fortune 500—three or four blacks in solid middle-management staff positions at corporate headquarters, and about three or four times that many at about the same level scattered in various functions in the Districts and Regions. We heard of only a few of the five hundred that had a black in what could be considered senior management. Of the black managers we interviewed none earned more than $200,000, but five said they earned in excess of $100,000. Of those included in the Heidrick and Struggles study, about a third earned $35,000 or less, a third earned in excess of $50,000—good salaries, but not great in corporate terms.

"Giving up that money. Giving up that money—that's the hardest thing to do," said a nut-brown, thin-faced manager. "If I had inherited wealth, of course I would quit this kind of organized life, but there's no way I can go back to making eighteen thousand dollars a year." This man worked as an assistant to a regional vice-president. He also commented on the amount of expense-account padding that nearly all corporate traveling people do simply as a matter of course. "When I'm on the road, I'm not even dipping into my salary."

The financial inducement is the grand inducement, and it is even more powerful when a manager dreams of the possibility of reaching the top. An article in the June 1981 *Forbes* revealed just how much some of the big boys at the top get paid. The top Chief Executive Officer listed was Thomas Pickens of Mesa Petroleum, who earned an estimated $7,865,831 in salary, bonuses, benefits, contingencies and stock gains. George T. Scharffenberger, of City Investing, earned $5,165,892 to place second in the top ten. Robert Anderson of Rockwell International placed tenth with $2,966,993—great money to dream about.

This does not take into account the financial reward that simply comes from running corporations with sales in the billion dollar range—and much of the income is tax sheltered in very ingenious ways.

Many of the benefits given to top-level corporate managers keep them from having to use their own money for such things as automobiles and life insurance, theater tickets and box seats at sporting events, three-martini lunches and city club memberships, financial planning help and legal help, home entertainment and relocation allowances. And many of these perks filter down to middle management, where black faces do show up. In addition, the benefits to all employees make managerial life more attractive. One company we know of needed a one-hundred-page, four-color brochure to outline all the benefits it offered its employees.

The woman we interviewed from this company kept the brochure on her coffee table along with recent copies of *Ebony* and *Cosmopolitan* magazines. The brochure contained information on medical and dental plans for the entire family, on life insurance and disability income, on profit sharing and stock options, on retirement plans and saving plans, on vacations and social service leaves, on tuition assistance and separation pay, on credit unions and health-care counseling for problem drinkers or drug abusers, on physical-fitness and weight-loss programs. It claimed that the new employee was not starting a job but starting a relationship, being ushered into a way of life. It should not be surprising that blacks from secretaries to vice-presidents find this life attractive.

Corporations satisfy a vast number of tangible needs. They do so as attractively, if not as snugly, as, for example, the civil services or the officers' corps of the American military. Our interviewees gave us many examples of how corporations also satisfy a wide variety of intangible needs.

A comprehensive list of these needs appears in Abraham H. Maslow's *Motivation and Personality*. American corporations are fairly good at satisfying what Maslow calls safety needs—security; stability; dependency; protection; freedom from fear, anxiety and chaos; form structure; order; law; limits; etc. Though the corporate environment is often filled with anxiety, the corporation itself is a haven from some of the other anxieties of the outside world.

Corporations are not so good, however, at satisfying the need for community and love, although we certainly found black managers who enjoyed corporate life because they did like the idea of *belonging* to an important organization, the idea of being included in a pleasant way of life.

An information systems manager in Detroit said, "I like working in a place where there is not a lot of bickering and pettiness. Actually I prefer being at work to being at home. People cooperate to get a job done in an atmosphere that is very cordial. If you want to know the truth, corporate America is the most peaceful place I've found. It certainly is more peaceful than either the home I was raised in or the home I have to go home to every night after work."

A very serious looking woman at a crowded corporate happy hour in Westchester County, New York, told us: "I like working with people from different backgrounds. I like managing people's careers. In the personnel function, you get a chance to develop managers and I take a personal interest in each manager that I help to develop. I get a great deal of personal satisfaction making the right fit for a particular job and then seeing that things run smoothly. Fitting managers in is like fitting pieces into a puzzle. We have seven thousand people in our division. We have the cash to bring them from other companies and it's my job to help orient them to our particular mode of operation. I enjoy doing this."

Another female manager, at the same interview, added that she liked getting dressed up each day and going downtown. "I love clothes. If I didn't have a good job, I wouldn't have the occasion to get dressed up each day and get in my car and go into the city.

"I've always loved dressing. It makes me feel good about myself, and it gives me confidence when I meet people if I know that what I have on is correct. In a corporation you can't be too way-out with your dress, but I find some way in the most standardized outfit to express how I feel about good-quality clothing.

"Don't get me wrong. I take my job seriously, but I don't take it so seriously that I can't take myself seriously. And to tell you the truth, I like being around well-dressed, nice-looking people, and the people in corporate America are about the best-groomed group of people you can find anywhere. So I like just moving around in the building, getting on the elevators—nothing tacky."

Another manager in the compensation section of a chemical company said she liked the contact with all kinds of people because it proves to her that she can relate to employees from the janitors all the way to the regional vice-president. "There are fourteen hundred employees in the region and I am in the benefits section. I like helping people. I enjoy seeing that people exercise all of their benefit options. It's my job to see that employees keep up with policies, procedures and changes that are important to them."

One public-information manager simply liked the fact that he worked for the largest company in the world. A few black managers we interviewed had vital staff jobs or decision-making line management jobs. However, even many of those at entry-level staff jobs seemed to enjoy working in an environment of power.

Another manager in the data center of a major corporation said, "I like being around these big white boys to see how they make decisions." One admiring manager in the pricing department of the wholesale division of a large chemical firm said he was particularly thrilled over the way that "a six-billion-dollar company [like his own] attempts to take over a four-billion-dollar company against the wishes of the four-billion-dollar company's board of directors."

He enjoyed reading about these battles between financial giants. Then lo!, his company made a tender offer to take over a smaller company simply because, it was rumored, his chairman didn't like the chairman of the smaller company. His eyes glowed when he talked about it. Being inside the raiding company did not give him inside information, but everything he read in the papers on this matter had added importance for him. When he went to work each day he felt himself a part of the take-over.

He added that he would not be dismayed if a bigger company tried to take over his company. It didn't matter to him who owned his workplace. He simply liked the excitement. Evidently everyone else in the office did too, because they talked about it with a tingle of excitement and humor in their voices. This was a more important game than Monday-night football.

This manager loved the Corporate Strategies section of *Business Week*, which was his favorite magazine. *Business Week* and *Fortune* and *Forbes* and *The Wall Street Journal* provided more enjoyment for him and filled more of his empty hours than *Playboy*, *Ebony*, ABC, NBC and CBS combined. He simply loved to read about money.

"I don't know," he said excitedly, "corporations have the power to shape the world and I do like being a part of that. I don't have real power but my job brings me in touch with all the big whiteys in the company. It's fascinating to me how they make deals.

"I remember I was in the chairman's office at a meeting and his secretary came in and said that the President of the United States was calling him. In Civics 101 I learned that the President of the United States was the most powerful man in the world and that people jump when he calls. The chairman of our company told his secretary to ask the President of the United States what he wanted, and to 'tell him I'm tied up, I'll call him back.' Wow! That blew my mind."

Belonging to something significant is indeed one of the intangible reasons why many people choose corporate life. Others choose it or find when they are in it that it satisfies another important group of needs. We, as humans, says Maslow, need opportunities to display our personal strengths. We like gaining a sense of achievement and a sense of adequacy, mastery and competence. Corporations certainly do give outlets for this sort of self-expression, even in jobs that are sometimes described as demanding, boring, repetitive, paper-pushing, overlong, stifling, unchallenging.

"I like the satisfaction of turning raw data into good results," said a financial analyst for a major cosmetics firm. "Most people in management are intimidated by numbers. I'm not, and so I get pleasure out of working with numbers in a way that will make them understandable to others."

"I like affecting the outcome of a project," said a surprisingly young black man who was product manager for a major convenience-food manufacturer. "I like seeing something happen because of something I did. When I'm given the opportunity to make decisions, I'm happy as long as I get support from senior management for those decisions. So far this has happened and so I get the chance to see what I've worked on materialize on a giant scale.

"For example, I had the major responsibility of repositioning one of our products in the product line. This gave me a chance to show what I could do. The product was sold in canisters and the consumer got just as much product as she would with a competing brand, but the competing brands were sold in glass jars and so the competing product felt heavier, which made the consumer feel that she was getting more. It was a question of perceived value. The last product manager thought that the light weight made our product more convenient to carry home, etc., but as soon as I became product manager I had the company change over to glass jars. In canisters we were selling fifteen tons of the product annually. This year I project that we'll sell eighty-seven tons of the product. Can you imagine how happy that makes me feel? I've been walking on a cloud for months," he said.

A salesman of office equipment said, "I like being out in the streets all day and my job keeps me running. I couldn't make it if I had to stay in an office, but a job in sales gives me a chance to move around and talk to different kinds of people."

In short, he liked his job, as did a great number of the managers we talked to. There were things about the job that they didn't like but they nearly all viewed careers in corporate management as symbolic of full participation in the life of America. They were in the mainstream, which is where most people want to be. This, in summary, is why they bothered.

VI

DIFFERENT STROKES

> Yes, we is all the same under God so we has the same prob-
> lems, but colored folk has special ones, too. It's the same being
> colored as white but it's different being colored, too.
> Then she repeated as though to emphasize the words: "it's
> the same, but it's different."

EVERYONE KNOWS SOME OF THE many truths that are buried within
this statement made by an elderly black woman to author Robert
Coles in the late nineteen sixties. For one thing black people look
different, and even this is a crucial, influential factor on corporate
life.

For example, John T. Molloy wrote in *Dress for Success*:

> It is an undeniable fact that the typical upper-middle-class
> American looks white, Anglo-Saxon and Protestant. He is of
> medium build, fair complexion, with almost no pronounced
> physical characteristics . . . Like it or not, his appearance will
> normally elicit a positive response from someone viewing him.
> Anyone not possessing his characteristics will elicit a negative
> response in some degree, regardless of whether that response is
> conscious or subconscious.

Physical appearance determines how people are treated, how the
world reacts to them and therefore it determines a person's way of
acting or reacting to the world. But there are some deeper
differences. Even when economic factors are similar blacks are generally reared with what might be called a different set of cultural
values.

In this area definition becomes elusive. These are things that everyone knows about but no one can measure, that cause the more scientific-minded person to try to either establish a means of measuring them or insist that they do not exist.

Among several of the white managers we interviewed there was a strong desire to deny the existence of significant differences. Understandably the pressure inside the corporation is for people to look at each other as if "we're all the same."

"What's the difference between a white internal audits manager and a black internal audits manager? What's the difference between a white male internal controls guy and a black female doing the same job?" asked Robert Collins, a white male who is a regional director of market planning.

He held his conviction so deeply that it made him red in the face to talk about it. "There is absolutely no difference." To him a manager was an entity trained to fill a slot the perimeters of which are set down in a job description. To him, anyone, including anyone black, who insisted that there was a difference was guilty of racism.

So a black manager who worked for such a man, and there are many white males like him, might look up from his or her desk at various times during the day, feeling different, but not knowing what to make of the differences; and certainly not knowing if they should ever be talked about.

The black manager might sense that the differences are affecting his or her career, but he or she doesn't know how or how much. Very often the differences affect the comfort level, but he or she will not know what to do about this because no one ever actually says that he or she is different.

Whites are often embarrassed to talk about racial differences, as if these discussions might reveal some embarrassing underlying assumptions of western civilization. Blacks certainly don't want to talk about them because the entire dialogue has been tainted by concepts of white racial superiority.

So it is possible to walk the corridors of many major corporations and assume incorrectly that racial differences must be inconsequential or else there would be at least some talk about them.

"I've never heard anyone in this company talk about racial differences, which would be all right if that meant that no one thinks about them. It would mean that everyone could be themselves, go ahead and do their jobs and that would be that. But it's not all right because blacks are still not given a fair and equal chance for most of the important jobs, because we're looked at as being different," said an EEO manager in Cleveland.

"The corporate climate is filled with the assumption that the black manager is a 'deficit model,'" said Dr. Price M. Cobbs, the coauthor with William Grier of *Black Rage,* to a meeting of the Black Alumni Association of Harvard Business School. "Most black managers with whom we talk tell us that they feel that they are viewed in their organizations as 'deficit models,' and that they are assumed to be incompetent until they prove the opposite."

Cobbs's impressions are based on fourteen years of consulting, during which time he has talked with over five thousand black managers and at least that many white managers in corporate America. This is certainly a large enough sample for us to assume that the attitude is pervasive. The managers we talked with confirmed Cobbs's contention; thus the silence inside corporations on matters of race must be filled with such typically western ideas as either 1) that blacks are not intelligent enough to make it in management, and those black managers who do make it are exceptions, or 2) that blacks have the wrong kind of cultural values to do as good a job as the typical white male can do:

"Sure, there is a perception on the part of many, if not most, whites in corporations that whites are more intelligent than we are," said a tall young black man who had finished Harvard with a bachelor of science degree in mathematics. "One of my managers asked me if I had gone to Harvard under a special 'black' program. This was his way to counterfeit my degree. Then he asked me if I had gone on a basketball scholarship. He was grinning but he was serious.

"This is certainly what goes on in the heads of some of the older white managers who didn't go to school with black kids. They came up in corporations believing that blacks were not managers because blacks were not smart enough to be managers. These kinds of beliefs are very hard to change. Even when there is a lot of evidence in your favor.

"I also think they have an emotional investment in believing that they are smarter than you—even ones who are very sympathetic to you. Often they won't give you an assignment because they don't think you're intelligent enough to handle it, and it could be the dumbest little assignment," he concluded.

"You'll always find yourself being second in charge behind a white guy; even if he's dumb they will trust him more," said a young woman who had graduated with honors from the University of Maryland.

"I'll give you an example," she said. "I remember that I had to fly out to Cleveland to deliver and explain a marketing plan that I drew up. My manager made me go over it three or four times in front of him so he could be sure I wouldn't forget what I was supposed to say —about *my* marketing plan. Then he took me to lunch and told me when I got to the airport I could check my luggage. I didn't have to carry it on the plane. He told me to be sure I got a baggage claim check, and not to worry because my bags would be flying out to Cleveland with me in the baggage compartment of the same plane, and when I got to Cleveland the baggage would be delivered to the baggage area, and there would be a sign telling me where the baggage area was. I just sat at lunch listening to this man talking to me like I was a monkey who could remember but couldn't think.

"Then he told me that near the baggage area there would be a sign marked 'Hertz' and I should go to the counter under the sign and ask for a rental car. It was funny. He had taken me to lunch to tell me this. I asked him if he wanted to tie my money up in a handkerchief and put a note on me saying that I was an employee of this company. In case I got lost I would be picked up by Traveler's Aid, and Traveler's Aid would send me back home.

"When he got my point, he got red in the face. He was very embarrassed. He was man enough, however, to admit that he had never felt the need to do all this with one of his white managers, and it did mean that he had an unconscious feeling that blacks did not know how to take an airplane. I should have told him to get me two bags of fried chicken wings and I'd take the Greyhound bus from Stamford, Connecticut, to Cleveland."

Another black manager said, "I had a manager once who would ask every one of my white peers the answer to a certain question, and it would never occur to him to ask me. He simply assumed that I didn't know. I remember once he wanted to know the capital of Burma. So he asked everyone around me. No one knew. He called his wife at home and got her to look it up in a set of encyclopedias.

"She came back with the answer Mandalay. He put that name in the report he was writing. At first I decided to let it go, and then I changed my mind. I went up to his desk and reached over his shoulder and crossed out Mandalay and wrote Rangoon just above it. 'Rangoon is the capital.' He looked up, surprised. 'Why didn't you tell us, Louis?' he said. I said: 'You didn't ask me. You asked the person to the left of me then you skipped over me and asked the person to the right of me.' I asked him if he noticed that he had asked everyone in the section except me, and it never occurred to him that since I was fresh out of the Vietnam War and had been in Southeast Asia, I should have been the one he asked first."

Geneticists, biologists, psychologists, sociologists, environmentalists and others have all had a hand at studying black people's intelligence and comparing it to that of whites. Surprising and definitive conclusions have been published and have changed forever the views expressed in former conclusions, which were, when they were first published, surprising and definitive.

During the second two decades of this century intelligence measurements, especially by anthropologists, placed the intelligence of black men halfway between monkeys and white men. Fortunately blacks have been doing so well lately that the scientific community is almost ready to concede that the average black just might be as intelligent as the average white. Groups of whites still score higher on "standard" intelligence tests, but in certain instances, groups of blacks score higher than groups of whites.

Sympathetic scientists explained the differences in scores by citing differences in nutrition, family disorganization, father absences, educational deprivations, levels of exposure to culture and responses to the testing process itself. And even when blacks score lower on "standard" intelligence tests they often function in real life situations indistinguishably from their white counterparts.

Unsympathetic scientists, however, have not simply given up. They argue that even when an individual or a group of black people scores higher than an individual or a group of white people, still the black gene pool doesn't score as high as the white gene pool. Not that any of them have ever given a "standard" intelligence test to a gene.

The perception of black intelligence has changed radically over the years. For example, once the owners of some National Football League teams seemed to agree that blacks were not smart enough to play organized football, and after this was proven to be untrue, they seemed to agree that blacks were not smart enough to play quarterback or middle linebacker. The second assumption proved to be untrue also.

"You know what it really is?" said a black manager in the public-relations department of a major electronics corporation. "The quickest way, one of the best ways to get promoted in a corporation, is to destroy as much of the competition as you can, so you have some ruthless white managers who get the edge on the black competition by playing on the prejudice of their superiors. While they are out drinking together, they plant doubts about the black guy's intelligence. They do it subtly: 'George is a good man. Great sense of humor. Ha-ha-ha. He's really a card, but do you think he's smart enough to handle the new job?' This is how it's done."

Many other managers agreed that there was a general perception on the part of whites that blacks were generally not very intelligent. "This is illustrated," one black manager said, "by how surprised they get in meetings when you come up with a good answer to a question or a good solution to a problem. They're stunned. It is also reinforced by how often whites veto the intelligent suggestions that the black manager makes. It is difficult for many white men to accept any idea that is not their own, and so sometimes you have to come up with an idea and give it to a white boy and make him think it was his idea, let him get promoted and hope that he will remember that he needs you to come up with good ideas, so he'll get you promoted right along behind him. But you have to be careful that he doesn't begin to think you're trying to move past him by giving suggestions directly to the unit head. You know what the irony is. The irony is that most corporate jobs don't even require that much intelligence."

Undoubtedly many writers on corporate affairs would agree that high intelligence, quick wit, deep intellect are not the qualities most needed to perform in most corporate jobs, especially those outside the research and development area. But many of these writers would insist that there are other qualities that the corporate manager must have and that it is in some of these qualities that blacks are lacking.

This usually brings them into the nebulous area of human values. In the stereotypic views held by most Americans blacks and whites seem to possess different values. There may be some truth in these stereotypic views, but the truth is certainly hard to quantify and impossible to apply to any particular individual.

There are blacks with solid, businesslike, no-nonsense sets of values and there are whites with more free-form, emotional, unstructured orientations to life. And so it is certainly foolish to try to make even these stereotypes fit. And yet we do worse than this, we apply the uglier kinds of stereotype to people of the opposite race:

Whites are cold, mercenary and hung-up. Blacks are lazy, criminal and in search of something for nothing. The overall point is that when one race looks at another in America, it sees some differences and it tries to name these differences. It tries to measure them, it tries to apply them to individuals and it often tries to deny them at the same time that it is trying to wrestle with them.

One of the ways that corporations try to wrestle with value differences is to hire black consultants to teach courses like the one we attended in Washington called "Black Values and Corporate Norms." The consultant who runs the course said:

"Since personal values are influenced by so many factors, it is natural that there would be some differences between the preponderant values of whites in America and the values that most often characterize black life-style. And yes," she said, "I've heard it said that blacks do not make good managers because their values are different from the values of white managers, who represent the norm in major American corporations."

Another consultant who gives a similar course said, "Yes, there are some differences. If there were no differences there would be no need for the kind of courses we give. And these kinds of courses are becoming increasingly popular."

"Yes," said still another consultant who also gives the same kind of courses, "there are some subtle but significant differences. The discussion of values tends to become quite vague because of a certain vagueness of definition, but it is certain that the cultural values that a manager holds will influence his or her effectiveness as a manager."

Values determine what a person considers true, right, good, worthy, desirable, ethical. They provide the standards and norms which control day-to-day behavior. Shared values provide an invisible link between people who have to interact in a certain situation, giving them shared assumptions and premises that inform their behavior without having to be verbalized or even recognized. Cultural values are usually so deeply accepted that the individuals who hold them are not at all aware of them, but any individual who holds other values is automatically judged to be wrong.

Values generally determine a manager's attitude toward causes and issues. They exert a powerful influence on the types of people a manager will feel comfortable with.

It is natural then that assumptions about differences in values should cause some problems for blacks trying to make it in corporate America. First there is an assumption that the values held by whites are the right values for the effective performance of corporate tasks, and there is the idea that any conflict in values will create friction in the smooth interpersonal relationships that are so important to the function of the corporation.

Values are hard to define. One study suggests that, at least on personality tests, whites seem to score themselves higher on responsiveness, dominance, compliance and thoughtfulness; and conversely blacks score themselves lower on all four of these scales. "But these scores are based on culturally conditioned perceptions and self-perceptions," said a black industrial psychologist. "That's the reason many personality tests are suspect as tools in personnel placement. They score perceptions and not actualities. They indicate how a person responds to a test and not how they respond to real-life situations. I'm not saying that there is no validity to the findings of these kinds of tests, but there are tests that show exactly the opposite—that blacks score higher in responsiveness, dominance, compliance and thoughtfulness." But this depends on how these terms are defined.

In racially mixed play groups, for example, it is most often the black male who rises as the natural leader of the group—so much for dominance. There are other tests which show that blacks are more sympathetic to others and therefore more responsive and that blacks have more anxiety about their jobs and therefore they tend to comply with rules and regulations more rigidly than whites—compliance?

In a study cited in *Comparative Studies of Negroes and Whites in the United States,* E. W. McClain "showed" blacks were more outgoing, less intelligent, less emotionally stable, more practical, more controlled, and more tender-minded emotionally.

McClain's study of college students "showed" that black males were more humble. Yet one of the corporate charges against black male managers is that they are too arrogant. McClain found that the black male college student is more adventuresome, but corporate studies show that white managers are more prone to take risks and more prone to feel secure while taking those risks.

McClain found that black males were more subdued but no one needs to be convinced that black males are not more subdued.

McClain found black females to be more suspicious, shrewder, more apprehensive and more anxious. Yet other studies found them to be more emotionally honest than any of the other three groups—white men, white women and black men. "Sisters are more prone to be quiet about what they feel. I think the idea of being shrewder is more a matter of historic stereotype and perception about what is going on in her mind when she is quiet. But she might be staying quiet because she is insecure being both black and a woman in a white man's world. You never know," said a black male manager.

Another black male manager showed less patience in his criticism: "What in the world is the scientific definition of 'tender-minded' and what the hell does 'humble' mean to a white man?"

The most important study of values as they apply to management functions was completed by Professor George W. England of the University of Minnesota in 1973. He studied the values of 1072 American managers in order "to make a contribution to the understanding of the way values affect corporate behavior." His reasons for undertaking the study are at the core of corporate concerns.

He asserted that personal values are important because:

1. Personal value systems influence a manager's perception of situations and problems he faces.
2. Personal value systems influence a manager's decisions and solutions to problems.
3. Personal value systems influence the way in which a manager looks at other individuals and groups of individuals; thus they influence interpersonal relationships.
4. Personal value systems influence the perception of individual and organizational success as well as their achievement.
5. Personal value systems set the limits for the determination of what is and what is not ethical behavior by a manager.
6. Personal value systems influence the extent to which a manager will accept or will resist organizational pressures and goals.

England came up with a complex scheme for measuring how important American managers considered each one of the sixty-six concepts below:

CONCEPTS USED TO MEASURE MANAGER'S VALUES

GOALS OF BUSINESS ORGANIZATIONS

High Productivity
Industry Leadership
Employee Welfare
Organizational Stability
Profit Maximization
Organizational Efficiency
Social Welfare
Organizational Growth

PERSONAL GOALS OF INDIVIDUALS

Leisure
Dignity
Achievement
Autonomy
Money
Individuality
Job Satisfaction
Influence
Security
Power
Creativity
Success
Prestige

GROUPS OF PEOPLE

Employees
Customers
My Coworkers
Craftsmen
My Boss
Managers
Owners
My Subordinates
Laborers
My Company
Blue Collar Workers
Government
Stockholders
Technical Employees
Me
Labor Unions
White Collar Employees

IDEAS ASSOCIATED WITH PEOPLE	IDEAS ABOUT GENERAL TOPICS
Ambition	Authority
Ability	Caution
Obedience	Change
Trust	Competition
Aggressiveness	Compromise
Loyalty	Conflict
Prejudice	Conservatism
Compassion	Emotions
Skill	Equality
Cooperation	Force
Tolerance	Liberalism
Conformity	Property
Honor	Rational
	Religion
	Risk

England measured these values in a racially mixed group but did not compare the white group to the black. In such an inclusive list there are so many ways that blacks could have tested differently and thereby provided ammunition for the claims that they did not have the right values to be good managers.

However, when John G. Watson and Sam Barone made a comparative test two years later, they found that black managers and white managers had very similar value orientations.

Black managers place a greater emphasis on organizational growth than do their white counterparts. This is the only goal of business organizations on which the two groups differed to any great extent. Concerning the concepts relating to groups of people, white managers seem to be more oriented to all groups of people than the black managers, as evidenced by the white managers' greater concern for customers, co-workers, and craftsmen. However, the black managers do show a greater concern for white-collar employees than do the white managers.

With respect to the personal goals of individuals, black managers place greater operative importance on influence, prestige, and security. With regard to general topics, change, risk, and rationality were more operative for white managers than the black managers, while emotions were a more operative concept for the black managerial group. Finally, concerning ideas associated with people, ability was a considerably more operative value for white managers. Trust, on the other hand, was a more operative value for the black managers.

It was once argued that blacks functioned less well in many situations because blacks had lower opinions of themselves, or weaker self-concepts. "Our findings," say Watson and Barone, "contradict the popular view that the black individual has developed an inferior view of self as compared to his white counterpart." The apparent change in blacks is undoubtedly due, at least to some extent, to the psychological effects of the black revolution of the sixties.

Also, when we look at the personal profiles of blacks participating in corporate management we see a far more elite group of individuals in relation to the general black population than white managers are in relation to the white population. They've also had to fight harder to get to where they are.

"Whatever the cause of their similarity," Watson and Barone concluded, "there does seem to be strong evidence that the two groups (black and white) have developed positive views of self. The evidence reveals the insignificance of skin color when evaluating the self concept of black and white managers."

WHAT ABOUT DIFFERENCES IN BEHAVIOR AND LIFE-STYLE?

For many years, social scientists and psychologists have been preoccupied with measuring racial differences of all kinds. *Comparative Studies of Blacks and Whites in the United States,* by Kent S. Miller and Ralph Mason Dreger, lists more than 1629 major studies proving that white people and black people are either different or the same in: (1) temperament (cooperativeness, conformance, imitativeness, achievement need, internal-external control, impulsivity, aggressiveness, intolerance-tolerance), (2) mental health, (3) proclivity to crime, (4) cultural values, (5) family organization, (6) occupational aspirations, (7) political ideology, (8) educational achievement, (9) language abilities, (10) intelligence, (11) biological characteristics and (12) genetic inheritance.

Taken in toto, the results of these tests are so contradictory that no real conclusions can be drawn. As we have said, conclusions reached in individual studies often depended on who did the study and what conclusions they were trying to reach: statistics, facts and test results can be used to support almost any opinion that a researcher wishes to support.

For example, blacks can be viewed as very "now-oriented," very unwilling to delay gratification, but they can also be viewed as the most patient, long-suffering, future-oriented people in America.

Tests can "prove" that blacks lack keen verbal skills and good verbal facilities, yet blacks are the most verbally inventive people in America. We have noticed, however, that some blacks do have difficulty verbalizing their thoughts around white people because they feel that they must use the same words and even the same tone of voice as whites or whites will judge them to be ignorant. "You can be as smart as hell," said one manager, "but if you don't sound like a white man, white men will judge you to be unintelligent. I speak slowly because I am a thoughtful, careful person, and unless I'm careful I will have these white guys finishing my sentences for me, very patronizingly, as if I don't have the brains to finish them."

Again the problem is a cultural narrowness, which would not be half as bad as it is if it did not destroy freedom and creativity. And most tests are used as tools of cultural narrowness. No matter what else they pretend to be, the designers of most of these tests are nothing so much as the police force for the repressive cultural forces.

If the differences between races cannot be measured then people's random sense of these differences may be as accurate as the results of tests. A junior high school class in New York City came up with a list of thirty-seven ways that whites and blacks are different. Their list is no less valid than the list arrived at by learned professors working under large federal grants. The problem is that everyone seems to have a list that he or she believes in, even while sometimes denying that such a list exists.

For example, some blacks we interviewed seemed to think that whites possessed a greater degree of professionalism. Whites, they claim, seem to identify more strongly with their jobs, which gives them an overall involvement. "They even look like what they do," said one black manager. "A white accountant looks like an accountant, a white lawyer looks like a corporate lawyer. After they learn each other's name the second question they ask is: 'What do you do?' They introduce themselves: 'I'm Bill Kerr, a marketing representative from XYZ.' They introduce each other that way: 'Sally, meet Lawrence Fisher, he's in pay and benefits at ABC.' The role adaptation is more complete. They wear their jobs all over themselves."

A psychologist we interviewed agreed. "But this may be true because whites have had significant jobs longer. It used to be that a job for a black person was something to do to earn a living, while to a white person it was often a definition of life: 'I'm a chemist.' I think that this will change as blacks get more significant jobs. I think it is already changing. I know of blacks who are eager to tell people who they are occupationally. You'll notice in places like Los Angeles, Chicago, New York and especially Washington, blacks do the same thing by passing out business cards, which is something that whites don't do as often.

"In Washington it seems that every black man who makes more than twenty thousand a year has a business card. I saw a dude dancing at the Fox Trappe, and right on the floor while he was doing the bump he was giving this girl his business card."

Some of the whites we interviewed say that blacks are a little too aggressive, while an almost equal number say blacks are not aggressive enough. "That's a problem," said a black sales manager who had played professional basketball. "In a sales organization a black person might be alternatively condemned for being too aggressive and for not being aggressive enough. The problem is they don't look at the results, the numbers, they look at the style. A white person might develop a certain style, or there might be a white style of doing things, and your boss might condemn the black person with better numbers for being too aggressive or not aggressive enough, because he doesn't understand his style. Case in point: on a basketball court, the white coach—in industry it's the marketing manager who is the coach—might never want his players to dribble into a corner, but he's talking about white players, whereas a black player might feel he *can* dribble into the corner; if they trap him he can leap straight up in the air and score.

"The problem in industry is that the black player doesn't get a chance to show his talent because every time he dribbles toward the corner the coach takes him out. Like they say the real problem with

American productivity is that they don't allow the best player to play, and they don't allow the player to improve on the techniques of the game. You've got these insecure white boys acting as coach and they want to diagram each play."

Some managers say that a surprising difference between black and white managers is that blacks tend to change companies more often. "It's not surprising," said an affirmative action manager, "when you look at some of the good reasons. It may be true that blacks tend to identify with the company less. They tend to think of it as 'their' company rather than 'my' company. This is because the company makes them feel this.

"Many blacks can't identify with a company because that company is not doing anything for the black community. Suppose you work for a company that is known to support right-wing causes. For a black person this is not a casual issue. It means to you that the leaders of your company don't really like black people. How can you identify with that?

"It depends on your level of social consciousness. You might be alienated by the fact that the company has a heavy investment in South Africa. Black and white people have different racial relationships to certain issues. And you're never going to have an effective society until you have a just one.

"And on a personal level, it may be a statistically verifiable fact that blacks tend to change jobs more often than white managers, for a number of good reasons. Qualified blacks are few in number and so they are recruited more heavily. Back when the government was forcing major companies to hire more blacks, you would have one company raiding another company for the few super blacks available.

"They change jobs more often because they are all constantly seeking upward movement and the signals that they are dead-ended are made clearer to them and so they jump, out of frustration. They tend to look around for another situation where they might find these opportunities. Frustration leads them from job to job, company to company, and often they find that opportunities in the second company are just as limited as in the first and so they move on to a third.

"There are a lot of reasons. A black person might feel that his relationship to a company is more tentative because of the greater likelihood of getting fired and so he would naturally establish a more tentative identification with any particular company. The black person is prepared for the worst and so he doesn't invest as much in a capricious situation as a white person would in a situation that is, for him, reasonably fair."

Another assumption is that blacks do not work as hard, but there is ample evidence that the exact opposite is true. "Generally," said a black female training officer with a major communications firm, "I think that black managers work harder on the job than white managers. Black managers seem to feel that they have to work harder. They know they're on trial. They know they're being judged by performance and so they become very results-orientated. Then blacks have this idea that working means doing something, while whites have been in white collar jobs long enough to know that work often means nothing more than spending time seeming to be doing something.

"It's almost like a guilt thing with blacks: 'I'm getting all this money—fifty thousand dollars—I have to show some tangible results.' Whites are better adjusted to the fact that they deserve fifty thousand dollars just for being there, and that most corporate jobs are not designed to produce immediately visible results.

"I know myself. I look around all the time wondering, 'What have I done today? What can I pick up and say that this is what I accomplished today?' I try to finish each day like this, even though I know that this is not what a corporation is all about.

"White people can be in a meeting all day and accomplish nothing but bullshit and they call that a productive day. Actually the meeting was nothing more than an opportunity for the boss to show his power. He stands, everyone else sits. He maps out the agenda that everyone else has to follow. He likes the idea that he can veto any suggestion that anyone else makes. He is controlling all of this expensive talent in 'his' meeting.

"After the meeting he wants to see who comes up and says: 'Great meeting, Bill. Super.' This shows him who is loyal to him, who is willing to lie and say that this meeting was a great meeting. I sit up in these meetings wishing that they would end so I can get back to my desk and do some work to justify my pay.

"With my old boss I used to say that the meeting was bullshit, but I've become a corporate sophisticate now. I just sit there without going to sleep. It still annoys me mostly because I am a loyal American in that sense so I can see why American industry is in so much trouble—calling meetings is one of the perks that go along with being boss.

"The right to waste subordinates' time is one of the perks you've earned by fighting your way to the top. I'll bet you that fifteen percent of all expenditures in American industry is wasted on perks that add neither to efficiency, comfort, productivity nor enjoyment. They are simply ways of differentiating status levels in the hierarchy—austere decadence. That's what I call it.

"Some of these guys in industry are more wastefully decadent than the European aristocracy; the only difference is they don't allow themselves to enjoy it as much. They have to justify it as a business necessity. Time is the thing they are most decadent with. Just take a guy who makes a hundred and fifty thousand a year—and there are plenty of these—he makes three thousand a week. That's six hundred a day. Put ten of these guys in a bullshit meeting that consumes an entire day and you've wasted six thousand dollars every time this happens.

"And here is this little black me, feeling that I have to produce tangible results because I would feel guilty about the hundred dollars per day I earn. Bullshit blacks don't work as hard."

Another black female manager agreed with this but for different reasons. "You have to work hard and be results-oriented or they'll fire you. The only hope that a black manager has is in his numbers. So you work to keep your numbers up. Productivity is a kind of security blanket. It won't guarantee that you won't get fired. It certainly won't guarantee that you'll get promoted, but it's the only thing you've got going for you in many situations—hard work.

"The ideal situation, to be completely cynical about it, is to have a dumb or lazy boss. Make him look good and you've got a certain level of security, if you know how to do it in a nonthreatening, non-put-down sort of way."

One of those hard-to-define differences that blacks have expressed pride in is an ability to loosen up and release tensions by dancing. "But you've got to be careful or even this will be used against you," said a young man on the legal staff of a Fortune 500 company in New York. "I'll give you an example of what I mean: I mentioned one day that I was going out dancing that evening, and that I loved to dance.

"This white guy on the staff would then call me 'Disco Al.' Everywhere I went he would say 'Hey, Hey, Hey. Here comes Disco Al.' Even in important meetings he would try to introduce me as Disco Al.

"Now if I hadn't gone to school with white guys it would have taken me longer to understand what he was trying to do. He was trying to undermine my effectiveness. How could anyone take an attorney seriously whose name was Disco Al?

"One day I got on an elevator and he was at the back of the elevator and he yelled 'Ladies and gentlemen, here comes Disco Al.' I walked on, turned my back on him without even acknowledging his existence and continued reading some papers I was reading. He stood back there chirping something about Disco Al, with everyone on the elevator wondering who the hell he was talking about."

In addition, corporate America created the first time in history that large numbers of black people allowed the making of cash to determine their primary relationships to most of the people they knew. For black people there had always been some more important reasons for their relationships—fun, kinship, love, spiritual closeness, history. Now they were in the mainstream. This is one of the things that made adjustment to mainstream life so difficult.

"Another assumption that can hurt black managers," said a white female manager who was secretly dating a black man, "is the assumption that black people have more fun. I know it's a cliché, but it's true. I like going to parties where most of the people are black because the parties are more fun. I work hard enough during the week and I don't want to have to 'work' during one of these boring corporate cocktail parties. But I know there are white people who think subconsciously: 'If blacks have more fun then it is just that we have more money.'"

A black female manager agreed to an extent: "I know I used to come in on Monday morning and I envied all the black secretaries because they were talking about this party or that party they had gone to on Saturday night, while I had been standing around all Saturday night listening to some boring fool saying things about the stock market that I had already read in that morning's paper. I had to go to create this image of being a serious corporate person."

For many very deep historical and anthropological reasons, one race in America seems to extoll a certain set of values while the other race seems to extoll another set. They overlap but they are not congruent and so they manifest themselves in different racial styles. These manifestations are what stereotypes, positive and negative, are based on.

Trying to use these stereotypes to judge potential job performance is useless because 1) the areas of overlap are far wider than the areas of difference even in behavioral styles, 2) stereotypic views that are brought to an employer's mind simply because of an applicant's or subordinate's race cannot tell the employer anything about performance potential and 3) there are very many individual style configurations out of which good performance of a particular corporate function can grow.

Saying that a person cannot be a good comptroller because that person possesses certain values makes as much sense as saying that the person cannot be a good comptroller because the person is a Libra, or saying that a person cannot be a good chief executive officer because the person is an extrovert.

All of this suggests that race is a very poor way of dividing people into groups, and it will make sense only as long as we react to people racially and defensively condemn the styles of their lives even when it might be healthier for us to adopt portions of these styles ourselves.

VII

MANCHILD
IN THE MAINSTREAM

WILLIS THORNTON DID NOT LIKE the title of David Halberstam's 1972 best seller, *The Best and the Brightest*, which was about the brilliant young men who came to Washington during the Kennedy presidency to run the country. He simply did not like anyone being called "best" and "brightest" until they had done something to prove that they were better and brighter than he.

Even before the black man Henry Aaron broke the home run record of the white man Babe Ruth, he had refused to acknowledge Babe Ruth as the home run king, because Babe Ruth had done nothing to prove that he was better than Josh Gibson, the legendary black home run hitter who lived at the same time as Ruth but was prohibited from playing major-league baseball. How can anyone claim to be the best at any particular thing until he wins the honor in free and open competition? History had proven that white men were best at seizing power, but were they really best at all the other functions that simply accrued to them because they held power?

This is the kind of thing that Willis Thornton brooded over while he was almost flunking out of Cardozo Vocational High School in Washington, D.C. His mother and teachers agreed that he had absolutely no sense of direction and almost no motivation. His father had nothing to say because no one knew where his father was. Willis was just another surly black boy until the civil rights movement came along. It was only then that he began to live.

He went South to join any marches, sit-ins, pray-ins, freedom rides, demonstrations, rallies and boycotts he could find. He enrolled in college in North Carolina simply to be where the action was. He still flunked quite a few courses but he read all of the black books he could get his hands on: *Black Rage, Black Power, Black Thought, Black Judgement, Black Thunder, Black Uprisings, Black Worker, Black Is, Black Like Me, Black Man's Burden, Black Boy, Black Cargo, Black Music, Black Rebellion.*

He read Fanon and Camus and Sartre and Malraux. He began calling himself an existentialist and wearing a beret. He was part true believer and part con man. He was not deep enough in the movement to rise to the top of it, and he was not interested enough in college to keep from getting booted out.

He moved back to Washington at about the time that Martin Luther King was bringing the racial struggle to the doorsteps of the White House. Willis managed to get into Howard University somehow, and he stayed on the fringes of the kind of activity that had done so much to awaken his intellect.

He did volunteer work for the Peace and Freedom Party, which in turn brought him into contact with many influential white people. He had never known great numbers of whites before. He was surprised to discover that they liked him and he liked them. He enjoyed arguing with them about some of the ideas that his new reading had set to burning in his brain.

One of the influential whites he met arranged for him to get into Harvard on a special program, and he, being ever the opportunist, decided that after Harvard College he wanted to go to Harvard Business School in order to try his hand at something he still called "bidness."

Before Willis Thornton went away to the Freedom Movement, he had been affectionately known to his friends as Nightmare.

Nightmare is now earning a high five figures as a corporate manager of marketing for a company in the Fortune Top 100. He is proof that a good manager does not have to come from a single kind of ideal background, that indeed a good manager does not have to be of a single kind of standardized character type.

At thirty-six he is more successful than most of his white contemporaries. His immediate supervisor, a marketing vice-president, who does not know him as Nightmare, calls him William, thinks he is an excellent corporate manager and a great "team player."

Nightmare loves his job. So far racial problems have not been so large that he could not overcome them, but he knows that continued advancement is more problematic. "I don't fool myself. The higher you go the more important race becomes. Above me everything is white." There are four blacks in the organization who are higher than Nightmare. Three of these are not in decision-making positions, however, they are in staff jobs, and the other, a black vice-president, has, in Nightmare's words, been pretending to be white so long that you can't even count him as a "brother."

Nightmare does not argue that his background is in any way similar to the backgrounds of the white managers and directors who are climbing the ladder with him. He rejects, however, the idea that his background represents the kind of "mark of oppression" described in the book of the same name by Abram Kardiner and Lionel Ovesey.

"I browsed through that shit up at the B-school, man," he said, waving his hands in disgust at the idea that "the Negro has no possible basis for a healthy self-esteem and every possible incentive for self-hatred." He was equally unimpressed by the assertion that the basic black personality is a "caricature of the corresponding white personality, because the Negro must adapt to the same culture, must accept the same social goals, but without the ability to achieve them."

Kardiner and Ovesey go on to name a group of pathological traits they say must characterize the life of the Negro: a conviction of unlovability, a sense of helplessness (fate control), uncontrolled hostility and a weak ego structure. "I have been that in my life, but I have never been only that. Never. You do come up under a lot of stress, but if you survive it you've also developed, along the way, some very healthy and effective coping mechanisms. For example, I can deal with uncertainty better than most white cats. I'm used to it. I can function under stress better. I can deal with crisis better, and I'm better motivated because I know what it is to live at Fourteenth and Chapin Street and I'll work like hell to keep from going back," he said.

Nightmare admitted that managers raised as middle-class whites have certain advantages too. "They are more standardized and therefore fit in with each other better. They are less prone to emotional extremes, more cooperative with each other, and compromise more easily with each other," he said. "This is what the corporation needs, what the corporation will always need. There are black managers who provide this as well as white ones, but there are other talents that it needs when the status is not quo—out here in the flux, out here in this confusion, you need more dudes like me. Dudes who can shoot on the run, who can think on the go, who are not bound down by a sense of how things have always been, who don't have to stop the action in order to analyze it, who can look for opportunities and seize them, who are hungrier and tougher."

He spoke rapidly, saying that he firmly believed that white people and black people are different. Raised as he was raised, it was not surprising that he would think so. "The question is, Must difference always imply superiority/inferiority? Can we really be a multicultural society which takes advantage of the proclivities of all of its people, or must we all either standardize and become alike or else be judged to be inferior and pushed back out into the margins of the economy? We all want to give our best to the country.

"In some ways it's all rhetorical because we are going to become a multicultural society. There is no choice, just as we are going to become—let me find a good word—a society that is controlled by two sexes.

"The only decision to make is, Is this going to be accomplished begrudgingly, in a way that will make America a second-rate culture because of the destructive animosity that exists between its people, or will it be accomplished progressively, making us the first multinational country?" he said, smiling. "I don't know."

He smiled, knowing that whether the listener believed it or not, there was something irresistible about his con. It had the ring of truth. It promised something to everyone. All they had to do was see things his way.

He said that he talked to the president of his company just as he was talking to the interviewer. He pulled no punches, and this was one of the reasons why the president liked him. "The only problem is the president has a reputation for avoiding tough decisions. Bringing a black man into senior management will involve some tough politics. I'm not sure he can face up to them, even though I think he's been grooming me for senior management."

Nightmare is certainly not a typical black male manager, but he is typical of a certain kind of black American male. As a manager he is an exception because he came out of the deepest jungle of our statistics on social pathology.

He believes that there are ways that America can benefit by using blacks like him. Because of their lives in the ghetto, they have lost something, but "white boys have also lost something by living in suburbia. They've lost some will, they've lost some heart. The blacks who have survived what I have survived have a contribution to make —one that cannot be found anywhere else in America. In order to win, America is going to have to use everything it's got," he whispered, smiling, feeling that his time was finally coming.

"Just as I said, the president of the company is afraid. He's not afraid of me. He is, understandably, afraid of what would happen if he forced me down the throats of senior management. He knows I can do the job. Senior management knows I can do the job. There's just a lot of fear that has to be overcome."

Several black male managers agreed with Nightmare's point of view as they assessed their own chances of making the breakthrough. They knew that some people from the black middle class had made breakthroughs. They had gotten important mainstream jobs in the mainstream.

But no black had made the big breakthrough, and Nightmare felt that it would be someone like him who would finally become the first black president or chairman of the board of a Fortune 500 company. He felt that America would soon be desperate enough to give him a chance.

Nightmare considers himself a black black, and by black he is not referring to the fact that his complexion is very dark, he is referring to his attitude and his orientation. He is referring to where he came from and to the fact that he is not ashamed nor willing to give up who he is. "Do you succeed, really succeed, by imitating white men, or by being yourself and waiting for the white men to become comfortable with who you really are?"

In this Nightmare was speaking about something that has only a little to do with style and diction—outward manifestations of what men like Nightmare hold on to in order to hold on to some more essential parts of themselves. "If Henry Kissinger can make it in America, speaking as he does, why do I have to start speaking like Walter Cronkite in order to be trusted in that inner circle of power? Am I not more fully American than Henry Kissinger? And I just may have some other qualities that he doesn't."

Nightmare is a student of the modern corporation. He owns more than fifty books on corporate management and he has read all of them, he said in his Manhattan apartment one evening. He looked tired. Part of his dark belly shone beneath a shrunken T-shirt.

He said that he has used books to transform himself, which is what the black manager has to do. "Read everything you can get your hands on about the way they function," he said. The book that struck him like lightning, in the same way that Fanon's books struck him during the sixties, was Michael Maccoby's *The Gamesman*.

This book, he explained, as he pointed into the air periodically with two fingers, did not transform him as the writings of Fanon had transformed him. He had already been in the process of transformation when the book was published. He took it down off his book shelf, which also held an expensive-looking turntable and stereo amplifier. The book simply froze "the darting, scattered fragments of my life so that I could really see them for the first time. That book was an eye-opener," he said.

"You're not going to understand why I lined over what I did. That's why I don't let people read my books," he said. There were notes in the margins of some of the pages. Some sections were heavily highlighted. Pale-yellow lines totally covered the black type on one page.

> The modern gamesman is best defined as a person who loves change and wants to influence its course. He likes to take calculated risks and is fascinated by techniques and new methods. He sees a developing project, human relations, and his own career in terms of options and possibilities.

In the margin alongside this passage Nightmare had written:

> He must see the possible positive benefits in everything that is required of him to do.

Farther down the page another passage was lined out with the same yellow felt pen:

> He is cooperative but competitive, detached and playful but compulsively driven to succeed; a team player but a would-be superstar; a team leader but often a rebel against bureaucratic hierarchy; fair and unprejudiced but contemptuous of weakness; tough and dominating but not destructive.

It was apparent that Nightmare was talking rapidly to keep from having too many of his lined passages read. On another page he had highlighted:

The gamesmen's yearnings for autonomy and their fear of being controlled contribute to a common midcareer uneasiness.

In the margin beside this passage he had written:

Make sure you have an alternate path when this uneasiness comes. The uneasiness will be increased if progress has been retarded by racism.

"This was a natural evolution for me," Nightmare said. "In the streets as a teenager, I was a little slickster. Then I started to believe, during the sixties, and I got hurt really bad. I thought I was going to go crazy. Then I got into Harvard because I was clever—I could do the job, but that wasn't the point—it was never in the cards for a guy like me to get into Harvard and then into the B-school. This whole damn thing has been a game. That's the only thing down here on earth right now, is a goddamn game. This shit isn't real. This shit isn't about nothing that's real. It's a game, and I'm a player."

He took his copy of *The Gamesman* back and slid it into its place on the shelf. He differed from the gamesman because he had fierce loyalties to those he had developed personal relationships with, including the president of his company whom he calls a "very decent cat with a good heart." In addition to fiercer loyalties he explained that he also had some deeper obsession.

"I am obsessed with winning. I want to win not simply for me and my own advancement but I want to win for my team, my company, my country. Everybody." He said he was also obsessed with the image of his own integrity. "I will never betray you," he said. "If we are together. If I give my word, I will never betray you." He leaned forward, pressing his case.

He seemed different from the gamesman because there seemed to be something more solid at his core. He seemed more passionate and therefore less opportunistic.

The irony of the lives of men with boyhoods like his is that for all the freedom that the streets offered, there were still rituals—rituals of manhood, rituals of personhood—that promoted values that left them more tradition-bound than men and women raised in liberal, extremely permissive homes.

Emotionally they were very much like those right-wing Republicans who are their own main adversaries in the fight to sway the liberal middle. The biggest evidence of this is in the way Nightmare complained about the excessive tolerance in a liberal city like New York. He had a habit of saying, "We're in our last days. Sodom and Gomorrah didn't have anything that New York City doesn't have right now." Regardless of constitutional guarantees, he said that the police and the fire department should burn down all of those porno places and peep shows. "If anyone ever dragged a kid of mine into child pornography, there wouldn't be a trial. I would pay the guy a visit and one way or another the shit would stop."

He argued that gay people are just morally lazy or morally weak. "They need to be kicked in their behinds and someone needs to grab them in their goddamned chests and told to either go out and find a woman or else take the ugliness back in the closet where it belongs. Unless someone does this, we're in our last days. This motherfucker" —he pointed to the ground under the building where he lived, he pointed to America—"this motherfucker is coming down."

Like a right-wing Republican he longed for "the good old days." Yet, because he was black, he couldn't just long for the past. There had been too much degradation in his personal and racial past. He wanted the future to be as the past should have been.

"I don't think that it will be true of our children. My kids will go to school with white kids. They will be raised with white kids and so there won't be a great deal of differences. All kids will gain something from the strengths of other traditions. Then people will be differentiated by individual talents and temperaments and not by race."

But something didn't ring true about his worried optimism. Statistics seem to say that white kids and black kids are not being raised together, that there are people who would let the public schools of this country go to hell before they allowed this to happen.

A few well-to-do blacks would be able to get their children into predominantly white public and private schools, but the majority of black kids will still go to neglected public schools, and find themselves growing up without the skills they need to take their places in the economic order.

We talked to Nightmare again at an outdoor café for the next session of the interview. It was apparent that he was glad to be out in sloppy gray shorts and no socks, strolling in the sun down Columbus Avenue. The interview seemed to justify his taking time away from corporate affairs in order to look at his life—itself a corporate affair.

"Most cats who go to Wharton or Harvard trade in their old lives and become imitation white boys. I'm a believer in the idea that people function best when they can be close to their natural selves on a job, when they don't have to transform themselves by imitation. I've been lucky enough, or smart enough, to be in company situations which allowed me to be that. I would say lucky because I've always worked for some fairly secure white dudes who weren't threatened by the fact that I didn't imitate them. What I did in B-school is refine my stuff, not give it up. I smoothed it out so I could fit in. I learned the vocabulary of la-di-da so I could hide behind words when I had to, but behind that façade of words I'm using my street sense. I'm kicking ass the way I know how.

"This company is loose, so I can use what I mastered in the street. I can be a con man, or I can kick ass, corporately, to get the results," Nightmare said. He admitted that had he been in any other company he would have been fired by now.

In corporate America it seems that the newer, rapidly growing high-technology companies that are "marketing-driven" are, in his word, loose. Their phenomenal growth over a very short time has created within them a different internal environment from the older companies in, for example, the public utilities field, in steel, and the automobile industry.

He said that the world had gotten really fucked up and it was no wonder that people were fucked up. He admitted that he had done something that most blacks needed to do but couldn't because they were too tradition-bound: "There's a stigma among black dudes about going to see a shrink—a psychiatrist. It looks like a sign of weakness. My problem is that I didn't go to see one early enough because I was in the middle of a sustained nervous breakdown. You've heard of walking pneumonia, well I had been having a walking nervous breakdown for a good part of my adult life. So I finally went to see this big black dude who was a psychiatrist. I needed someone to give me some objective data on me. This dude came off the streets just like I did. He had studied in Germany and so he had the academic shit down, but he hadn't lost his basic blackness and so he didn't come at me from the point of view that I was sick or crazy.

"He just gave me a reading of myself. He explained the things in my background that made me what I am. See, that's why you can't go to a regular white shrink. He has a white standard and he can't help you to deal with where you're coming from because he doesn't know where you're coming from.

"I met this psychiatrist at a party and we were trying to hit on the same woman. I got hostile and he got hostile and so some of the people there had to cool us out. And this motherfucker gave me his business card and told me anytime I wanted to kick his ass then give him a call—'If I ain't home leave a message on my answering machine, faggot.'

"See how ridiculous this all is: I pulled out my business card and told him if he thought he could kick my ass then give me a call and if I wasn't in the office 'leave a message with my secretary, you big punk.'

"Anyway, I saw on the card that he was a psychiatrist and I had this brother working for me who was having some trouble. This brother was freaking out. The white people were getting to him and so I called the shrink and asked would he meet me and this brother for a drink without saying that he was a shrink—just say he was a friend of mine. We were going to talk to this brother and help him cope. So that's how I got to know the shrink. After that we used to go out for drinks and the shrink would give me a reading. I mean, I never went into his office and stretched out on his couch or any of that phony shit.

"He told me that one of the things that might hold me back on my job is a weak or brittle ego structure—yeah! yeah! yeah!—he said, really. For example, he said, 'I bet you have a hard time taking instructions. You always want to do things your way. You take instructions because you got to, but it burns you inside. And you have a very hard time taking criticism because whenever someone criticizes anything you do, you feel that they are criticizing you. You personalize everything,' he told me.

"'A corporation is a team,' he told me, 'and you are an individualist. That's natural, coming from your background. Everything you've ever gotten in life you've gotten it for yourself, and the only person you could honestly thank for ever helping you is your mother, who brought you onto this ball of dirt. After that it's been you, you, you.'

"We talked about his background too, which made it cool since he wasn't putting me in the position of being a sicky and he being the almighty doctor. I didn't pay him either, but I did get him some consulting work with the company because he was a hip dude. He ran some classes for black managers. The white cat I was working for accepted the fact that he would be better for some of the black employee problems, better than a white shrink.

"Anyway, we would just go out and rap until all hours of the night. Some people might have thought we were weird because we were always together and we would turn down dates with women just so we could talk about black male things—see, that right there is very different for black males. We are never, ever, really deep and honest with each other.

"He told me a lot of stuff, man. How I had had to become egocentric in order to survive all the shit that was trying to destroy my ego and destroy me [to not be victimized by the "mark of oppression"]. I had to believe in me. I had to trust me. Now this helped me up to a certain point, but as I moved up in the corporation this was a liability. I wasn't alone anymore.

"My loneliness made me a workaholic. It gave me a very dictatorial management style. It made me very suspicious of other people, especially white people, and so it made it difficult for me to accept help. He told me I had difficulty delegating responsibility. Now this cat was telling me all these true things about me and he had never seen me on the job.

"So I learned of some stuff that is in black backgrounds, especially black male backgrounds, that put them at a disadvantage in a corporation. This was a heavy cat, man. He had done a lot of consulting with the U.S. Army and so he knew his shit." Nightmare paused to hear a reaction to what he was saying.

"He told me that to some extent I believed in 'fate control,' that I believe that a person's destiny was not controlled by himself but was controlled by fate, and this gave me a slight touch of come si, come sa, which meant I was more inclined to accept and adjust to things rather than try to make them better.

"He told me some fantastic things. He even interpreted my dreams. Just before I was to get this promotion and big raise, I used to have these dreams about being shot, or about being killed in an automobile accident or dying in a plane crash. He told me that black people are very often like that when they're on the verge of success. They are so fatalistic that they fear that something will happen to rob them of the success. It was amazing. I had never been able to get that close to another man before, without feeling, as I said, that some fag was coming out in me.

"I didn't agree with everything he said, though. I mean, he said that the fact that I loved to buy expensive shoes and suits was a manifestation of an insecure ego. I don't believe that. I think this is a manifestation of a little bit of the peacock in the black man, which should be in all men. It's also the black man's desire to have an individualized style. Blacks like to be individualized, whites like to be standardized—they used to anyway. Now they are seeing that too much standardization destroys creativity and personality, while blacks are discovering that too much individuality destroys organization and cooperation.

"We discussed the idea that in the urban black male's background there is also often some gang experience, so he has been used to blending into an organization. He has had experience following a leader, but the leader always had to be somebody he respects.

"But very often in the corporation the leader, his boss, is not someone he respects, because he doesn't respect the process by which the boss came to be the boss. He has become the boss without winning the right to be the boss. He might have gotten to be the boss because he kissed someone's ass, or he married the daughter of the chairman of the board, or because he had a Nordic appearance. This is what I mean: who is best and who is brightest?

"The competition has to be open and fair. Then if I get beaten I can truly respect the person who has beaten me because, first of all, I can learn something from that person that will aid my growth. But look at the other side: Suppose you know this white cat who when you were coming up together, you outsold him, you outperformed him. You went into his territory after him and did a better job. Yet here he is sitting in the boss's chair telling you what to do. You have to listen to him because of the structure, but you don't respect him. The whole deal is fraudulent and so you lose respect for the entire system. This is what has happened in America: too many people have spotted the fraud. I mean, Watergate, what was that?

"That's why it's hard to get people motivated. That's the problem with productivity, and this has nothing to do with color. White people too have seen the fraud and so it's very hard for them to really believe in the system."

Nightmare looked out at the variety of pretty girls passing along the avenue. He commented on them. He didn't agree with those black male managers who felt that sexual jealousy and sexual competition are at the basis of much of the tension between the white men who run corporations and the black men who want to get the chance to run them.

He is reminded that there is a school of psychologists who say that subconsciously all male competition is for the attention of the female of the species, women's liberation notwithstanding. Does this mean that the white man does not want the black man to advance for fear that this would make the black man more attractive to women of both races?

"I know what you're saying, but I think this is bullshit. I can't believe that a white man sits at his desk and thinks like this. This might have been true a long time ago, but there's every evidence that during the sixties the white man would rather give you a white woman than to have you take some real power off to where he didn't have one of his women watching it.

"I think that the sexual thing only clouds the issue," Nightmare said, displaying annoyed impatience with the opinions of other black male managers who felt that this sexual thing was too deep in western history for it not to play an important part in a mixed sexual and racial environment today. "People don't care that much about sex these days," Nightmare said. "The question is survival."

His feeling was that sex had been so organized and bureaucratized, like so much else in modern life, that much of the passion had gone out of it. So there could not be much passion in the sexual competition between white and black men anymore. "It's power and money, nothing else."

Even the vocabulary of sex, he argued vigorously, is corporate rather than erotic. "A love affair is called a relationship. People get together to fulfill needs. A lush word like lust has been replaced by a computer pip like horny." He laughed cynically.

In such a brave new world, he argued passionately, it seems absurd to talk about the white man not wanting the black man to have white women. But not all the black men we talked to agreed.

"It's subsurface," another manager had said earlier, "but it's still there. For one thing the guys who run corporations came up during the fifties and it's like a religion to them. They're not comfortable with racial mixing on a sociosexual level. You can't tell me they are, and you can't tell me this doesn't influence the way they think.

"You also have to remember that when you talk about corporate life, you're talking about every little town in America. You're not just talking about busy people in cities, but you're talking about the 'redneck' who worked his way up, who has a daughter going to integrated schools and a wife who may not be appealing to him, or he may not be appealing to.

"The race/sex thing is too deep in history to say it has disappeared just because people are struggling to become high corporate dingdongs." This manager subscribed to the idea that the sexual tension between black and white men is still strong enough to put black men at a disadvantage in any sexual environment that white men control.

"Sure it's a problem," said a black secretary. "They especially don't like to see a black manager in a position of authority over a white woman. I remember there was this brother in our section who went out and hired a pretty blond secretary. You should have seen how all the white men in the section watched him—like hawks. Every time he came out of his office to speak to her some of them would stop what they were doing and listen, and God! you could see them squirming when she went into his office and closed the door.

"They tried everything," the secretary said. "They tried to talk her into quitting. They used to make jokes about it to make the entire thing ugly. Pretty soon the girl did quit and the black guy got transferred."

The part of America's nightmare that includes a black man is, more often than not, a sexual nightmare. This, no doubt, is the reason why some of the black men we interviewed wondered if the emphasis on sexual harassment in corporate America will be used against them. By mid-1981 sexual harassment ranked along with declining worker productivity as the hot issue in many major corporations. It brought out the paranoia in more than one black male manager we interviewed. It brought out caution in others and resentment in more than a few.

Sexual harassment was bound to come up as a major issue because so many women were moving into the labor force, especially into high-mobility jobs where they depended on the fairness or the favor of men to determine how rapidly they would rise.

Some women have used sexual attraction and favors to get what they wanted—or thought they deserved—from men for as long as there have been men and women. Some men have used superior social or economic positions to extract sexual delights from women in circumstances too numerous to mention. The extremes in each case have been outright prostitution and outright rape. Between these extremes are the shaded variations that make the problem so complex. Corporations are right to be concerned, because a tone has to be set that will make the workplace as fair as possible for both men and women.

Errors are going to be made that will affect many people's careers. As we will see later, black men have good reason to fear that many of these errors will have negative effects on their already fragile corporate lives.

"You know there aren't going to be many sexual-harassment charges filed by black women against white men. I think that even if you do have a lot of mixing between white men and black women it's done under conditions where both of them, but especially the black woman, have too much to lose to risk filing charges," said a black female who has a white lover in the company she works for. "I think a few people know we're close, and a few people actually suspect that we are going together, but it's not a public thing," she said.

This woman lives forty-five miles from her job and there is very little chance that anyone who works with her would ever see who her visitors were. "I'd rather keep my business to myself," she said. "I started dating white guys in North Carolina, actually, and then when I came up to the Midwest region I dated a few black guys in the company and then I found this one man that I liked and he was white and so he and I have been friends for about seven months now."

It is likely that there will be even fewer sexual harassment charges filed by black women against black men. Most black managers do not have enough corporate power to really harass in any heavy way. Whatever happens between them is usually handled privately.

Most cases of harassment will, undoubtedly, involve white women and white men. This is true because of numbers and the power of white men in corporate America, and the willingness of white women to file such charges. "Between these two groups there are the greatest number of possibilities," said a young white salesman who said he didn't have enough power to harass anyone either. We interviewed him with a black salesman in a northern Virginia suburb of Washington, D.C.

The black salesman added that there were several secretaries in his office that he wouldn't mind harassing. They laughed, but there was no way of knowing how serious either one of them was. "I'll give you a switch on that," the black salesman said. "There was this guy in the office they called Lance, a white guy, and they called him Lance because he tried to lance every good-looking woman he could find. He was a young good-looking dude and he was supervisor for all of the customer service reps, who were mostly female. The men who worked for him turned him in for sexual harassment because the good-looking women were getting all the promotions."

A black female social scientist, who is a professor and human resources consultant, said: "Black men have the most to lose in this because they justify any white fear that social contact will mean sexual contact. It doesn't matter that white men and black women have been doing it for generations. For the black man it can be deadly." She had set up her consulting company when she learned that major corporations were beating the bushes to find experts who could help them with their human resource problems. She said that one corporation alone had enough problems to keep a good consultant in business for years. "Black men disregard the vulnerability of their positions and do take on white women who work for them as lovers. Now these women might be jockeying for promotions or they might not be. It might just be a matter of mutual thrills, but it really angers black women, who are experiencing a shortage of males in the first place. Black women get angry but they don't try to turn the brothers in, in most cases, because they like to see black men advancing in the corporations. So the black woman just looks at him as a fool and handles her rage internally—even in cases when the white woman gets promoted ahead of her by a black supervisor who has a touch of vanilla fever," she said, laughing.

"But I think this is going to end. I think that black women are going to stop handling the entire matter on an emotional level and they are going to start looking at it more as a matter of unfair career competition. These are women who have begun to see things in career terms rather than racial terms, but you'd be surprised how difficult this transition is and how few of us have actually made it— the transition from group-mindedness to individual-mindedness and career-mindedness."

She went on to explain, with a mixture of regret and self-mockery in her voice, how she and other women have tried to maintain commitments to something larger than their own careers. She explained that if women give in to this kind of selfishness then everybody in America will be pursuing "self" and there will be no keepers of the hearth. She laughed at how lonely life can be for the keeper.

"Another interesting case is one I had to investigate in California last year. This black guy was making it with a white woman who reported to him. They had a heavy thing that everyone knew about. This black guy was up for a promotion and he was competing with two white guys for this promotion. One of the white guys went to the white woman who was going with the brother and told her that she either make a charge of sexual harassment or he would expose the entire situation and get her fired.

"She panicked and made the charges because she felt that her career was really in jeopardy, but their affair had been so open that she couldn't make the charges stick, so both of them lost out. She was transferred out of the branch and the brother was not given the promotion. His career is dead-ended.

"Then there have been several false charges of sexual harassment lodged by white women against black men. There is a significant fear among black men that this sexual harassment thing will be unfairly used against them. Corporate America has always been very political, but this sexual thing is complicating the politics even more; you'd be surprised."

Black men sense that their image in America's eye is not totally negative. They know that lurking below the surface is an image similar to that which Norman Podhoretz partially revealed in his 1963 essay "My Negro Problem—And Ours." Podhoretz wrote:

> . . . just as in childhood I envied Negroes for what seemed to me their superior masculinity, so I envy them today for what seems to me their superior physical grace and beauty. I have come to value physical grace very highly, and I am now capable

of aching with all my being when I watch a Negro couple on the dance floor, or a Negro playing baseball or basketball. They are on the kind of terms with their own bodies that I should like to be on with mine, and for that precious quality they seem blessed to me.

In *Soul on Ice*, Eldridge Cleaver discusses how those white men who concede "the body" to the black man will forever deny that he also has a mind that equals theirs, for to make this concession would be to give the black man a two-to-one victory.

More pertinent to our discussion, however, is another passage from *Soul on Ice*:

> The Class Society has a built-in bias, which tends to perpetuate the social system. The Omnipotent Administrators, wishing to preserve what they perceive as their superior position and way of life, have, from a class point of view and also on an individual level, a negative reaction toward any influence in the society that tends to increase the number of males qualified to fulfill the functions of administration. When it comes to anything that will better the lot of those beneath him, the Omnipotent Administrator starts with a basic "anti" reflex. Any liberality he might show is an indication of the extent to which he has suppressed his "anti" reflex, and is itself a part of his lust for omnipotence. His liberality is, in fact, charity.

"Okay, okay, okay, okay," Nightmare said after our long discussion of sexual harassment and its various effects on black and white careers. I admit that. I used to date a lot of them. They were easier to get along with. They didn't hassle me as much. I was getting hassled on my job and I didn't want to be hassled on my off-duty time, so I started dating white women.

"I was making good money and so if I wanted to run down to Barbados to relax, it was better for me to take a white woman. If I had taken a black woman she'd have considered me a marriage candidate. She'd have been negotiating with me to make a commitment, and she'd have been uptight about her morals and about what I thought of her. She'd have tried to act marriageable and I wanted someone to act free and loose for some hot fun in the sun.

"The white woman, she doesn't want to marry you. She just wants to have some fun like you. It's easier. She can give herself without feeling demeaned because the bottom line is she's still white and you're her social inferior and she doesn't have to get into a status battle. To her you're still an M&M, not the chocolate candy by that name. An M&M is a Madison Avenue Mandingo.

"For a long time I found white women easier. I didn't have to approach them or woo them. They approached me and wooed me. That's what I needed at the time. But then I got tired of that and I swung back across the line, but I found it hard to get into sisters because there was always so much tension between us.

"So what I tried to do was to find a black female psychiatrist I could talk to like I talked to the other psychiatrist, but when I went to this one black woman, she couldn't deal with me on a conversational level. She kept trying to set herself up as a mother-confessor to the prodigal son.

"She was very directive, and superformal. I think her education went to her head. I got less understanding out of her than I did out of this white Ph.D. psychologist I was fucking up at the B-school.

"You know," Nightmare said, "if you want to talk about what might work on the white man's mind even more, I'll tell you something that occurred to me when I was reading the book *Games Mother Never Taught You*.

"A fact that might work on his mind more is that black men are the Sunday gladiators of the American Republic. The football field is the coliseum and the action is piped into American homes by TV with these gladiators earning all this big money to be symbols of masculinity for the civilization," he continued.

In the book that he referred to, author Betty Lehan Harragan attempted to analyze this situation:

It is no accident that 80 percent of the businessmen who comprise today's chief executive officers told *Fortune* magazine some years ago that football was their favorite spectator sport . . . College textbooks often introduce business management subjects to inexperienced students by using the illustration of a football platoon . . . Top Management in business feels an intense affinity to the head coach of a football team; their problems seem almost identical . . . Sports metaphors abound in business talk, as might be expected.

To illustrate her point Harragan shows these parallels:

Back-up team or bench strength: Full complement of trained, duplicate players who sit on the sideline bench prepared to enter the game at any moment to replace players who are hurt, tired, or otherwise removed. In management, the upper three levels of hierarchy contain several strong executives who are fully trained to take over the top job at any time. By extension, smart supervisors move to train subordinates for their jobs to pave the way for their own advancement to higher levels. Considered a sign of a well-managed company or department.

Coach: The boss. The unquestioned decision maker for the team. Not a player. One whose job is to motivate and help players perform well together. A current fad in management training, as in "the best manager considers himself a coach."

Disqualified player: One who has been ousted from the game as a penalty for a personal foul. The severest penalty for prohibited acts traceable to loss of emotional control under stress, as illegally tripping or hitting another player in anger. Significantly, women "disqualified" from management are usually described as "emotionally unsuited."

End run: Moving around the lightly defended ends of the line to avoid massed opposition in the center, as when women create new jobs for themselves rather than competing with men for an existing "man's" job.

Huddle: Get together with selected coworkers before a meeting to devise ways to get one's point across against opposition; make a deal with collaborators who stand to benefit from cooperation. Literally, the team get-together before each play on the field when quarterback gives secret signals that tell each player where to position himself, what to do, to facilitate the play.

Jock: A male professional athlete; a thoroughgoing competitive team sportsman. The "jocko mentality" pervades highly competitive, nonregulated industries.

Monday morning quarterback: A pejorative term describing player or spectator who delights in explaining how something "should have been done," or "How I would have done it." An after-the-fact analyzer who points out the obvious—that something should have been done differently since the attempted move failed.

Punt: A quick kick of the ball in desperate circumstances when it's necessary to get out of an untenable position. A gamble against great odds.

Quarterback: A key player who calls the signals, i.e. tells other players what to do, and how. Absolute authority figure on the field as delegate of coach.

Tackle the job: Approach a task with single-minded concentration, as "Let's break the back on this." Overused cliché supposed to rev up team players.

"You see what I'm saying," Nightmare said. "If football is the metaphor for corporate competition, how does the white man feel about the fact that black men, who are only ten percent of the American male population, make up seventy-five percent of the superstars in football and about thirty-five percent of all professional football players?

"I think this works on his mind in subtle ways more than the sexual thing, but I don't think it's all negative—the way it works on his mind. I think it makes him curious. See, Vince Lombardi is the patron saint of CEOs, the master coach. But I think one of these guys is going to be like Hank Stram, when he was coach of the Kansas City Chiefs, in the AFL. Remember? The AFL was the *other* league. The NFL had all the great teams and all the great players.

"Secretly Hank Stram began drafting all these niggers, picking them up from Grambling and Southern while the NFL was bidding for the talent from Notre Dame and Michigan State.

"Hey, it's a documented fact. Then they started having interleague games and Hank Stram turned all these niggers loose on the NFL's glory boys. The niggers killed them. Check the record. Check out the Super Bowls. The NFL has never recovered.

"Corporate life is like it was with baseball before Jackie Robinson. You're going to get a crazy Branch Rickey–type white boy as a CEO, who is going to come out of the dugout in a losing cause and signal for a bad black dude like Cliff Alexander, or me. He's going to say: "I don't care if I get booed. I don't care if they make threats on my life. I'll tough this one out. I want to win and I'm going to field the best player."

Nightmare leaned back, pleased with himself, pleased that he had been able to get a lot of things out of himself. He is not a typical black male manager, nor has his life been usual. It seems instead to be the hyperbole which expresses the essence of many men's struggle to find and maintain a sense of self in the corporation.

VIII

BLACK WOMEN, WHITE WOMEN AND THE WAY IT IS

"THAT'S THE PROBLEM. That's it," said Jackie Howard, a black woman who worked as regional manager of health services for an electronics manufacturing company. "As I see it, the black man confronts the white man too much," she continued, attempting to get a good hold on the idea. "The black man confronts the white man—or let me say in the brother's defense, if I care to defend him—men in general confront each other all the time. With them it's a battle of egos. The problem for the black man is that the white man is bound to win these confrontations.

"Of course the white man is not going to confront the brother to his face. He doesn't have to. He can use the system against him. That's how the brother gets beaten down, eventually. I know in our region there are some beaten-down brothers, and so the sisters are the ones who are pushing, but I'm not sure I agree that the black woman will outdistance the black man in corporate life."

Among blacks, men had a considerable head start in the mainstream, at least ten years, but as soon as the black woman came in, a myth grew that she would soon overtake and pass the black man. "Just as we've done in so many other areas," said Lorraine Oliver, a supervisor in the customer-relations department of a major cosmetics firm.

Some black women believe the myth, and a good number of the black men we talked to also believed it. "The sisters are doing fine," said Eugene Harris, a sales manager for an office-products company. He named two black females in his company who were about to pass him. He was more sad than bitter.

"I have to have lunch next month with my supervisor so he can tell me that I've reached my peak in the company. I know that's what he's going to say. I think that's one thing the sisters should be aware of: they are behind black men right now because they came in later, and so they are moving up faster, but they might reach their peak just as we've done. It's easier to get promoted when you're on the lower levels. When you get into middle management, that's when it gets rough. Most black women have not come to this point, so some of them are being manipulated into thinking that the black man ain't shit, again," he said on this, his last lunch before departing on a five-city trip to brief five branch managers on a new productivity audit.

He was subdued and "beaten down" in a way that the next few black female managers we interviewed were not. They were full of energy and optimism. Some were disappointed about their personal lives, but they were much more positive about their chances of making good careers in corporate America.

"I don't blame the sisters," Harris continued. "What happened is this: Black males were in corporate life first. When the sisters joined, they immediately came in to help the black male with the black agenda—getting fair treatment for black managers across the board. But many sisters soon discovered that the black agenda was really the black male agenda.

"What it was, I think, is that the black male found himself ahead of her for once in his life, and he wanted to stay ahead. He helped other black males, but in a lot of cases he didn't take her seriously. First, he was as chauvinistic as the white man. Second, he didn't always trust her, for some of the same reasons that men, in general, don't trust women. Third, he was suspicious of her for the reasons that black men are suspicious of black women," he said, inadvertently displaying the kind of thinking that forms the basis for most of our prejudices, our likes and dislikes, our concepts about social reality and our misconceptions, which either poison us or help us make sense out of the world we have inherited.

"So, naturally, she jumped ship and decided to go for herself. She got the white boys to help her. Then you had a lot of black dudes saying that she was aligning herself *with* the white man *against* him, saying that the white man promoted her and favored her because she could be counted twice on the EEO report, favored her because she was no real threat to his dominance because, since she was a woman, he could manipulate her.

"If she wouldn't go to bed with the brother, or if she was cute, or if she hung out with the white boys, he accused her of sleeping with white dudes. He still talked to her but there was definitely a separation. See, this is history repeating itself. That's what's been happening all along to black people," he said, laughing.

In several companies there was evidence of a great deal of tension among black male and female managers. It was subdued but it was there. "Sure," said Marvin Kelly, who is part of a target marketing team for the same office-products firm as Eugene Harris, "I heard footsteps behind me. I felt threatened by the sister coming up behind me. I mean, this is natural. I think she has an easier time in the system than the black male. I don't know," he said. "I agree that she does have two strikes against her: she is black and she is female, both. But together those strikes will get her in the game because they keep her from swinging for a home run. She is less ambitious. She uses that last strike and just tries to hit a single."

Weeks later a black female listened to these ideas. "Isn't that sad," she said. "But that's where we are."

Clark Puryear, a college recruiter, said that the myth might become reality because "there are many more black women on college campuses than black men. Just from the point of view of sheer numbers, it might prove true."

To better understand the different problems facing male and female black managers, we attended a conference for black female managers at a Washington hotel, where we met Roberta Mosley, a social psychologist who was a keynote speaker at the conference. "Women seem to be much more realistic," Dr. Mosley said. "Black women don't come in with the expectations that they're going to become presidents of these companies. A lot of these little black guys—especially ones from the better business schools—come in thinking that they're going to zoom to the top. When they fail, they're disenchanted and they get frustrated, angry and somewhat apathetic," she told the group in a session on corporate goal setting.

This was one of many groups of corporate black women who held meetings and seminars in order to decide what to do about their careers. Such meetings were becoming extremely popular. Black men held meetings too, and there were other meetings attended by black men and women, but it seemed that the women were much more intent on planning and strategizing in group settings. The men were more often loners. This conference, though, was unlike the others in that it was scheduled for an entire weekend. The twenty-three women attending had come to wrestle with their problems until dinnertime Sunday night.

"I'm not saying that I believe the myth either," said the small bright-skinned social psychologist during the luncheon break on Saturday. "But I can see why some people believe it. Women in general, I think, find it easier to conform. Women orient themselves to the world as it is. Men see visions of how the world ought to be," she said, still searching for the right handles to give the women, in order for them to hold up their experiences long enough to take a good look.

"You'll notice in all the literature by white women on corporate life that there is very little criticism of that life," she said. "In the book *Managerial Woman,* the first chapter is called 'The Way It Is.' This is what women are interested in finding out. There are many ways that black women do not tune into the woman's movement, but there are many ideas from the movement that are applicable, and I think that this is one of them.

"Women follow rules with less felt sense of loss of ego or face. They find it easier to say: 'I don't know. I'm uninformed. Tell me.' The women's movement seems to be now telling women: 'Your way is not the best way. Give up your way and learn to do it as a man does it. After all, his way must be better than yours; this is the reason he has dominated you for so long.'

"This all comes out of western psychology, pioneered by Freud. White women have been taught that they are without something, a penis, if you're a Freudian, and the movement has been trying to tell them that they must operate as if they had one—have balls, if you will.

"To the extent that the black woman buys into this, directly or indirectly, she is likely to feel: 'Hey, guys, don't blame me. I'll show you I can be just like you. I'll do exactly what you do.'

"Whereas the black man says, despite the fact that he has not built an IBM or an Exxon himself, 'Hey, since I've been here I've learned some things about this system, and I know some things about myself, so let me try to do it my way.' The black man dissents more, and so he doesn't seem to adapt as easily. It's harder for him to adapt."

This is one truth, but there are others. It could be argued that men adapt better and this is why they wear their corporateness so totally. In some companies it was the women who were the splashers, because the men were either tired or felt that career advancement was an individual thing and that any identification with a group, especially a disrespected racial group, could do their individual careers more harm than good.

There was something enticing about the social psychologist's ease of generalization. However, "the black woman is also used to making do," she continued. "This has been the lesson that history has taught her, so she might seem less impatient about racial discrimination. She will put up with a situation until she can do better."

By this time, five of the women attending the conference had gathered around Dr. Mosley. "I also think there is some truth to the idea that black women are not as threatening to the white male power structure, and therefore just on a one-to-one basis white men have an easier time accepting them. The black woman can disagree with a white man without his feeling the same loss of face that he would if a black man, who worked for him, disagreed with him. She can suggest things to him. She can even manipulate his superiority complex into a desire to help her master some of the new territory she has to master. He will let useful information drop because he feels, 'You're just a woman, you really don't know what to do with it.' Black psychologists are having a field day with this idea that the black male's physical presence, and all it conjures up in terms of stereotypes, images and very primitive male competitiveness, puts the black male at a disadvantage as long as the white man thinks in terms of 'we/they.' "

As long as no one interrupted, the words continued to roll out of her pleasant face. Her generalizations, formed out of archetypes and stereotypes, suggested that a price would be exacted from those women who dared to be exceptions. It was apparent that she liked to generalize about matters that could not be gotten at by statisticians.

"Until the white man accepts the black man as an American like himself, until he recognizes the black man as a member of the team, as one of 'us Americans,' he is going to use the system to keep him down as a competitor.

"On the other hand, he might not see the black woman this way, because there again arises this idea that she is less ambitious," she said.

One woman winced but held her peace in the face of this idea that black women are not serious contenders in the same way that black men are. Evidence suggests that the seriousness is equal in intensity if not in style. The difference in style comes, no doubt, from the acceptance by most black women we interviewed of the difference between themselves and men.

Most of the black women we interviewed had not accepted even a part of androgynist theory. They insisted that men and women are different. They were women and they wanted equality, not similarity. One of the women listening to Dr. Mosley commented, "I think we're just as ambitious as men, we just don't show it." This generalization too had to be qualified, because in its way the ambition showed everywhere—in demeanor, in time commitments, in worried brows.

The woman who had held her peace said: "I think there is a perception that women in general are less ambitious than men, but I think that this is just a part of the woman's strategy. She knows that nothing turns a man off faster than a woman who is too openly ambitious, but believe me I want to be chairman of the board just as much as the black man does."

"Do you really?" asked Mosley. The women waited for her to continue, but she didn't. It seemed that the psychologist was much more comfortable speaking in front of an audience than going one on one with these younger women. She was older and somewhat old-fashioned. This was apparent from the beliefs that seemed to underlie the modern surface of her argument.

She had a husband who had grown children by another marriage. Both her daughters and her son were out of college. She had been married all of her adult life, and though she was successful her career had not consumed her life.

She had given us two interviews before inviting us to the weekend women's meeting. She had admitted that her world was far removed from the transitional world in which her young female clients were doing battle.

At the conference the women had a section of the hotel dining room cordoned off for themselves behind a folding wall. Behind that wall there was probably more hustle and bustle, more of a din than there was in the kitchen. From the level of energy and activity it was hard to believe that even the WASP male's positions were safe from these women. They were about business. They were about their careers.

There was an eagerness and an earnestness about them. Having corporate careers seemed to give them a tremendous sense of accomplishment. They seemed optimistic. They were far from satisfied, but they were happy to be on their way. They seemed to have no regrets that they were not yet superstars of the corporate world. Their egos seemed not to put rain clouds above their parade.

They undoubtedly knew intimately what their mothers and grandmothers had had to go through, and so their mood and energy seemed to reflect how far they, collectively, had come, rather than how far they had to go.

Joyce Ivory, a tall, brown-skinned feminist from Chicago, wanted to figure out how black women could stop defining themselves in relation to men. It did no good to tell her that men define themselves in relation to women. The idea she wanted to get across was that men go ahead and define themselves and then women have to fall in with that. "Women ought to do the same," she said in an office she had rented for a black feminist newsletter that she wanted to publish.

Joyce Ivory's anger had a soft aura, as if it were an argument against a vulnerability to men, and as if she intended in time to overcome it with her newsletter. Sandra "Sandy" Wilson, on the other hand, was not a crusader for female self-definition. She had simply struck out into the no-man's land of her female self after the breakup of a marriage which, she said, never should have been.

"I got married simply because I was cute and men liked me and would date me and want to give me things for any one of the number of reasons that men like to give cute women things." Sandy Wilson said she was very happy because she finally belonged to herself. "I like going to work every day to my own neat, orderly office. I block out time for myself—a week, let's say—and I know there are goals that I want to reach before that week is up, and I want to put as much of my time as possible into the accomplishment of those goals, in a manner that represents my *best* effort." She talked excitedly and moved her hands around in the air like yellow butterflies in her own neat little office.

"And so during the week," she continued, "I try to make sure that nothing in my personal life will detract from either my time or the attention that I can devote to the accomplishment of those goals. During that time I won't accept a date with any man because that date or that man is bound to bring out concerns that have nothing to do with the accomplishment of those goals," she said rapidly.

"I work from, say, eight in the morning until seven at night, in the office. Then I might plan a period of exactly one hour or two hours, or whatever, that I'm going to spend at home that night. I'm glad that I don't live with anyone—a husband or a boyfriend or a female roommate. I'm happy that I don't have a child; because what I want to do is devote my entire self to the accomplishment of these tasks.

"So I can come home and get something to eat, or maybe I'll go out to eat because the company pays me well enough to go out anytime I want to. If I go out to eat with someone, it will be either someone who relates to my career so we can gossip about that, someone who relates to these goals I have set for myself, or someone who will not bring up any distracting topics. I'm not interested in being either upset or stimulated in any way.

"Then I can be home by nine o'clock. I can either choose to look at some television or just have the television on. I might talk on the phone to someone concerning the job. I might call home and talk to my folks, if I feel that what they say is not going to upset me in any way. They know by now that the only thing I want to handle during the week is: 'Hello, how are you? Fine. I love you. Good-bye,'" she said, shaking her bobbed hair like a girl in a shampoo TV commercial.

"Then I will decide if I want to tackle the two hours of work I scheduled for myself, or whether I want to fall asleep and get up at five in the morning and do the work. This would depend on how fresh I am.

"These are the kinds of things that make me think that I really don't want to have children. I couldn't devote this kind of time to what I want to do. This is why I'm glad that my boyfriend is in Washington, D.C. He lives there. I have no desire to move to be closer to him and he's so deeply involved with his thing that he certainly wouldn't want to move up here. We see each other twice a month.

"If I get transferred to California and I couldn't see him, I don't think it would matter that much, and I don't think I would spend time writing long letters, or spend a lot of money calling long distance for very long. I think that the relationship would just fade away.

"I think this is what it means to be totally devoted to your job. There are plenty of people who run a routine just like this. They haven't got it down as smoothly as I have. They keep trying to make things fit into their lives that won't fit in. I don't want to be super-mom. I don't want to do all this corporate stuff and have a child too, I just want the corporate life.

"It's not that I want to be a vice-president of the company. I'm not even looking that far ahead, although I'm making choices that will make that kind of career path possible should I choose to take it. I'm not burning any bridges behind me, but for now I'm very happy just accomplishing these tasks that are assigned to me.

"I get a great deal of pleasure out of going to meetings and listening to what other people have to say, and of saying my two cents' worth. Just getting up the nerve to speak out in meetings is an accomplishment for me, and I'm proud of myself for doing that, especially if the meeting is based on departmental targets for the entire year in a situation that involves millions and millions of dollars.

"A lot of the things that others don't like about corporate life, I love. I like writing memos and knowing that these memos that I write will be read by some of the higher-ups in the company. I don't know. They might throw most of the memos in the trash can, but one time I saw one of my memos attached to a report that my supervisor was sending out to the field and I felt like I wanted to frame that report and put it on my bedroom wall at home. I really did.

"When I get to be a supervisor, I'm going to love having people working for me, and I'm going to try to develop in my people the right kind of attitude that will help them advance their careers. I have to do a lot of paper pushing, but I don't really mind. I get pleasure out of getting that paper work done. You might not believe it, but I wake up in the morning happy that I've had a good night's sleep so I will have the energy to go in and tackle the pile of paper work that I have to clear away."

She grew serious for a moment: "I didn't always love my job. I think est [Erhard Seminar Training] gave me an experience of myself. It helped me to center myself and to eliminate a lot of the garbage in my life so I would have the space that was necessary for me to do what I needed to do," she said, speaking earnestly about est, the popular, shortcut method for finding a fragment of the self to believe in.

Sandy Wilson had used it to journey away from the rich but confusing entanglement with the complicated emotional relationships that are the soul of black life. She wanted her life as orderly and uncluttered as the office she worked in, as orderly as the long corporate corridors outside her office and the rows of similar offices that stretched from one end of her cantilevered building to the other.

"I was married once. That was the lowest point in my life. My ex-husband made me feel that there was something wrong with me for being like I am. He was a college professor—Afro-American studies, and he would try to keep me up half the night talking about the same ideas over and over, and he made me feel guilty for not being involved with anything other than my job.

"He wanted to have a child, and he said that his schedule would permit him to spend a great deal of time with the child and so I could still have the child and pursue my career, but try to imagine me keeping the schedule I just talked about and raising a child at the same time.

"I love children, children are great, but I think I may have gotten all of my maternal urges out as a teenager when I had to raise my younger brothers and sisters. And I got most of my need for a lover relationship satisfied during the four years that I was married. I hated myself. I let myself get fat. I disliked the confusion that my ex-husband was bringing into the house in the form of a lot of noncorporate people who felt that they were superior to corporate people, and I bet I make more money now than any two of them," she said, laughing.

"The only way I would ever get married again would be to a corporate man who wanted his life set up exactly as I have set mine up. I wouldn't even accept a second date with anyone who is not about what I'm about. I don't like to be around anyone who questions any of the decisions I've made about my life. Anyone who does this automatically reminds me of my ex-husband and thus reminds me of the most miserable time in my life, and so when this man calls me up for a second date I tell him, 'I don't like to schedule dates because a date obligates me and I don't really like to be obligated to another person. I like to be free to fulfill my obligations to myself.' I tell the guy that if he calls back and finds me in the right mood, I might let him take me out to dinner.

"Most guys don't call back. The one or two who persist are, by their persistence, telling me that they are willing to play it my way. So when we go out on the date, I control the conversation to make sure he doesn't take it off into some area that I don't care to deal with.

"Except this one guy, who is very persistent, who stays on my mind a lot and so sometimes when he calls I might be feeling a little down and so we'll go out and he'll listen to my problems whether they be job-related or related to some kind of loneliness or home-sickness, or something that one of my brothers and sisters said on the phone that upsets me. He's slick. He knows that sooner or later he's going to catch me at the right time, and then he's going to work his way inside, and get this fantastic sexual relationship started, and then he feels that he's going to be in control.

"I do get lonely living up here surrounded totally by white people —nice people, and I could have a white boyfriend at the drop of a hat —but this guy, he's black and I insult him, but he still doesn't go away. It's an interesting little battle. I don't think I'm going to give in to him," she said, as if she were in control of herself enough to know that the option was totally her own. As if he had almost no power in the decision.

"He's corporate but he looks at corporate life differently than I do. I have no noble corporate ambitions, no grand schemes, but he has a corporate Reggie Jackson complex. He wants to be a star and he'd like to get this sexual thing started because he thinks that he could then get me on his team. He promises that he can make me a corporate star too, but the trick is that I might become a star before he does—just by concentrating on what I can manage, doing a good job, getting excited about the interactions between people, trying not to think of them as either black or white.

"This is me. This is Sandra. I'm sure the president of the company doesn't go home thinking about how much Sandy Wilson has contributed to the company, but I think about it. I get ideas in the middle of the night and I jump up and write them down. I think each day about how much my little efforts contribute to the overall strength of the company.

"When I make the President's Club, or the Golden Circle, I feel proud, and all of the plaques I get I hang on the wall in the office and then I get duplicates and hang those on the wall at home. Every time I see one of our products advertised on TV, I feel proud, or I listen to the commercial and think of ways that I could make the commercial better or make the product better. This is what I like doing."

There is no way to tell how many women have freed themselves in the way Sandy has. It seemed that Sandy had done what Joyce Ivory wanted to advocate in her black feminist newsletter. Joyce Ivory said no. Joyce's office was cluttered. The walls were covered with posters advocating dozens of causes or advertising dozens of art shows and concerts by socially conscious artists. Joyce Ivory said she still wanted to "wrestle with the problems of society. If feminism means anything to the black woman, it must mean this," she said.

There was evidence that most women we interviewed still wanted to wrestle with social and human problems in the way that most corporate men and some women, like Sandy, did not want to do. Because they are concerned about other things. These women might seem to be less single-mindedly ambitious.

Women are, in the words of a data control manager in Cleveland "traditionally the keepers of the hearth and the culture. Whatever we give up will be lost to generations. We want to be successful corporate managers but we must be other things too. It's a shame that men don't realize that they must be other things."

The answer for such women seems to lie in changing the corporation so they can be these other things and still hold serious corporate jobs alongside men who have been liberated enough to be other things. Being totally job orientated seems to be more difficult for black women than white women even though black women have had a longer history of working to support themselves.

The difference might arise in the fact that the two groups of women have stood in very different relationship to the American economy, and thus to corporate life.

Many white women have been involved in corporate life as wives of men who ran corporations. This history endures for many of them who are still wives in what might be referred to as old-fashioned marriages.

The white American marriage, which is to say the archetypical American marriage, was designed so that the wife supported the husband's efforts in the economic world, and even when it functioned imperfectly it was more supportive of white male ambition than all but a few of the best of those fragile things called black families.

From the black side of the tracks we used to hear white men say, as no doubt some still do, "A good wife is worth a million dollars." In the ideal American scheme this worth could be calculated in two columns. First, on the very practical level she was his helpmate, his capable support, his confidante; second, on the symbolic level she was the inspiration for his working so hard to make that million dollars—for God, country and the little woman.

This is the famous, or infamous, pedestal upon which she was placed. It is certainly true, as the women's movement has been telling us, that this family system's smooth functioning depended upon the suppression of many of the rights of women. It is equally true, as we learn from some of the literature of the movement, that many women went mad under this suppression.

But it is untrue to say that the white woman was kept in her role simply by the superior economic power of the white male. On a crude level we can agree with Reuben Hill and Howard Becker's statement, in *Family, Marriage and Parenthood,* that "money is a source of power that supports male dominance" because "money belongs to him who earns it, not to her who spends it, since he who earns it may withhold it."

But in the ideal American marriage women were also acting out role behavior that had some relationship to biological functioning. No doubt the roles had been distorted in male-dominated civilization, but the roles had a great deal to do with how the people involved defined manhood and womanhood. Thus eager, happy support was "natural" from someone who believed that was what she was put on earth to do, in return for the provision and protection she got from her husband.

Working hard, succeeding and coming home to "the little wife" were a husband's obligations. Staying at home with aid and comfort was the "right" wife's obligation. We learn from John Cuber and Peggy Harroff's *The Significant Americans* that influential Americans were nearly always married to the "right" wife.

Even the conflicts between these couples were controlled. "At worst," the authors wrote, "there was some private quarreling, nagging and 'throwing up the past' of which members of the immediate family, and more rarely close friends and relatives, have some awareness. At best the couple is discreet and polite, genteel about it in the company of others."

Other couples in this mid-sixties study of male-female relationships between white adults who were clearly successful in business and the professions, "did duty" for each other. Others were passively congenial to each other, with the husband pouring most of his passion into his work, and his wife pouring hers into community activities. There were some who were wrapped up in each other, the wife cheerfully supporting the husband and believing that to be the price she paid for the salary he made and shared with her. This is the way the system was supposed to work. We know of course that it did not work this way for most black families, and this has more than a little to do with the crisis of black families today.

Only a few couples in the study lived up to the ideal expressed by one among the 437 upper-middle-class adults who participated: "Her femininity, easy charm and wit are invaluable assets to me," the ideal male interviewee said. "I know it's conventional to say that a man's wife is responsible for his success and I also know that it's often not true. But in my case I gladly acknowledge that it's not only true but she's indispensable to me."

His ideal wife kept files for him and accompanied him on trips just to be there to support him. She was his home-office manager, his gal Friday and the mother of his kids.

Despite the fact that the number of ideal marriages in the study was small, the majority of the marriages held together. When they were not held together by mutual acknowledgment of the dependency of each on the other, they were held together by tradition, practical convenience, social sanctions, punitive divorce laws and severe, built-in restraints on the economic activities of white women.

Despite the fact that many of these forces are not as instrumental in holding together the marriages of corporate men today, we found that most of the successful managers are married, and most of the black managers who are doing well are also married.

Some of them are in new marriages, two-paycheck marriages with both partners on nearly equal economic levels, but the greater number are in modified versions of the old-fashioned marriage. The modification is that the wife works. Traditionally, black women *have* worked. "I don't think there is enough black club activity and this sort of thing to sustain a black woman day in and day out," said Clarence Warren, a happily married black marketing director living in the Boston suburbs. He explained what was traditional about his marriage.

"My wife works as a schoolteacher, and I know some other corporate wives who work in real estate. These two professions seem to give the woman the flexibility of time that will enable her to help her husband deal with the demands of his job." His marriage was very much husband-centered, in the American tradition. But it was also wife-centered, in an equally traditional way, because he was bringing flowers home to her after his three-day marketing conference in Mexico City.

She is out of the house during the time that the kids are in school and she is back home well before her husband returns. It produces a stable situation for the husband and gives the wife a sense of independent success and accomplishment that does not compete with his.

"There's no doubt that it is much tougher for a black wife to fit into this pattern since she had no role models: her mother was not a corporate wife. My wife is very much in sync as far as her role as schoolteacher and mother, and she's a great wife. I would say that much of my success I would attribute to her support. When I have a problem she sits up all night and listens even though she might have to go to work tired the next day.

"I call her to tell her the result of deals that we've discussed at home, that involve my job but that she's given me advice on. I think it is unquestionably an asset for a man to be married—to the 'right' woman of course," he said and smoothed down his pencil-thin mustache. This conversation was, of course, from a man's point of view. It did not acknowledge how much harder it is becoming in the modern world to be the "right" woman, and how much harder to decide, "right" for whom?

Was his wife content to discuss his deals, or would she rather be involved in deals herself? Did she really like the flowers, or would she have preferred to be a marketing director herself, on her way home from a convention in Mexico? There are very few women today who are not troubled by these questions.

We agree with an unbylined article in the New York *Amsterdam News,* America's largest-circulation black newspaper:

Many women derive great satisfaction from a full-time career as mother and homemaker. . . . Not every woman is interested [however] in being a housewife, any more than every woman is interested in being a teacher or a doctor.

Many women abandon outside career goals for home-centered life because of pressure to fulfill their role. It is not an easy compromise to make. Feeling trapped in a lifestyle at odds with their real interests and goals, many women become increasingly overwhelmed with frustration and anger as the years slip by.

This, of course, is only a part of the problem. To the extent that this has been, and to a great extent still is, a white society, life is harder on black people. To the extent that this has been, and to a great extent still is, a male-dominated society, life is, during this transitional time, bound to be more confusing for women. Think then of black women in corporate management for whom life is both hard and confusing. These are the two strikes that the ambitious black woman has against her.

There seems to be no doubt that the percentage of black male managers who are married is lower than the percentage of married white male managers. The percentage of married black female managers is lowest of all. "I was in a black corporate women's group nine years ago," said Eunice Lewis, a big-eyed manager of employee relations for an oil company. "At that time nine of us were married and one wasn't. Today eight of us are divorced, and one is questionable. It's unfair. It's unfair, I tell you, that my career, which is so positive, should have such a negative effect on my personal life.

"I think that men don't worry about this because they have not been taught to place such a high value on personal life. They don't have to worry as much about how personal decisions affect others—affect children, for example," she said angrily even though she didn't have children.

"The thing that we are discussing now is the very reason why I don't have any, and yes, I'm very angry about that. I had a little twerp tell me that I was too selfish to have children. When a woman worries about herself she is regarded as selfish because she has to be consciously selfish to put herself and her needs first. This all came up because I won this T-shirt with 'ME!' printed across the front. This guy told me he hated that shirt and it showed that I was too selfish to be involved with anyone.

"Men can put their needs first without even being conscious of being selfish. They just do. They don't need a T-shirt to remind them. 'ME!' is written all over everything they do. Therefore, they go about being selfish without ever being accused or self-accused." She softened the tone of her voice as she said this.

A frequent pattern for the black female manager's life seems to be as follows: An early marriage to a man she has since divorced, who either did not advance as far as she did or who advanced but attempted to retard her advancement. She has a child who is, at present, about eight years old and in a private school. She dates someone who is not committed to her and she has some problems about giving herself up to a noncommitted relationship, while at the same time she has the desire to be in a committed relationship.

Eunice Lewis fits the mold, except that she has no children and no one she dates regularly. Five times during the interview with her, she mentioned that she earned almost fifty thousand dollars a year. Several times she simply said "a woman at my economic level," as if she were telling about a source of pride and a curse, a charm upon which her self-worth was based but which had also driven away the weak or soft portions of what she desired for herself. "A black man can't deal with a woman at my level," she kept saying.

The problem is that women know there is something to look for besides success in a career. Fulfillment for them is not confined to that single criterion. Marcia Henderson, a manager in the real-estate division of an electronics firm, told us: "I used to call my grandmother in Alabama every time I got promoted, and I used to notice that my grandmother, who loves me madly, was never very happy about my promotions. This really made me unhappy and so one day I asked her why. She said, 'Child, you keep getting promoted you gonna lose your husband.'

"She was right. I lost him even before my next promotion. Then every time I got another raise or promotion my grandmother would say, 'You done lost one husband, you keep on going and you ain't gonna get another one.'"

The consensus among women we interviewed was that a black man cannot deal with a woman who makes more money than he does, and this is why it is so difficult for a successful black woman to get a man.

Some men commented that a black woman will not marry a man who makes less money because she is tied into an upward-mobility mentality which will make her abusive to a man if he doesn't make as much. " 'I can get along without you,' is the first thing that comes out of our mouths," said Roberta Mosley, the psychologist who spoke at the conference we attended.

"We say it all the time. 'I'm making my own money. I don't have to put up with this.' We become very intolerant," she said. She had her afro hairdo combed in another style. Her grown daughters had probably given up wearing afros, as had all but one of the women in the group.

Roberta Mosley spun her theories out over the women as she moved playfully in front of them, her body moving freely under a loose-fitting robe-type dress. "If we marry a man who makes less than we do, we feel that we are marrying beneath us," she laughed. "It has something to do with the feeling of being used. It has something to do with, for God's sake, that this man has not taken care of his responsibilities. We are a little bit tired of all these brave Mandinka warriors who have trouble getting out of bed to go on the hunt, much less bring back the game." The other women at the conference swung in with her and began to laugh.

"And it is true that the black male ego cannot deal with it, often times. He might have difficulty feeling like a real man. He'd rather date a secretary, someone he can dazzle with his eighteen-thousand-dollar-per-year salary, or a white woman he can dazzle with his supposed sexual prowess." She made a gesture that broke the women up with laughter.

"This is a very complex problem and it is not going to go away. It may be a lot worse before it gets better. It's created a lot of angry black women and a lot of black men who've just tuned out. A woman wants a man to take care of her *for once,* and yet she doesn't really need to be taken care of and she'll let him know it if she gets angry. Black males and females define manhood in very traditionally American ways, so you have this black man who wants to feel that he is bringing home the bacon. If he's not actually doing this it's a form of castration. Very often this is a man's way of giving love: by providing for the material needs of 'his woman and family.' Often he does not know of any other way to give love. It's a mess.

"This is an interesting dynamic for the corporate black woman. It is interesting to look at how she feels that she is giving love. If she goes out and makes a salary, isn't she just like the black man? She might feel that she is giving love by helping him, or even taking the leadership in meting the bill collectors each month.

"He wants her to give love in the more traditionally American feminine ways, by being submissive, by serving him, by being cuddly and Doris Day cute.

"He doesn't feel loved, just as a woman doesn't feel loved if all the man is doing is bringing home the bacon. So what we have to do is figure out what it will take for each of us to feel loved. Very often the black man will feel that he is giving love by making love, but a woman might feel that he is doing nothing more than using her again. It's a mess, I tell you. She feels that she is simply being used sexually, and because of her history, nothing turns her off faster. She would rather not acknowledge her need for sex; in many cases, she would rather be celibate than to feel she is simply being used sexually. The trade-off is missing. What is he giving her for this prize—her body—that she is giving him? He certainly isn't giving her help with her career problems. He's usually too wrapped up in his own career problems—and God help you if your career is going better than his. He's not going to help you at all. He might end up attacking you. The poor woman might have to ask him to help her with the housework and the kids because he is still caught up in the role of this being a woman's responsibility, and so by doing the dishes or cooking once in a while, he feels that he is doing her a favor. He still wants that freedom to run the streets, corporate style, that his father had, but he wants you to account for your time in the streets because you are 'a woman,' and this you must do in order for him to feel that you are 'his woman.' So quite rightly the woman asks: What is he doing for me? Oh my God. My daughter, myself.

"From the man's standpoint, he can ask the same question. I'll give you an example. I have a lot of clients who are professionals. I counseled a woman who was very much in love with her husband and she couldn't understand his deep resentment toward her. He had helped her get a professional degree and through his friends he had helped her get a really fine job, but then all of a sudden he started pulling away. She couldn't understand it, so she blamed it on the same thing that you blame it on: the black man can't deal with a woman who makes more money than he. I listened for about three sessions to what she was saying and then I made a suggestion.

"I suggested to her that since she was making such a good salary why didn't she try bringing home gifts to him. She hit the roof. At first she was completely turned off to the idea, and she disliked me for suggesting it. The idea: her bringing home gifts for a man. But she eventually tried it and it worked. Here's why: Successful men bring gifts to their women; why shouldn't a successful woman bring gifts to her man? Women still want to *be* the gift. She wants to bring her tired body as a gift. She is forgetting that a man's path is strewn with more bodies, white and black, male and female, than he could ever possibly want. He couldn't continue to consider a woman's body a gift. He might even begin to consider it a duty and an obligation—work.

"He says: 'She's not bringing me gifts, she's not cooking for me or ironing my socks. She's not making the home comfortable for me. She's not helping me with my problems.' Quite rightly he asks: 'What in the hell is she doing for me? What do I need her for?' and he takes off. This is also an interesting dynamic: How do black men give love and feel loved?

"It's very very complex. We, as black people, have skipped an entire era in the history of the western world and we want to be modern but we still want to have some of those things that took place right after the age of chivalry. We want the little house with the white picket fence, the little apron and the hubby coming home to the two point two children named Dick and Jane and the dog named Spot, but we would be bored by that even if we got it. This confusion is where much of the anger of black women comes from, and we can live without bitterness and anger only when we stop blaming history and each other for what happened to us. We have to dust off the considerable advantages we have and get out into the market place."

Among the people we interviewed there was not a great deal of bitterness over the tremendous progress that white women have made in the corporate mainstream. It is simply a fact that most blacks resign themselves to with some sadness and no surprise.

Most of the black women we interviewed agreed that presently

(1981) more energy was being expended fighting sexual discrimination in corporations than fighting racial discrimination. The campaign to end racial discrimination highlighted the sixties, but it was a campaign against sexual discrimination that dominated the seventies.

Many black women complained that the war against sexism has been of only marginal benefit to them. They still had that racial strike against them. They were of the wrong sex during the sixties and the wrong race during the seventies, losing in both decades.

"For a number of reasons sisterhood has not been a powerful resource for the black woman in corporate America," said Roberta Mosley, opening the conference's afternoon session. "In some companies I've been in, black women have been included in women's caucuses only because it would have been conspicuous to exclude them.

"I think, however, it's a waste of time to say, as I've heard some black women say, that these little white girls are just like their daddies when it comes to race. I think it was simplistic to think they'd be otherwise, but even to spend time deciding if this is true or not is a waste. I think it would be more productive to look at what white women share with other members of the 'protected classes' under Title VII of the nineteen sixty-four Civil Rights Act, and to look at the differences and advantages that white women have—advantages that they cannot share with you women, and in many cases would not share even if they could."

For tactical reasons, or perhaps because they believed it, white women used to say that the gender hurdle was higher than the racial one, that white men would admit black men to positions of power before they would admit women of any race.

For example, a white woman in the communications industry said in the *Harvard Business Review* as late as 1978: "If the choice for a person to fill a job were between a black man and a woman, there is no question in my mind how it would go. Corporate America would choose the black man."

Coming as late as it did in the seventies, this statement from so knowledgeable a woman must be viewed as a result of willful blindness. In 1978 a woman had already been chosen as chairperson of the board of one of the major TV networks, and a woman was soon to be named president of a major film studio, while no black man was even a senior vice-president in the industry.

By 1978 there were ten times as many white women as black men on the boards of major companies. "In the companies I consult with," said William Anderson, a management consultant with a small black-owned firm in New York and Washington, "the numbers of black male executives have remained pretty much the same over the last five years. A few black females have been added, but white women have made quantum leaps into the system and they are in many more diversified functions.

"In the beginning, in their anxiety, white women might have believed that black men had an easier time. Now all you have to do is look at the numbers." He stacked the questionnaires he had used in his session in a pile on a rear table of a large auditorium in the federal building where he was conducting the session for several federal departments.

The numbers show, as blacks contend, that white women are moving up much faster than other members of the protected classes. For one thing, there are more of them. For another, white women have never been totally out of the mainstream, even though they have not been in the water either. We can view the majority of white women prior to 1970 as people on rafts being pulled along the stream by fathers and brothers and husbands.

They were not, generally, economically more deprived than white men. Often, in fact, they enjoyed more of the benefits of the system than the white man who went out to work in it. In 1970 it was estimated that women controlled 80 percent of the nation's private wealth, but women were seldom elected to membership on powerful boards of directors, and the top jobs in industry, politics and public service were closed to them.

Of course, not all white women were housewives. Many worked, and they were usually confined to the dullest, most sedentary tasks, almost always under the supervision of men.

Numerically they dominated such professions as teaching, library work, nursing and certain social service occupations. However, most of the supervisory positions in these professions were held by white men, and often in these professions, as in other jobs, women were paid less for equal work.

As far as numbers are concerned, white women cannot be called a minority group since they outnumber white males. It is in the lack of power, and the resultant discrimination, that they qualified, along with racial minorities, for protection under Title VII of the 1964 Civil Rights Act. It is generally known that several congressmen voted for their inclusion not because they wanted to give them equality of opportunity but wanted to overload and therefore undermine the entire act by making it cover almost two thirds of all American citizens.

White women who wanted or needed to enter the labor force needed the protection of this act, because in many ways they had been treated as inferiors. They were in this respect like racial minority groups. The similarities were even more striking in those cases where women accepted the ascribed sense of their own inferiority. That internalized sense of inferiority often retarded full development of individual women's potential, as it did with individual members of racial minority groups.

But not since Salem, Massachusetts, in the sixteen hundreds, have American women been hanged for nonexistent crimes, whereas blacks have been in the twentieth century. They have not, during this century, been subjected to as harsh penalties under the criminal justice system. Law and custom has restricted them from many public and private facilities, but they have not been categorically relegated to facilities of inferior quality.

White women were not spat upon for trying to enter certain public schools, but custom, law and quotas barred them from many of the better schools and colleges in the nation. The treatment of white women has always been a strange mixture of chivalry and condescension, of kindly protectiveness and cruel manipulation.

The white woman was often subjected to cruel stereotyping, but usually this was no more harsh than the stereotypes that the culture ascribed to white men. The big difference was that the woman's ascribed characteristics were used to bar her from certain positions and privileges and to make her accept as her lot certain roles in the industrial order—the roles of wife and mother and emotional supporter for husband and family.

In many cases the myth of the contented housewife was as blind and cruel as the myth of the contented Negro, and often, like the Negro, a white woman had to distort her personality to conform to an image of herself that was designed to keep her subordinated.

But her position was never as bad as that of the black man or woman in America. "That's why it has been relatively easy for her to get accepted in the mainstream," said Carla Lewis, a black female manager with an insurance company. "You can see it now. In ten years there will be no comparison between her status and the status of other members of the protected classes. Paths are opening up for her. I don't know what you can say about it."

She said she had absolutely no animosity toward white women. In a corporation you use whatever you've got going for you in order to win. The white woman has this easy identification with the white man. "She's using it," Carla said. "In the name of sisterhood, I don't think there's going to be much reaching back. At this point it might be easier to get help from a white male than a white female." Carla spoke in her office with the door closed. She did not seem particularly unhappy. She had adjusted to life as it was.

"White women are just doing better than we are. I think they will continue to do better. One very simple reason is that there are more of them, and they are generally better educated, in greater numbers than are other minorities; thus, they have more usable skills as a group. All they had to do was transform Wellesley and Smith from finishing schools for wives, which is what they were a dozen years ago, into finishing schools for up-and-coming business types.

"It's not just a matter of *formal* education. White women are not discovering the nature of corporate life for the first time. Many of them have been around this kind of environment all their lives. At least the ones who are now highly successful in corporations. All they are doing is changing their place in the system.

"They know the subtle nuances of the system. They know how to interact with the system. They have more respect for the system because they know it is their system. They can use it more effectively because they trust it and it trusts them. They can organize and protest without raising the fear that they are trying to overthrow anything."

In addition, white women are capable of more effective subordination because many of them grew up with genuine awe for powerful white father figures, and with envy for their brothers, who were closer to their fathers than they were allowed to be.

Black women often comment on this apparent natural deference that white women have for powerful men in corporate life. Often the black girl didn't have a father, and when she did, she seldom was able to hold him in awe because she learned, often in painful ways, too much too soon about the limitations of his power to provide for or protect her and her mother.

Jacqueline Clarke, the director of public relations for a major liquor distributor, told of a meeting that white and black female managers held with the top management of their division. During the meeting a white female who was spokesperson for the group, "a militant libby right out of *Ms.* magazine," began laying it on heavy, vigorously expressing her views to the bosses.

Suddenly the biggest boss present said that he didn't think that women should curse. The white woman continued talking, continued sprinkling her monologue with profanity until the boss said, "God damn it. I said I don't think a woman should curse, so sit down and shut the fuck up."

The woman promptly sat down and started sniffling. Crude as this example is, it does display something about the freedom of interchange between white men and white women. The boss would have found it more difficult to exact this kind of deference from a black subordinate because the exchange could have been loaded with all sorts of racial overtones.

By expressing himself this way he might have given the impression that he was a racist, and he didn't want to do that; and, on another level, the boss could never be quite sure how the subordinate would react. A black man might go "crazy" and launch a physical attack before the security guards could get to the conference room. A black woman might turn into a "Sapphire" and let loose with a verbal attack that could scar the boss's ego for months.

"There is a comfort level that is missing, and it's missing because of the history that white men have created in order to justify the dominance that they have exercised over black people for so long. Black people continue to be victims of that history.

"White women seem to know more about what to say to the president of the company and how to say it. Deference is not a problem with them because it is not fraught with implications of submission to someone who might hold all sorts of demeaning racial stereotypes about you.

"White women are much more able to be demanding of the system because they are basically not interested in making radical changes in it. They are much more able to go to their fathers and brothers to talk over problems."

Tom Murphy, a white male, who is director of equal opportunities in the western region of a major chemical company, said that in the white woman's demands there is an implicit "whine." "If you don't take care of me, who will?" He said that white men are very vulnerable to white women's whines. He laughed. "We've been used to responding to them."

Murphy had been so vigorous in fighting for equality of opportunities for women and minorities around corporate headquarters in the Southeast that he had been shipped out to the field. He hadn't changed his stance but he admitted that he was tired.

"Where's it going to stop?" he asked. "I have nothing against equal pay for equal work, but I agree that the white woman, as a class, was never economically deprived. If we're going to do some good, economically, for some of our staggering social problems in this country, giving white women jobs is not going to help one bit."

The force of Murphy's argument was reduced by his knowledge that women did not receive equal pay for equal work. Earlier he had mentioned that he had read somewhere that on the average they got $.57 for the same work that a man gets a dollar for.

He was ambivalent. It was evident, nonetheless, that he viewed the demands of white women as coming not from alien creatures but from family members trying to wheedle something more out of him. He was tired, he kept saying. He was one of those white men who battled for women's rights while trying to get women to please see his side of the argument: hasn't he done enough?

Whenever the answer was no there was no place that he could hide from the continuing demands; for, after all, he does have to live with, sleep with and father white females.

A chairman of the board of a major American company is usually isolated from signals to change his stance on racial questions. He can live for months without a single close personal image of the effects of racism. He hears about racism as an abstraction, secondhand. Whereas every day he is bombarded with signals that he needs to change his way of thinking about gender. His wife tells him and certainly his daughter tells him. "And they are very vulnerable around the effects of sexism on their little babies. 'No. No. Go out and change the world but my little baby has to have that executive job," said Tyrone Giles, a black consultant. "They turn flip-flops when they think about their daughters' careers being ruined by sexism. They also know that emotionally they are vulnerable to their daughters' revenge. If he doesn't change his stance the daughter can start dating a black man. Little girl is just as determined as daddy to have her way.

"You know what a white senior vice-president told me? He told me that his daughter had been denied a promotion for a certain job. 'You know what they told her?' he said. 'They told her she wasn't ready. God, what do they want? She's been in the business five years. She has an IQ of 156.' I looked at him and said to myself, 'I was in the business for ten years and I have an IQ of 158, and that's why I'm a consultant. They wouldn't even promote me to the job that she wanted to be promoted from. I couldn't get a job like hers for myself much less am I able to get one for my daughter, sister or wife," he said.

Giles's final comment underscores our conclusion that the black woman is the most unsupported of the four groups in our corporate drama. More than any of the others she must depend on herself, but this is not the only reason why the myth that black women might outdistance black men in the corporate mainstream might remain only a myth, unless corporations make significant changes. We are not speaking simply of double discrimination.

The main reason may be that women, even women who are successful in corporate terms, are more likely to seek alternatives to the corporation, as it is. Many say that they cannot find a sense of self-fulfillment in being wife and mother, but they are, at the same time, discovering that corporate managerial careers often give no more than an illusion of self-fulfillment to those who commit themselves to the sixty to seventy hours of work that corporate careers often demand.

It is not simply the time that has to be spent. It is the psychological atmosphere that pervades that time that can be so deadly. The women we talked to seemed more violated by the impersonality of this atmosphere, apparently, since much of their conditioning, if not their nature, stressed interrelatedness, personalization and merging of the self with other selves.

In the women we interviewed there seemed to be a greater yearning for alternatives since it seemed that fewer of their needs as women were being gratified in this game that men have set up. They seemed to want looser arrangements so that they could take care of some of the personal needs that were important to them. This desire was intensified, no doubt, by the fact that they did not have "wives" to take care of some of these things for them.

Nor do they have "wives" to build a family life for them that would give them some of the things that are missing in the workplace. Few black women we interviewed attempted to deny that there were significant differences between men and women and that there were gifts that women could give in corporate situations but most felt that these gifts would be underappreciated in the narrow male culture of the corporation.

Most felt that women were just as ambitious as men but as one branch operations manager for an electronics firm said: "Ambitious for what? Sometimes it seems that men want to get ahead just for the sake of getting ahead. Women seem more concerned about the quality of life that you will have when you get to where you want to go." This seems to point to the flaw inherent in any culture that denigrates those qualities which are usually called feminine, those softer qualities that men cast out of the workplace because they used to be able to find them at home where wives and girl friends waited, those softer qualities of grace which all books on Japanese management praise as the qualities which make the Japanese workplace and Japanese workers so productive.

IX

WADING, FLOATING, SPLASHING AND DOGGY STROKING

DESPITE AND BECAUSE OF all we have said, black managers do find managerial styles and personal life-styles which allow them to function about as well as everyone else does in the mainstream.

The managerial styles are, at bottom, very similar to the styles white managers adopt in order to cope. They are, however, different in proportion, and often they are more "colorful," either more sadly or amusingly so.

In order to discuss these styles and to divide them into categories, we can use the controlling metaphor of this book—swimming in the mainstream:

WADERS are new entrants to the mainstream of corporate life. They come in for many reasons, one of the more compelling being that corporate life seems, in many ways, more attractive than alternative careers. The pay is now higher than in most professions. For blacks, the prestige and even the titles have tremendous psychological importance—manager for General Motors, director with Exxon, sales rep for IBM.

Most waders expect, after a while, to shove off and swim toward midstream and then start swimming upstream. In the beginning most do not know that the stream is so full of turbulent currents and stagnant pools, so full of well-tailored flotsam and jetsam, so perilous with undertows and eddies, so crowded with false promises and poor drainage that it is much more difficult to swim than the wader at first imagines.

American corporations in this decade are so varied. The automobile and steel industries are struggling to survive. The oil industry seems to have more power than the government, whose job it is to try to enforce Equal Employment Opportunity regulations.

Corporations that overexpanded during the rich sixties are looking for ways to retrench with the least possible pain. Inflation and recession are chipping away at financial resources. Organized labor wants more but seems able to produce less. The national educational system grows less and less able to produce the kinds of young people that the corporations need. All of these factors have made wading in more difficult.

Corporations need the government for so many things, and yet they complain about the vast number of governmental regulations. To them it seems that every little governmental commission, board, authority, administration, department, office, division or agency has the power to create rules and guidelines that have the force of law.

Future shock has become present shock, producing an enormous variety of anxieties. Those on top fear they may not remain there. New young black faces are a threat to them. Those struggling to get to the top fear that the whole system might come tumbling down before they get there.

Such anxieties are understandable in a consumer oriented society, whose greatest and sometimes only recreation comes through things that come at very high prices.

Some waders dream of power, of having a billion-dollar company behind their schemes, or millions of dollars of corporate money behind their pet projects. Some waders seek only the security that a corporation can give to self and family. They dream simply of the ability to make a $270.00-a-month car note, a good house with good schools, an occasional shopping spree and a few thousand dollars for the Caribbean vacation that was once only a once-in-a-lifetime quiz-show dream.

These are the kinds of impressions that we got when we talked with eventual waders at several graduate business schools.

Not all waders, however, are college fresh-outs. "Many of the people we see are not necessarily fresh out of college," said a trainer who runs a management orientation program for waders for the American Management Association. "Many, in fact most of the ones we see, are people who have been with the company for a good number of years and have worked their way into supervisory positions. They have a lot of experience with the company but not a lot of experience as managers."

These people might never get more than knee-deep in the managerial mainstream. They are really foremen rather than managers in the Harvard Business School sense. They are, nonetheless, waders, despite the fact that nearly all will remain waders for the rest of their careers.

They differ from the other large group of waders who are men and women fresh out of college or business school. Going to graduate business school was like wetting down before coming into the water.

"If we're going to call them waders then I would definitely say that they don't always know what they are wading into. The M.B.A. is the ticket, for sure, or a technical education," said a corporate college recruiter for a major chemical firm. "You've got to realize that jobs are not as plentiful now as they were in 1972. I was not a recruiter then, but I imagine that even in a company like ours there were good possibilities for the liberal arts graduate in the management training programs. I still think there would be these opportunities in sales and marketing in companies with this kind of focus. But if you want to move up (into midstream) it is almost certain that you're going to have to get some business education."

An advantage now is that many companies allow you to do this while you're still on payroll. Others grant leaves of absence.

A 1974 article in *Business Week* painted a rather rosy picture of the situation that confronted the black M.B.A.: "Corporate competition for black M.B.A.s is keen. The *Black Wharton Graduate Directory* reports that the average starting salary for the 33 blacks who graduated from the school last month (June 1974) is $16,500, about $700 above the class average."

News like this had black candidates flocking to graduate schools of business. Many of them already had a few years of corporate experience and were looking for a way to silence the frequent comment that they did not get promoted because they didn't have the qualifications. "I picked Columbia Graduate School of Business because I knew that with a degree from Columbia no one could say that I didn't have the training," said a young female manager who finished Columbia in 1976.

If an M.B.A. was the price, hundreds of black managerial aspirants were willing to pay it—sometimes as much as ten thousand dollars in tuition, twice that in room and board and two years of drudgery and sacrifice. "I thought that a B-school degree would give me an edge on the competition," said the Columbia graduate. "I didn't know at the time that the average starting salary for the black B-school graduate was higher because the black graduate was usually older and had several years' seniority over the average white graduate."

She was aware, however, that her company would pay for a good part of her education and guarantee her job after graduation. In the early seventies it seemed that the entire graduate-school establishment was in a hurry to get more blacks qualified for significant positions in management. Many of the schools banded together so they could recruit more effectively.

Six business schools took a grant from the Ford Foundation and formed a Consortium for Graduate Study in Management. Ten other schools formed the Council for Opportunity in Graduate Management Education. Several other groups were formed. The idea was to prepare black people to be successful waders. "It gave me more confidence," said the Columbia graduate; "it made me think that I was going to get a more significant job in the company, and it made me sure I would never hear again that I was not qualified."

Upon graduation several major corporations wooed her, but she went back to her old company, expecting to do much better than when she had left. Eventually, however, she came to agree with a study by Professor Edward P. Layear of the University of Chicago: "Although blacks are able to get comparable starting positions, they do not keep pace with whites in their climb up the occupational ladder over their lifetime." Three years with her original employer was enough to teach her this all too well.

An article by George Stevens and Penny Marquette in the August–September 1978 issue of *MBA* magazine amplified this conclusion. "The truth is that most minority MBAs who have entered organizations have not become managers, if manager is defined as an official who controls a budget, supervises others, and makes decisions. Many minority employees who are called managers actually hold no authority and little responsibility."

It seemed to many of the waders we talked to that they had forced themselves through the narrowing experiences of business school for nothing. By 1980 they were hearing that the corporations were searching more vigorously for something other than the M.B.A. "The guy who is all technique is not the answer to any corporation's prayers," said a manpower recruiter in Fairfield County, Connecticut.

Wading in in the right way is important but there seems to be no single right way to wade in. Some wade in knowing that they will not get to midstream, nor do they have a burning desire to swim upstream. They join that group inside the corporation whom we call FLOATERS.

The young woman from Columbia accepted this name for herself because, for the time being, that's all she wanted to do—float. She had been promised big things by a product manager before she went for her M.B.A. The product manager had told her she would have a significant job when she returned from school and she would be part of the team that would eventually run the marketing effort for the entire product line.

Almost none of the promises, except the high salary, were ever fulfilled. At first she became angry, then bored. She was given little real responsibility and no power to make decisions. She reported to her boss as if she were his administrative assistant rather than a manager. The people who were supposed to be working for her knew of her powerlessness and so they usually went around her and spoke directly to her boss. They actually worked for him rather than her. There was nothing else for her to do, she thought, but float.

Many black managers, like the Columbia graduate, size up the corporate situation and realize that they either can't swim against the corporate currents or don't want to. They turn faceup and float, knowing that as long as the government keeps pressure on the companies to have blacks in management they will not get fired. They are rocked about, splashed by the splashers and jostled out of the way by the passing swimmers, but they hang on.

Some black floaters ensure their survival by becoming experts in certain specialized areas—especially if the company markets to great numbers of blacks. They become black experts. In a sense, some of these black managers are actually swimmers, but they are swimming in a special tributary of the mainstream.

When the dollar volume in these special areas is high enough, the black manager may reach a position of considerable power and influence, but his or her power is rarely, if ever, transferrable to the main branch of corporate activity.

Floaters are not necessarily the most inactive people in corporations. They make valuable contributions. Some of them are even more productive than swimmers, for the act of swimming has little to do with actual productive activity. It is simply the effort a manager makes to get ahead in the stream.

Floaters, then, are the solid core of the corporation. Most of their activity is not directed toward advancing their careers; they are more dedicated to getting the job done. As far as getting ahead is concerned, much of even their best work is analogous to treading water.

They perform the routine, unglamorous but necessary tasks of the corporation—shuffling paper, writing reports and memos, gathering data and routing information—the day-to-day concerns that make up most of the average manager's career. "Craftsmen" and "company men," as Michael Maccoby describes them in *The Gamesmen,* are usually floaters rather than swimmers.

> The craftsman holds the traditional values of the productive-hoarding character—the work ethic, respect for people, concern for the quality and thrift. . . . He sees others, co-workers as well as superiors, in terms of whether they help or hinder him in doing a craftsmanlike job. Most craftsmen whom we interviewed are quiet, sincere, modest and practical. . . .

> In the company man, we recognize the well-known organization man, or the functionary whose sense of identity is based on being part of the powerful, protective company. His strongest traits are his concern with the human side of the company, his interest in the feelings of the people around him and his commitment to maintain the organization's integrity. At his weakest, he is fearful and submissive, concerned with security even more than success. The most creative company men sustain an atmosphere in their groups of cooperation, stimulation, and mutuality. The least creative find a little niche and satisfy themselves by feeling that somehow they share in the glory of the corporation.

Most of the blacks we interviewed fit these categories.

No doubt most floaters once thought that being a good craftsman or company man would get them promoted. They thought that promotions were based on job performance, and many of them were good at their jobs. They were better than the swimmers.

Black floaters were in a particularly frustrating position because corporate tides would not carry them upstream at all. Inside the companies they were stagnant, but to outsiders they were men and women of high salary and some prestige. They were very often misunderstood by outsiders, because how could they expect sympathy from schoolteachers, civil servants, and blue collar workers who earned far less than they did, who did not drive to work in shiny cars, who did not dress up each day in suit and white collar?

The inside floater does not have nearly as much prestige as someone we will call an outside floater. An older black manager at a chemicals firm headquartered in the Northeast is an almost perfect example of the latter. It is almost as if he floats around on a rubber raft. The raft was supplied and inflated by the corporation, which has no desire to see him sink or drown.

He knows that he is not advancing his career but he is happy. He earns $57,000 a year, which is exactly a thousand dollars for each year of his age. His children are grown. He has a 6 percent mortgage on his home in the nicer section of a black community thirty miles from work. The company is not likely to transfer him. He knows that.

He came to the corporation from the Urban League and so he acts more like a social service person than a hard-driving corporate manager. He could also be mistaken for a Baptist preacher. He is always seen in the black community and at public gatherings because he is the chairman of the board's chief public-relations person to the black community.

He encourages the company to buy blocks of tickets to support black events and he gives these tickets out to younger black employees. He also acts as an adviser to them when they have adjustment problems. They respect him because he is the best source of human warmth in the corporation. Even the chairman drifts into his office whenever the chairman wants to talk to someone with "feeling."

The chairman also imitates his speaking style on occasions when he wants to deliver a stirring speech, and generally respects him— but not as a productive component of the corporation.

Many younger black men and women managers are floating also. Many are quite happy with their jobs because they prefer the human side of industry. They are well aware that many of their jobs were created especially to meet the company's EEO targets.

Some of these men and women remember when their parents earned less in a year than they earn in a month. Admittedly they find it frustrating to be paid and not utilized, but this is far better than being both unpaid and not utilized. Many of them construct for themselves alternative means of fulfillment. Some become customer's men (or women).

A young and handsome office products salesman in Washington, D.C., is an almost perfect example of this kind of floater. He knows all the secretaries of all his customers by their first names. He brings them flowers because he knows all of their birthdays. He calls this salesmanship but it is really his method of humanizing his job. Whenever he finishes his appointments he would rather make "cold calls" than go back to his office. For this reason his "numbers" are higher than those of his peers, but he doesn't get promoted as fast as they because while he is out floating around among his secretaries, they are back at the office politicking.

He defends his behavior pattern by saying, "Man, I was hired to sell machines, right? Well, that's what I do. They better promote me." When they don't promote him he calls their actions "racist." In a strict sense it is not racism but politics, or rather his lack thereof, that keeps him from getting promoted, but the reason for his failure to play politics is racial without being racist. He simply doesn't like to be around white people all the time.

He knows that his manager does not like his style. He is also hiding, for he fears that the more he is around whites the more likely they are to see things about him that are not corporate.

He knows that his branch manager doesn't like the way he sells products, even though his numbers prove that his is a very effective method. They want more control over his behavior. Since he feels that he cannot work his way into a position of control, he doesn't want to be around those "bastards back in the office" who want to control him.

The "bastards back in the office" use his effectiveness reports to register their disapproval. They say he has poor interpersonal skills.

When he has to come back to the office to deal with these reports, he becomes a SPLASHER, because he feels that the attacks on him are racially motivated, which is only partially true.

A splasher is a manager who makes waves, who stirs up a commotion. He is the angry black of the corporate mainstream. More often than not he came out of the civil rights era and he tries to keep his racial militancy alive in the corporation. Many of them were anticorporate before they came in, or at least they had serious doubts about becoming a "corporate nigger." Some were very procorporate life until they found out what it was like. A third group thought that the transition would be easy and when their personal ambitions crashed into the realities of life on the inside, they adopted anticorporate rhetoric: corporations thrive on racist suppression in South Africa, corporations profit from starvation wages in South America, Asia and the Caribbean. Others say that major corporations destroy the earth by strip mining, using herbicides, or dumping toxic waste.

Their personal maladjustment makes them more self-righteously moralistic. They are adept at putting a finger on all that is wrong with corporate life, but their splashing is far too isolated to achieve any results. They represent points of view that the corporation needs to hear, and it is often only from them that the corporations hear these points of view from within.

Other blacks in the corporation called splashers crazy, until they needed them to help protest a personal racial injustice. The splasher is always glad to have the opportunity to strike out at the company. Splashers are frequently good performers, because they are often more aware, better educated, and more sensitive than other corporate types.

They do not dedicate their entire intelligence and all their efforts to performing their corporate jobs as the jobs are structured. They are forever looking for ways to do things differently. Often they are splashers because they hold jobs that do not challenge, but the company does not trust them enough to put them in jobs that offer significant challenge.

Sometimes they start splashing because they find the waters of the mainstream too chilly, they find other managers too mechanistic. They are not content to suppress their feeling that the company should be a more humanistic environment, but their reasons for splashing are seldom taken seriously because, on the one hand, they are vague, and on the other hand they strike at the very basis of the corporation's way of dealing with its people.

Such splashers are seldom able to begin to formulate any alternatives because they are too overwhelmed by day-in-day-out aggravation over having to continue doing things in the manner that has alienated him or her in the first place.

We know of a splasher whose original mission was to humanize the corporation. Since he couldn't get help, he set out to do it himself. He earned the nickname "Memo" because he was forever firing off memos protesting anything and everything. When the company resisted his suggestions, he charged the company with racism.

During the nineteen sixties he would take white women back to his bachelor pad and launch into tirades against racism and (for their sake) sexism in the company. Ironically, sometimes the white women joined with the black and got him appointed director of affirmative action and EEO. His vague discontent had then been crystallized— in the wrong place, of course, but now the company could deal with him.

He forced the company to promote a few minority workers and women. He got the company to deposit some of its money in minority banks. He got it to put some different kinds of food in all company cafeterias—soul food in the South and Mexican food in California and Texas.

All of his actions were significant, but somewhere along the way he lost the reasons for his ever becoming a splasher in the first place. He and the company assumed that if he saw something wrong, the something must be racial.

A SCUBA DIVER can be a subsurface floater or a subsurface swimmer. The essential fact of his or her corporate existence is that he or she socializes downward. The scuba diver in corporate life is more comfortable with the cleaning ladies and the contract maintenance people than with peers and superiors.

Scuba divers are often guilty around older black people who work at menial tasks in corporate offices. In this they are like a certain kind of splasher who identifies with those lower on the social scale. The difference is that the scuba diver never brings his true self to the surface of corporate life either in conformity or in protest.

The cleaning ladies are usually quite proud of the scuba diver. "He's a very nice man," said a contract maintenance woman of a black accountant. "He has gotten up without getting uppity. He'll invite you into his office to have coffee. Sometimes the girls get together in his office and we have a big time with him. He's such a nice little fellow," the woman said with a soft West Indian lilt.

The black secretaries love him too, because he does not act as if he is above them. He goes out to lunch with them. His own secretary is black. He has always had a black secretary, whose promotions he will fight for far more fiercely than he will for his own.

He is a humanist, but one who quietly resents the consciousness of status and level that helps make the corporation an uncomfortable place for those who perform necessary and important functions on the lower levels of the corporate hierarchy.

Generally he does not make waves. He is too proud to spend his life complaining because that would imply that "they" have something he wants. He accepts racism as an Eskimo accepts snow. He doesn't like it but he knows he has to live with it.

Because he does not spend a great deal of his time cultivating an image compatible with high aspiration, he has limited his ambitions to whatever hard work will earn him. He doesn't have a great emotional investment in the company, but his personal pride makes him a hard worker. Many whites recognize something in him that they like. He is no threat.

"I really don't want to be president of this company," one scuba diver told us sincerely, "even if they were ready to allow a black person to do that. Comfort is more important to me than power or prestige."

SNORKELERS, unlike scuba divers, lurk just below the surface of the corporation in a kind of antisuccess solidarity with other black employees who are going nowhere. They complain but, unlike the splasher, they don't make waves. They hang together, sometimes to reinforce their own sense of insecurity, and sometimes because they enjoy bitching.

Swimmers gravitate toward power, and when they associate with peers they plot mutual political advantage or size up the competition. In contrast, snorkelers form cliques with the powerless, cliques oriented toward mutual ego protection.

The main topic of conversation of a group of snorkelers who used to party together in and around Chicago was the racism of the regional vice-president. They did not organize to do anything about him, but they seemed to get a great deal of mutual satisfaction out of telling the same stories about him over and over whenever they got together.

There was the story about the white woman who got promoted because she was sleeping with him. There was the story about how one of them wrote a marketing plan that he took all the credit for. There were also the stories about the little racial remarks he liked to make at sales conferences. These stories were comforting to the group. They were rituals of solidarity. They were used to form a warm human bond to keep "us" distinct from "them."

The member of the group who told us about their activities said that she wanted to start socializing with some of the whites in the company but she was afraid that others in the group would talk about her. Given the uncertainty of finding genuine white friends, she didn't want to risk losing her black friends.

One of the more amusing black corporate characters is the DOGGY STROKER. Doggy stroking is dog-paddling—furious churning with the arms and legs without developing much forward movement.

Delmar Johnson, a regional operations manager for one of the top five electronics firms in the country, is a perfect doggy stroker. He is moving ahead but he has had to expend more energy than most swimmers. When he says, "All I talk is business," he means it. He has the company logo in every room of his suburban home.

He has never been married. A love affair with anyone but the company would take too much time, and there is no woman who would fit into his plans.

He is as tall and as dark as Nightmare, and he comes from a very similar background, but he tries to let none of his background come through in his diction or his demeanor. "The great big black nigger holds his coffee cup with his pinky finger sticking straight out like Lady Ann holding her teacup," said a scuba diver in his company. "He rides around all winter with skis on the back of his Mercedes and the nigger can't even ski."

He speaks with a mouthful of air, making sure that he pronounces each syllable of a word. Sometimes he even pronounces three syllables of words that have only two. Because he is so careful with his speech, he makes grammatical errors that he would not make otherwise: "Frankly, I doesn't talk anything about politics or religion. Those are two subjects I avoids," he says when he is asked about anything controversial like racism. Then he laughs in the preplanned manner of a person in a TV commercial.

"He sounds like a Republican around white people and a Democrat around blacks," said one of his black peers, who also claims that the doggy stroker would never hire a black secretary and wouldn't sit with a black colleague in the cafeteria unless it was the only other doggy stroker in the regional office, a black female who also "speaks with her lips folded in" so they won't seem too Negroid.

"They usually try to get a white person or two to sit with them. Then they are as happy as puppies. If a black person happens to sit down they become silent. They eat fast and leave."

The scuba divers in the company hate them. The snorkelers call them phonies. Swimmers respect them because they are making forward progress without being really competitive. Hip young white people either laugh at or are annoyed by them. Older whites wonder why all Negroes can't be more like them.

In all fairness it must be pointed out that the company Delmar works for is much more rigid and conservative than Nightmare's. He and Nightmare are about the same age but Nightmare is no farther ahead than he, even with the advantage gained by going to Harvard Business School. Delmar went to a college in Florida whose name he does not mention. He has had to work harder to prove himself and he has done this.

Nightmare can say "Easy" when he departs; Delmar must say "Ciao." Nightmare says, "What's happenin?"; Delmar says, "Lovely day." Nightmare says, "That's ba-a-a-d" when he likes something; Delmar says, "Golly, that's super."

Any characteristic or action that might be called Negroid Delmar avoids. He adheres rigidly to rules and regulations. His style is totally inflexible. He works hard and has a very clinical approach to his job. He is harder on his black subordinates in order to prove to his white peers and superiors that race means nothing to him. He came to work on Martin Luther King's birthday and he was the only supervisor, black or white, who reprimanded black subordinates for not showing up to work on that day.

Back during the period of "tokenism" there was the tendency

among many black managers to hold up the subtle nuances of white middle- and upper-class life as the standard for all people to imitate, but these managers had been raised to aspire to this and so there was some comfort in their imitation. Delmar imitated what he thought was proper behavior because he was ashamed of nearly everything about himself that was obviously "unwhite." He could not do anything about his color, but he could avoid anyone else of the same color.

He did as much as he could about his mannerisms, but this sudden adoption of the "ways of white folk" made him socially clumsy and made him "talk funny."

He believed in racial uplift, but he had a very narrow view of what he wanted to lift black people toward. Whenever he had to deal with them, he insisted that they be businesslike, even on those occasions when a white male would have allowed them to be relaxed. He was proud that he had made even his mother be more businesslike. Even though he was making more than $50,000 a year, he insisted that his mother sign a promissory note when she needed to borrow $200 from him.

He insisted that his brother pay him bank rate interest on a small loan that he had been prevailed upon to make to him. "We've all got to stop being so slack," he said of his known and unknown kinsmen.

X

SWIMMING
IN THE MAINSTREAM

THE JOURNEY THAT THIS BOOK represents was begun in order for us to examine corporate life and black lives within it. We must then end the journey by talking about both. Some black managers fit into corporate life very well. We can call them SWIMMERS because they have mastered the technique that has enabled them to avoid and surmount turbulent currents, stagnant pools, all the flotsam and jetsam, the undertows and backwaters. The question arises: How did they do it?

"Without hesitation I would say that performance is key," said Reginald Bishop, an older swimmer who believed very much in the meritocracy. He was not the highest-ranking black we interviewed, but he wore his situation as comfortably as any. The highest-ranking black we interviewed agreed that performance was the key, but he was an engineer who by sheer brilliance had made himself indispensable to his company and highly marketable to any other company in his field. His company had to promote him to keep him.

"Unless you're willing to work hard and unless you're capable of outstanding performance," said Bishop, "you haven't got a prayer." This man had made it up through the ranks in financial management, which is a specialty too, one in which there are definite criteria for judging outstanding performance. He was brilliant with numbers. He was needed as assistant controller, financial services, and so he was made assistant controller, financial services.

"You've got to know how to play the game," said Herbert A. Carter, a vice-president of personnel. This man had no specialized skill except his ability with people. He had developed a very pleasant personality that was a combination of understatement and extreme self-confidence. At the age of only thirty-nine, Carter had been made vice-president of a Fortune Top 100 company.

Joyce Cooke, a district operations manager, and the highest-ranking black woman we interviewed extensively, said, "You've got to be totally preoccupied with your job. You've got to sacrifice. You've got to decide that this is what I want, and be willing to make the sacrifices necessary to get it. God knows, if there is something I know how to do it's sacrifice."

We also knew of black women who had risen higher under special circumstances, who had succeeded because they were needed to do special jobs for the company. A female Ph.D. in industrial psychology had been hired by a major electronics company to work in human resources planning, and two women we knew of in the cosmetics industry had advanced significantly in the special markets section.

Human resources planning is important work and the special markets sections of major cosmetics firms are tremendous revenue producers. These three women were certainly doing well, but we wanted our long interview to be with a woman in the main line of a company's business who had made it up through the ranks in open competition with all others in the company. "You simply have to be clear and remain clear on exactly what *you* want," Joyce Cooke said. She had been in her job sixteen months. The expectation in the company was that she would soon be groomed for the position of vice-president of major accounts. (She thought so too. This was apparent from the way she denied she'd heard the rumor.)

Information on how to swim successfully came from a great many sources, but especially from the three swimmers already quoted in this chapter and from Michael I. Timmons, a financial planning manager (B.A. Princeton, M.B.A. the Wharton School of Finance). A senior vice-president of his company had pointed him out as a "comer" and the person to interview instead of one of the three black vice-presidents in the organization. "Mike has a better handle on what corporate life is all about," said the senior vice-president.

These then were the four swimmers we interviewed most extensively. Reginald Bishop, the financial whiz, and Joyce Cooke, the district operations manager, seemed to be from the old school. They were managers who believed that the best way to be swimmers was to work harder than everyone else, pay strict attention to corporate policies and procedures, be extremely cautious, be more dependable, loyal to the organization, and more diligent about setting up beneficial relationships with people who would rely on their expertise and ability to deliver results.

They were steady strokers who preferred rather calm, familiar waters in which to demonstrate their strengths—mainly their ability to produce for the team, thereby inducing members of the team to look out for them.

The other two swimmers were more inclined to focus on corporate life as a game. They were creatures out of a book like *The Gamesman*. They were convinced that working hard might not be nearly so important as working smart. Many books identify this kind of manager as a representative of the new trend in business executives. These managers seem to focus more on getting ahead than on getting a particular job done. They put career above company, self-fulfillment above respect for the status quo.

They believe in taking the shortcut if they see no personal advantage in taking the long way around, but they often work as hard as more traditional types. For the most part they get their tasks done, and well. But the reason for good performance has almost nothing to do with pride of accomplishment, and almost everything to do with building an impressive work history for the next leap forward.

As we have said, Michael Maccoby calls them gamesmen, and Elwood Chapman, in his book, *Scrambling: Zig-Zagging Your Way to the Top,* calls them scramblers. The March 9, 1981, edition of *U.S. News & World Report* says that with them the "me generation" has entered the executive suite. "Young managers working their way up the corporate ladder have different ideas about work than their elders—and many firms are listening," said *U.S. News.*

"A new breed of manager is bringing subtle but important changes in ways that corporations deal with their rising young executives. Loyalty to the corporation, deference to superiors and other tried-and-true ways of getting ahead are low priorities of these young men and women managers."

They are no longer financial analysts, lawyers, general managers, IBMers, Xeroids, Bell Tellers. They are careerists. They work in the corporation but they work for themselves, and they would jump in a minute for a more fulfilling situation in another company.

They are in step with Eugene Jennings's model of a mobile manager, who uses a rearview mirror to remind him of what he has done successfully and a telescope to tell him what he must prepare for in the future. "At any given time he is addressing himself to the past, present and future. He thinks and acts in triple time. He utilizes this trifocal orientation for personal gain."

The past is meaningful because it has contributed to his present skills, the future because his vision of it motivates him to make the most of his present experience. He knows that image is often more important than reality.

People inside and outside corporations are often amazed at how successful this new generation of managers can be, even when they leave a string of failures behind them. We know of one such manager (white) who as a district manager presided over the fall of his district from second to ninth place in the company. He was promoted from district manager to a job as head of Canadian operations, which he left after three years. Canadian operations were profitable when he got there, but were operating in the red when he left. He was promoted from Canadian operations to head of a task force at corporate headquarters, which wasted more than $27 million before being disbanded by the board of directors. He is now a senior vice-president.

No black manager could get away with this, but our two new-generation swimmers have seen that politics, personality, contacts and attitude toward self and the job are often more important than competence and performance.

The black manager must be both traditional and "new breed." The black manager's corporate situation is usually even more existential than that of the white manager of the new generation. The climate in most corporations is not racially open enough for blacks to insist on all of the options and opportunities, to exploit career possibilities as new-breed white managers can.

Blacks must "prove" themselves in situations where white managers are assumed to be capable. Blacks must seem more grateful for opportunities. They must not appear to be scrambling or gaming. They must, in short, appear to have mastered and accepted the traditional attitudes and values of business life.

However, just to be assured of an average rate of career advancement blacks need to know at least as much as the white scrambler knows and uses to accelerate his rate of advancement. In order to survive, black managers must be aware not only of the options and the possibilities in a corporate situation, but also of the traditional requirements for acceptance in that situation.

Richard America and Bernard Anderson's *Moving Ahead* is an effective guide for mastering both the traditional and the new. The book surveys the essential steps in a swimmer's career, from wade-in to middle management to upper middle management, which is usually where even the best black swimmers peak. Although the book's twenty chapters cover almost every aspect of career progress, they do so in a very skeletal way. One is tempted, while reading, to graft the flesh of experience onto these corporate bones, to dig deeper for the human answers to these important questions. For example:

HOW IMPORTANT ARE THE RIGHT CREDENTIALS?
Moving Ahead says:

Engineers with M.B.A.'s, it appears, do about as well at getting promotions and responsibilities in technical industries as those with Master of Science in Engineering (M.S.E.)—up to a point. However, it is widely believed that a B.S. in Engineering, combined with an M.B.A., is of greatest value for any management career, technical or nontechnical. . . . Career flexibility and movement to the high levels appear to be enhanced with a solid M.B.A., as is generally assumed. Black managers with engineering undergraduate degrees appear to do as well in management as their white counterparts. On the subject of the relationship between education and black life in corporate America, this is only the beginning.

"No doubt education *is* key," said Reginald Bishop. "Good education is the first ticket you have to punch if you hope to make it in corporate America—the M.B.A. if possible, or an engineering degree, or a combination, which is what you find a lot of younger black managers coming out of school with. They want to make sure."

Mike Timmons said, "Business education gives you some initial exposure to the field of business, which most of us don't get at home since our parents were not in business. This is why I would suggest the M.B.A. The right education also gives you credibility.

"You're going in with a credibility problem, so I think it does matter where you did your training. You can't wear your degree on your vest to show everyone, yeah, I went to Harvard, I went to Yale, I went to Stanford, but the word circulates on you. They had the word out on me before I came in the section and that did end the credibility problem to some extent, but not entirely. It was still a case where I had to be forceful about showing that my training did me some good. Immediately they began putting me on special projects. I think this was to test me, but it may have been because they had confidence in me. I simply read it as a matter of my boss saying, 'Here, you went to Wharton, handle this.'

"This is one of the ways that Wharton worked to my benefit because I did handle it, and I insisted on the right to present it to the corporate pricing task force. This gave me early exposure to top management. I'm sure that when they talked about me they mentioned Wharton to assure each other that my doing such a good job was not a fluke. The CPTF itself gave me other jobs, which I handled well.

"The executive vice-president of the company was head of the CPTF, and so I got to know him. I think he wanted me to fly out to the West Coast for this purpose—he wanted to feel me out. Then sometime later my immediate supervisor said to me, 'You know, you've got a godfather. Someone is looking out for you.' He didn't tell me who. I asked him if it was the executive vice-president. He said no. So I just assumed that it was someone the executive V.P. had appointed to watch my progress.

"They say that going to the right school gives you contacts. That's true to some extent. You have a lot of people out in the field who were classmates, and when your name comes up there's an immediate stamp of approval. If they disapprove of you they invalidate their own degree, unless they can say that you were a goof-off at school and all you did was chase women. I did chase women, but none of them knew about it.

"If there is someone in the organization who had gone to the particular school you went to, they will tend to think automatically that you're all right. You get that immediate stamp of approval.

"The top management of some companies is dominated by graduates of certain business schools, and when you come into this kind of situation you have instant credibility, rapport on a certain level because each business school teaches you to think in a characteristic way.

"But I think that for the black graduate, one of the biggest benefits is that it gives you confidence. And you'd either better come into a job with confidence or you'd better get it quite early on."

Joyce Cooke agreed that confidence was most important because, more than anything else, she had suffered intellectual intimidation when she came into corporate life twelve years before. "No one had heard of North Carolina Central University, which is where I went to undergraduate school. Howard is the only black school which has gained wide credibility and sometimes even Howard graduates feel this intimidation. I know one who pronounces Howard very fast so that some people might think that he said Harvard," she said. She had asked to be interviewed in her home because that was one of the few places she said she felt really relaxed. She did not, however, seem very relaxed even there. She seemed, by nature or because of experience, very cautious.

"I was very nervous in meetings. I wouldn't speak up because I was afraid of embarrassing myself. Outwardly I knew I had the knowledge but I had been made to feel inadequately prepared. I used to tell people that I went to school in North Carolina and they would ask whether I went to Duke or the University of North Carolina. They would say this knowing that I hadn't, but I would say that I went to North Carolina Central in a very apologetic voice.

"I didn't know until I came to the Northeast that there was such a stress on where you went to undergraduate school. I'm glad I came into industry before I went to graduate school or I might have gone to business school in the South and that's not the best situation. I'm not saying that you can't make it under those circumstances, but it will take you longer for both internal and external reasons.

"I could say that gaining self-confidence was the main reason why I started graduate school. I started at night and then I took a year off to complete my M.B.A. I knew as much about my job and I was doing as good a job before I took the year off, but there were two reasons why I wanted that M.B.A. First, I thought that my lack of graduate education would catch up with me—no, three reasons—second, there's a place on your performance evaluation which pertains to self-development and efforts to improve self, and third, because I felt that having the M.B.A. would give me confidence."

"We take the view that blacks do have to be better educated," said the director of a graduate program for black M.B.A. candidates. "This coincides with the view among major companies that they would like to find more qualified blacks. The argument that there are not enough qualified blacks for business has some validity, and it is also fair to say that major companies are committed to upgrading and increasing the pool of trained black business talent.

"I'm not going to say that the commitment is not genuine. I think that corporations as entities are not racist. The commitment is real as to funding programs that help blacks acquire those skills that are sorely needed in business. There is a scarcity of available talent. They recognize this, and they know that black America is an underutilized resource.

"They give the money but this does not always mean that they are fully receptive to the candidate who returns to the company after acquiring the M.B.A. There is an assumption that the white graduate with the right credentials is equipped to do the job. With the black graduate there is a wait-and-see attitude.

"But there's nothing that anyone can do about this. I think that what you have to do is be really sharp, and I suggest to all of our students that they should improve their communication skills. Often it's not how much you know but how well you can communicate.

"There is a surprise effect when they find an extremely articulate black person. That person is more highly regarded than an articulate white person. That's why it's doubly important to speak the language of business with as much facility as possible, which means you have to work at it, speaking and writing.

WHAT IS THE BEST WAY TO BEHAVE DAY IN AND DAY OUT?

"As hard as it might be and as unrealistic as it might seem," said Emmett Rice in the October 1979 issue of *Black Enterprise,* "in my experience it is always better to act, to work and to perform as if there were no such thing as racial discrimination." Mr. Rice is not in corporate life, but as a governor of the Federal Reserve Board he is in a very similar situation.

A black female pricing manager said that it is better never to forget that you are black. She launched a diatribe against all those blacks who try to "forget who they are and where they came from."

Joyce Cooke said she is extremely conscious of race, "but I bend over backward to try never to say that anything that happens to me occurs because I am a woman or because I am black."

A female manager for a major transportation company brought in her lawyers three times when she felt she was being discriminated against because she was a black woman. All three times the company backed down because she could prove that there was some substance to her charges.

As much as the last three managers might seem to disagree with Emmett Rice, not much disagreement is evident in their day-to-day job performance. "You don't think about it day to day," said Mike Timmons, the Princeton and Wharton scrambler, "because it's not operative on a daily basis. Race does not enter the picture during day-to-day interactions with people on matters that are basically colorless. When promotion time comes, when assignment time comes, when evaluation time comes, that is when you have to be aware. Otherwise, I think it is better to forget all about it.

"I think that to some extent whites are more accepting of the blacks' professionalism than many black managers want to believe. I think that in some cases blacks have a very defensive attitude when the racial question has nothing to do with the situation.

"I think that too many blacks fall back on hard work for their salvation, and then when they don't get promoted they feel that they were not promoted because of racism. They were not promoted because hard work does not necessarily win promotions.

"I think they know this going in, but they work doubly hard so they can have something to blame white people for. They know they are inept at the politics of corporate mobility and so they know they are not going to be promoted if they don't play politics, but they are reluctant. Or they are very uncomfortable or they don't have the personality or the social graces to position themselves, so they put their nose to the grindstone in order to convince themselves that the system is racist.

"I get the feeling sometimes that white people are ready to open up but black people are reluctant to make the effort to meet them halfway," he said.

Activity for its own sake is often valueless. Activity, the swimmer must understand, should be geared to some step-by-step plan for getting from where the manager is to where he or she wants to be. The manager should look up from each task and take time to answer these questions: Why am I doing this? What difference will it make as far as my objectives are concerned? How does this work fit into the objectives of those who can impact positively or negatively on my career?

It is characteristic that those who live in capricious environments, who do not control many of the variables, or at least feel that they cannot control many of the variables, work hard because hard work gives them an illusion of control.

Those who have been made to feel inferior find themselves in a similar bind. They find themselves driven by a compulsive need to prove themselves on every single project. They feel inadequate or unaccepted and so they gain some measure of temporary self-assurance by doing perfect work. The self-assurance is only temporary because they are driven into the next project with the same compulsive need to prove themselves.

Each project seems like the first one. Good things that they've done in the past do not relieve the compulsion. Their work is never good enough because deep inside they feel that they are not good enough. They often drive their subordinates in the same way, and for the same reason, or they sometimes refuse to delegate work. They are forever looking over the shoulders of subordinates to make sure the subordinates will not embarrass them with work that is "inferior."

They become workaholics. They burn all the time but they don't burn out. They simply do not get promoted, while others who have not worked as hard pass them by.

In order to work smart, one of the first things a manager has to do is set up a system for honest feedback, because otherwise the manager's supervisor might feel that the manager is working hard on the wrong thing. The work the manager is doing might have little relationship to what the supervisor really thinks is important, little or no relationship to the manager's effectiveness as a manager, or little or no relevance to the manager's long-range career objectives.

"I'm not saying that you should be in corporate life for personal aggrandizement, or that you should do your work with the idea in mind: What is this doing for me and my career?" said the Princeton and Wharton scrambler. "I don't think you should underestimate the importance of being a team player. Play hard for the team while you're on the team, play as hard as you can for the team, but remember that your play should also enhance your future marketability.

"You have to think about the overall success of the project rather than your own personal aggrandizement, but be sure you get the credit for your contribution. But even more important than the credit is the experience. I think that some people look at hard work in the wrong way. They might not want to change companies because they feel that they don't want to leave their record of hard work behind and move to a company where they are not known.

"But if you've worked smart the hard work has added to your own development as a professional. You've actually put the hard work into yourself, improving your skills, your marketability, your credentials and credits and your personality. Every project is a growing experience. In doing a good job you get a fair exchange: the company gets something out of it and you get something out of it."

IS EXTENSIVE, RACIALLY INTEGRATED
SOCIAL INTERACTION NECESSARY FOR SUCCESS?

"To reach middle management," said Joyce Cooke during our long interview in her living room, "I don't think you have to do a lot of socializing with your peers. This may have been true some years ago but in most companies now it doesn't have to be. The kind of social contact that you have across racial lines is usually enough to gain the off-site familiarity that you need with the white people you work with.

"I remember they used to say that you had to live in the right place so you could have your boss over for dinner because he wanted to check out your spouse and check out the way you ran your home and raised your kids. I think that now if you have him over, it's just to promote this off-site familiarity that will break down certain barriers to communication that you might have on-site.

"I don't think that social life means as much as it did before because you're actually working such long hours that you get plenty of opportunity for social interaction during those long hours, particularly if you consider business lunches, off-site meetings, development seminars with the mandatory cocktail party or trips out of town.

"It seems that social and business life have merged. There are cocktail parties in the company that I don't usually attend, but I don't think that I'm missing a great deal. To tell the truth, I'd rather be around white people when they're sober, and since I don't have a husband to tote around to these parties, I don't want to go alone.

"The wives of the guys don't want this single black woman loose at the party, especially if you're the woman that her husband sees every day at the office or makes business trips with.

"For a black woman, socializing with white men is something you have to do with great care to avoid even the appearance of anything sexual. To that extent you turn down invitations that you otherwise would accept.

"For example, if one white man asks me out for drinks, I'll usually always refuse. If there are two men going, I might say yes, because there is some value in going out with these guys, but if you go out alone with one of them there is an almost automatic assumption that something sexual is going on, unless it's during the day at lunch.

"I've just never developed any social rapport with white women. First, because there are not a great many white women in the company at my level. Then we all work so hard that when we're not working we're holding together the other parts of our lives. This is the main thing, but I know many of these women socially because in the company, as I said, social and business life merge to a great extent."

Purely social interaction, then, is polite, infrequent and not too deep. The business that is discussed on social occasions is specific because the social occasion usually arises in a specific context. This is to say that the social occasion has a theme. It may be related to an off-site meeting with managers who work in different regions, or it might be the kind of theme party reported on in *The Wall Street Journal*: "The woman student at the Harvard Business School ticks off a list of parties she attended lately—a boat trip with First Boston Corporation, dinner at New York's Russian Tea Room with American Telephone & Telegraph, harbor-view cocktails with E. F. Hutton & Company—just your ordinary cutthroat social situation," she says of the typical party. Cutthroat? Yes, because she and her classmates are competing for jobs at the parties, and their hosts are competing for employees.

"Party giving has become a new wrinkle in the effort of corporate employers to recruit top students who are getting masters' degrees in business administration. Certainly other business gets discussed at these theme parties, but as social occasions more and more become extensions of business activity, there are fewer and fewer barriers to black participation in them."

Cooke said she has been to several resort weekends for business meetings. It seems also that managers are so mobile in many modern corporations that they are not in one operation or location long enough to develop deep friendships with coworkers. Many managers seem to carry on friendships by telephone with networks of other managers spread out all across the country. The telephone, rather than the cocktail party, seems to be the main element keeping the social side of business life together.

The authors of *Moving Ahead* write:

> There appears to be a broad assumption that white managers and executives spend many pleasant social hours entertaining one another and establishing understanding and confidence that are valuable in business and that make all the difference in the world in the competitive position of white managers relative to black managers.

> We strongly suspect that, while there is clearly more intra- than interracial social contact, most white managers would also report a sense of social exclusion. It is our impression that most white managers really have very little meaningful or professionally useful social contact with their colleagues in most companies. The sense of social deprivation that many black managers say they feel therefore may be an unnecessary burden and may be largely a fantasy. In actual fact, they may be suffering scarcely any real social disadvantage compared with most of their peer competitors.

> Among our non-random sample of forty-five managers, one-fourth say they have found church, private club, and other social contacts with white managers to be professionally helpful; a few say they have not; and almost half say they have not tried such contact. Most are ambivalent about social contacts off the job with white associates. They recognize the intangible value in social interaction, but many perceive risks and find the setting unnatural or unpleasant to some degree.

The Princeton and Wharton scrambler takes exception to this

point of view. He carries on an active social life with ex-classmates and with others in his company. He admits that his motives are extremely utilitarian. "I like to know how they think, how they operate, which will give me a sense of what is possible and what is impossible in my situation.

"I know that when I go out to dinner with a coworker that coworker is sizing me up and I'm sizing him or her up. Neither tells a great deal about our personal plans. When you're strategizing about your career, you certainly don't want everyone in the company to know what you are thinking, and in most cases I don't talk about any business specifics or even any personal specifics.

"In career strategy what you have to avoid is being preempted, upstaged, undermined, excluded or diminished in importance, so you can't give out the kinds of specific information that will allow anyone to do that; but at the same time I think too many blacks isolate themselves from social contact with white peers. This kind of broad social interaction is absolutely necessary.

"I'm not at all uncomfortable socializing with whites. It gives me a chance to size up how they think—generally and specifically. I can determine that Bill is this kind of person and Jane is this kind of person; therefore I know what I can expect from Bill or from Jane within a particular job situation. I enjoy socializing with whites.

"Because I know they are doing the same thing—sizing me up. It's all a game. The evening has some of that in it, but it also has some genuine friendship in it, which is also useful for sizing up those factors in the environment that will have positive or negative impact on your plans. It gives you the facility to anticipate strategies and counterstrategies. It gives you a sense of the environment you are working in and how to further your own ends in that environment.

"There is also a lot of genuine respect that can grow out of this kind of interaction. Living in New York City makes it easier, because you're not operating in a goldfish bowl, as you would be in a town even as large as Washington. You don't always want everyone in the company to know who you're going out to dinner with.

"With people inside the company, I've found it's better to establish arm's-length relationships. With corporate people outside the company it's safer to get a little closer because you can both talk more freely and this will enable you to sniff out insights that will make your intuitive judgments about corporate people that much sharper.

"You can get a panoramic view that is valuable and necessary. I'm not married. I don't know if I could carry on this kind of life if I were married. I'm sure I couldn't, because I eat out about five evenings a week, and I usually have dinner with someone I can learn something from.

"Whenever I go to cocktail parties, I remain very businesslike because I am a bachelor. I usually corner one of the top officers in the company, or I corner the wife or an older woman so the sexual factor doesn't enter the mind of anyone who is watching my performance. I stand very straight. I don't laugh too much or too loud. I have only one drink and I leave early," he said.

Reginald Bishop is married and has two children. He lives in a white neighborhood where neighbors are as friendly with him as they are with each other. His kids have no problems in the schools. He and his wife fulfill their social obligations to people who invite them to dinner by having dinner parties or cocktail parties themselves, especially around the holidays. These parties are usually small and they contain a mix of blacks and whites, fellow employees and outsiders. The Bishops describe these parties as low-pressure.

In his company there is a lot of socializing, but he feels that he is not excluded to any great extent. There are people he gets along with well and so he visits their homes and they visit his. Other people form other social circles.

Whenever the comptroller hosts a party to which everyone in the department is invited, Bishop receives his invitation just like everyone else. His wife, a schoolteacher, knows some of the other wives in the company and numbers several of the white ones among her friends. He knows that there is racism but he tries to live as if it doesn't exist.

"When we moved into this house," he said in the living room of his modern suburban home, "kids painted a KKK on the mailbox but the police were very cooperative. They found the youngsters who did it, and the fathers of the boys made them come over and paint the mailbox and the pole.

"That happened five years ago and there hasn't been any real trouble since. People more or less accepted the idea that we were here," he said. Reginald Bishop seemed to fit very well into the informal structure of the corporation.

Some black managers complain that because they do not socialize with whites on a frequent basis they are excluded from the informal structure of the company. They argue that the informal structure is a sort of "shadow corporation" that conforms in some ways to the organizational chart but differs from it in important ways.

The organizational chart delineates lines of authority and responsibility, divisions of labor and function, and the official network of who reports to whom with respect to assignment of task and coordination of work. In the informal structure, they say, social connections are important because they are the basis of agreements, deals and mutual support.

In the grapevines that link the informal structure, news of extreme importance is relayed, much of the jockeying for position takes place, rivals are talked down, destructive rumors can be started or stopped and favors can be traded.

In certain companies the grapevine is still important, and unless a manager is permitted into the informal organization he or she will never really learn the ropes. However, many of the companies that have hired blacks are newer high-technology or marketing-oriented companies in which even the formal structure seems to be in constant flux. Lines of authority and responsibility shift so rapidly that no one can keep up with them. As a product planner for General Electric told Raymond Corey and Steven Star, the authors of *Organization Strategy: A Marketing Approach*: "Under the old organization, each department was headed by a closely knit management team. I was on the general manager's staff, and knew what was going on at all times. Now, I frequently don't know why a decision has been made, or—worse—even that it has been made at all."

Managers are constantly shifted around. Specialists are brought in on a project-by-project basis. Units are reorganized to meet changing market conditions, new technology or new management objectives that a powerful informal structure is much less likely to develop. "You barely get to know people before you find yourself moving on," said a corporate director of marketing who had worked for four companies in a total of seven different locations in twelve years.

"People are extremely detached from each other. I imagine there is an inner circle within the company at upper middle management levels, but below that I don't think so, and many of our top people have been raided from other companies. They are so new to the operation that I don't think they form a real group."

In all companies good social connections are important, but often they can be developed without participating in the extensive informal structures that are deeply ingrained in traditional companies. Most newer, well-managed companies are ones in which in-company social life is so fluidly merged with business life that those who avoid an extensive social life don't miss much. Andrew Souerwine in *Career Strategies* makes a distinction between these companies, which he calls "open systems," and the more traditional companies, which he calls "closed systems."

CLOSED SYSTEM	OPEN SYSTEM

CONTROL

The power person assumes that he has control and exercises his power over others to change their behavior. He keeps reminding his subordinates of his position.

The power person assumes that his subordinates know he's in the power role. He believes that he cannot exercise complete control but that subordinates control their own behavior and, therefore, the achievement of organizational objectives.

Control comes through discipline —the use of rewards and punishments, the exercise of fear and threat. "Let them know where the power is." "They won't do it on their own." "When the cat's away, the mice will play." "That's my job: to keep them in line." "I reward those who do well; those who don't do well know they're in trouble with me."

Control comes through training and development and through counseling of subordinates. If people know what needs to be done and how to do it, they will direct their own behavior. Self-control is the major determinant of direction of behavior. If an individual gets out of line, peer pressures and social sanctions will bring him back into the fold. There is a high correlation between a person's performance and the rewards he seeks.

Reporting forms, budgetary con-

While the power person has a

trols, rules and regulations, and procedures manuals let a worker know what is expected of him and keep the power person informed when anyone gets out of line.

healthy respect for necessary controls, he is skeptical about control systems as the ultimate solution to most organizational problems. His faith rests more with people than with systems.

GOALS

The power person accepts the idea that his goals are probably different from those of his subordinates, and he tries to work within that diversity. To find areas of mutual support is to deny the difference in roles and demands between the power person and the subordinate.

The power person strives to establish common goals for himself and the people under him. He accepts the idea that support for each other's goals will be necessary if the goals of each are to be reached.

Orientation is to the present. There's a job to do now. Training and development is done to develop those skills needed now. Crises are avoided by making sure that people know what and how to do what's needed now; future goals are too hazy to respond to now.

Orientation is to the present *and* how it relates to the future. Training and development is used to provide opportunities for personal growth. Crises are avoided by preparing people for the future issues before they arise.

DECISION MAKING

The power person expects to make the decisions, especially the important ones. To ignore this is to abandon his role and to display weakness.

For developmental purposes, individuals at all levels should have an opportunity to make decisions about those aspects of their function that affect them directly. However, decision making by subordinates should be kept within boundaries that protect both the individual and the organization from severe consequences.

COMMUNICATIONS

Communications are unilateral. Relevancy of issues is decided at the power level. Whatever is communicated comes at the convenience of those in power. Feelings and social climate are unknown and/or disregarded.

Communication requires a mechanism for feedback. What's relevant is a function of the person receiving the communication. Communication is an ongoing process where feelings and social climate must be analyzed and understood.

Concerns are primarily upward: "I relate best to power, and my job is to do what my boss wants done."

Concerns are upward, downward, and horizontal, particularly where related functions may have a bearing on achievement of objectives: "I must respond to what is demanded of me, but I do this best through open communications with people at any level directly involved with my objectives."

Techniques are *directive;* control comes through carefully structured communications, job descriptions, and organization charts. Find out what needs to be done and then mold the person into the appropriate shape needed.

Techniques are nondirective. Jobs and organizations are structured to use people's strengths and permit achievement of personal as well as organizational goals. There is a reliance on "subtle signals" to provide direction and interest.

Dissension and conflict must be discouraged. To show disagreement and to raise questions about management decisions is a sign of not being a good "team player." Consistency is a central value.

Dissension is a natural human behavior. Conflicts should be confronted openly and in an atmosphere that conveys that the conflict will be resolved for the good of all. Differences in policies and procedures will be tolerated if it is for the good of the organization and others.

Needless to say, most black managers fare better in open systems, but it is simplistic to speak of an entire company as either open or closed. The marketing division could be open while the manufacturing division might be closed. The Los Angeles branch might be more open than the Kansas City branch. Classifications are helpful but they cannot be applied rigidly. Everything in business seems at one time or another to take on the fluid aspects of a game.

It is also apparent that closed systems are not good places for a majority of managers, black or white, male or female. In this book we have shown how the treatment of blacks in these systems is symptomatic of the treatment of all managers.

Managers said repeatedly that the system had to be made more human. They were not speaking simply of the inhumanity of cutthroat competition although that is a factor which, taken to extremes, has a negative effect on the productivity of a corporation. They were not speaking of the long hours of routine or repetitious work, nor solely of the devastating effects that the managerial life often has on spouses and children, nor of the anxiety and stress that sometimes ruin the health and sometimes kill.

The fear of being fired, the drive to get promoted so that one's level in the hierarchy and one's salary level will shore up one's sense of self-worth, the sacrifices of personal conviction and individuality—these are all part of the problem. However, the root of the problem lies in how the corporation views itself and its people. Make no mistake about it, corporate managers do belong to the corporation they work for. The problem then is that often the corporation does not even think of them as people.

Some of the most influential books on corporate management state that corporate managers are not viewed as total human beings: ". . . complex work organizations are viewed as social machines with almost-human parts," writes Wilbert Moore in his award-winning book, *The Conduct of the Corporation*.

Viewed from a humanistic perspective, this is a startling book. "Affection for one's employer or fellow worker is not required; in fact, sentimentality may impair rational judgement, impersonal performance, and orderly procedure. Devotion to duty has only a remote or negative relation to devotion to people."

The book is wry, ironic and also straightforward and serious, which makes it very sad. "It is really remarkable what money, in the form of wages and salaries, can do in dissolving apathy and antipathy. I do not say that money alone makes the world go around, or that our mechanical model powered with money is precisely a true one, but it is true enough for enough people to be taken very seriously. It is a noteworthy social invention, a testimony to human ingenuity in the almost non-human use of human beings."

There are so many things that are not just morally wrong about this view but logically shortsighted as well. First, money has lost much of its power to dissolve antipathy, if indeed it ever had this power. It dissolves apathy but it does not necessarily get people to work toward any goals but their own monetary ones. It creates apathy—especially in a situation of limited resources, which all situations ultimately are. It forces antipathy underground—but make no mistake about it, people destroy each other directly and indirectly for a greater share of the finite resources.

Nothing illustrates this better than the treatment of blacks during this period of hard times. The mechanical model supposes that relationships between people are based on rational judgment instead of emotions. This is not true. By suppressing softer emotions like devotion to people and sentimentality, we leave the field clear for the baser emotions that surround the competition for money.

Corporations are cauldrons of greed, anger, pettiness, mutual sabotage, frustration, alienation and other emotions that short-circuit the machine in all those places where human compassion, some sentimentality, and some devotion to people do not win out.

Many people—black and white, male and female—bring these human qualities to the corporation and manage to maintain them. They bring them in from the larger society where they have been valued and preserved by minorities and women.

But what happens as more and more of these people are pulled into the corporation? What happens as more and more of them clamor to be a part of the system in order not to be exploited by it, to paraphrase the epigraph by William Blake that we used in the beginning of this book?

The corporations must learn to value what they bring. The corporation is safe, and we are safe as humans, only to the extent that no force is strong enough to make us into ciphers in a world created by logic without imagination, and in procedures that grow in some lopsided way out of the perceptions of one now-powerful group's (white male's) view of reality.

BIBLIOGRAPHY AND REFERENCES

BOOKS

Albrecht, Karl. *Successful Management by Objectives*. Englewood Cliffs, N.J.: Prentice-Hall, Inc., 1978.

America, Richard F., and Anderson, Bernard E. *Moving Ahead*. New York: McGraw-Hill, 1978.

Andrews, Kenneth R. *The Concept of Corporate Strategy*. Homewood, Ill.: Dow Jones-Irwin, Inc., 1971.

Bernard, Chester I. *The Function of the Executive*. Cambridge, Mass.: Harvard University Press, 1966.

Campbell, Angus, *et al. The Quality of American Life*. New York: Russell Sage Foundation, 1976.

Carr, Albert Z. *Business As a Game*. New York: New American Library, 1969.

Chapman, Elwood N. *Scrambling: Zig-Zagging Your Way to the Top*. Los Angeles: J. P. Tarcher, 1981.

Cleaver, Eldridge. *Soul on Ice*. New York: McGraw-Hill, 1968.

Corey, E. Raymond, and Star, Steven H. *Organization Strategy*. Boston: Harvard University Graduate School of Business Administration, 1971.

Cuber, John F., and Harroff, Peggy. *The Significant Americans*. New York: Appleton-Century-Crofts, 1965.

Drucker, Peter F. *Concept of the Corporation*. New York: New American Library, 1964.

Du Bois, W.E.B. *The Souls of Black Folk*. Chicago: A. C. McClurg & Co., 1903.

Ewing, David W. *The Managerial Mind*. New York: The Free Press, 1964.

Feinberg, Mortimer R., with Dempewolff, Richard F. *Corporate Bigamy*. New York: William Morrow, 1980.

Frazier, E. Franklin. *Black Bourgeoisie*. Glencoe, Ill.: Free Press, 1965.

Freudenberger, Herbert J., with Richelson, Geraldine. *Burn-out.* Garden City: Anchor Press/Doubleday, 1980.

Gelber, Steven M. *Black Men and Businessmen.* Port Washington, N.Y.: Kennikat Press, 1974.

Gill, Gerald R. *Meanness Mania.* Washington: Howard University Press, 1980.

Glazer, Nathan. *Affirmative Discrimination.* New York: Basic Books, 1976.

Greiff, Barrie S., and Munter, Preston K. *Tradeoffs.* New York: New American Library, 1980.

Grier, William H., and Cobbs, Price M. *Black Rage.* New York: Basic Books, 1968.

Harragan, Betty Lehan. *Games Mother Never Taught You.* New York: Warner Books, 1977.

Heller, Joseph. *Something Happened.* New York: Knopf, 1974.

Hennig, Margaret, and Jardim, Anne. *The Managerial Woman.* New York: Pocket Books, 1978.

Hill, Reuben, and Becker, Howard. *Family, Marriage and Parenthood.* Boston: D. C. Heath, 1948.

Jennings, Eugene Emerson. *The Mobile Manager.* Ann Arbor: The University of Michigan, 1967.

Jones, Reginald. *Black Psychology,* 2nd ed. New York: Harper & Row, 1980.

Kanter, Rosabeth Moss. *Men and Women of the Corporation.* New York: Basic Books, 1977.

Kanter, Rosabeth Moss, and Stein, Barry A., eds. *Life in Organizations.* New York: Basic Books, 1979.

Kardiner, Abram, and Ovesey, Lionel. *Mark of Oppression.* New York: New American Library, 1980.

Kent, George. *Blackness and the Adventure of Western Culture.* Chicago: Third World Press, 1972.

Kerner, Otto, *et al. Report of The National Advisory Commission on Civil Disorders.* Washington: U.S. Government Printing Office, 1968.

Kerr, Clark, and Rosow, Jerome M., eds. *Work in America.* New York: Van Nostrand Reinhold, 1979.

Kreps, Juanita M. *Women and the American Economy.* Englewood Cliffs, N.J.: Prentice-Hall, 1976.

Lerner, Max. *America As a Civilization.* New York: Simon & Schuster, 1967.

Maccoby, Michael. *The Gamesman.* New York: Bantam, 1978.

Martindale, Don A. *The Nature and Types of Sociological Theory.* Boston: Houghton Mifflin, 1960.

Maslow, Abraham H. *Motivation and Personality.* New York: Harper & Row, 1954.

Miller, Kent S., and Dreger, Ralph Mason, eds. *Comparative Studies of Blacks and Whites in the United States.* New York: Seminar Press, 1973.

Mills, C. Wright. *White Collar.* New York: Oxford University Press, 1951.

——. *The Power Elite.* New York: Oxford University Press, 1959.

Molloy, John T. *Dress for Success.* New York: Warner Books, 1975.

Moore, Wilbert. *The Conduct of the Corporation.* Westport, Conn.: Greenwood Press, 1975.

Myrdal, Gunnar, *et al. An American Dilemma.* New York: Harper & Row, 1962.

Ouchi, William. *Theory Z, How American Managers Can Meet The Japanese Challenge.* Reading, Mass.: Addison-Wesley, 1981.

Parker, S. R., *et al. The Sociology of Industry.* London: George Allen & Unwin Ltd., 1967.

Pascale, Richard Tanner, and Athos, Anthony G. *The Art of Japanese Management.* New York: Simon & Schuster, 1981.

Presthus, Robert. *Men at the Top.* New York: Oxford University Press, 1964.

Purcell, Theodore, and Cavanagh, Gerald F. *Blacks in the Industrial World.* New York: The Free Press, 1972.

Reisman, David, *et al. The Lonely Crowd.* New Haven: Yale University Press, 1950.

Schneider, Stephen A. *The Availability of Minorities and Women for Professional and Managerial Positions 1970–1985.* Philadelphia: University of Pennsylvania, 1977.

Shorris, Earl. *The Oppressed Middle.* New York: Anchor Press/Doubleday, 1981.

Souerwine, Andrew H. *Career Strategies.* New York: American Management Association, 1980.

Terkel, Studs. *Working.* New York: Avon, 1975.

Toffler, Alvin. *Future Shock.* New York: Random House, 1970.

Yankelovich, Daniel. *New Rules: Searching for Self-Fulfillment in a World Turned Upside Down.* New York: Random House, 1981.

Yates, Jere E. *Managing Stress.* New York: American Management Association, 1979.

PERIODICALS

"Affirmative Action and Charges of 'Reverse Bias.'" *Library Journal,* April 15, 1976.

Albery, Dr. Michael. "Procedures in Industry and Business." *Advanced Management,* March 1952.

Alderfer, Clayton P., *et al.* "Diagnosing Race Relations in Management." *Journal of Applied Behavioral Science,* April–June 1980.

Allen, Frank. "Chief Executives Typically Work 60-Hour Weeks, Put Careers First." *The Wall Street Journal,* August 19, 1980.

Antonovsky, Aaron. "A Study of Some Moderately Successful Negroes in New York City." *Phylon,* Fall 1967.

Beckham, Barry. "From Campus to Corporation: The Challenge to Adjust." *Black Enterprise,* February 1980.

Benson, Carl A. "Mobility and Career Development for Black Professions." *The Personnel Administrator,* May 1975.

"The Black Manager: How He Fits into the Corporation." *Employee Relations Bulletin,* December 7, 1976.

"The Black Message: Business Must Do More." *Business Week,* January 22, 1972.

"Black Professional Women." *Black Enterprise,* November 1971.

"The Black View, The White View." *Black Enterprise,* March 1972.

Bonaparte, Tony H. "Problems of Black Managers in Business Corporations Today." *Advanced Management Journal,* January 1972.

Bowen, Jr., Charles P. "Let's Put Realism into Management Development." *Harvard Business Review,* July–August 1973.

Boyle, M. Barbara. "Equal Opportunity for Women Is Smart Business." *Harvard Business Review,* May–June 1973.

Brashler, William. "The Black Middle Class: Making It." The New York *Times* Magazine, December 3, 1978.

Bremer, Otto A. "Is Business the Source of New Social Values?" *Harvard Business Review,* November–December 1971.

Brown, Robert W. "The Black Tax: Stresses Confronting Black Federal Executives." *Journal of Afro-American Issues,* Spring 1975.

Chayes, Antonia Handler. "Make Your Equal Opportunity Program

Court-Proof." *Harvard Business Review,* September–October 1974.

——. "Corporate Mobility." *Black Enterprise,* March 1973.

Coles, Robert. "It's the Same, But It's Different" in T. Parsons and K. Clark, eds., *The Negro American.* Boston: Beacon Press, 1966.

Collins, Eliza G. C., and Scott, Patricia. "Everyone Who Makes It Has a Mentor." *Harvard Business Review,* July–August 1978.

Cobbs, Price M. "Corporations, Credentials, and Race." *Harvard Business School Bulletin,* March–April 1981.

——. "Corporate Culture." *Business Week,* October 27, 1980.

——. "Corporate Mobility." *Black Enterprise,* March 1972.

——. "Court Turning Against Reverse Discrimination?" *U.S. News & World Report,* July 12, 1976.

Cunningham, Mary. "How the Corporate Culture Stifles U.S. Productivity." Washington *Star,* May 10, 1981.

Curley, John. "More Executive Bonus Plans Tied to Company Earnings, Sales Goals." *The Wall Street Journal,* November 20, 1980.

Daniels, Lee A. "The New Black Conservatives." The New York *Times* Magazine, April 4, 1981.

Davis, George. "Bitters in the Brew of Success." *Black Enterprise,* November 1977.

Dennis, Ruth E. "Social Stress and Mortality Among Non-White Males." *Phylon,* Summer 1977.

Denton, Herbert H., and Sussman, Barry. "Blacks, Whites Agree Blacks Have Gained, Differ on What's Ahead." Washington *Post,* March 24, 1981.

——. " 'Crossover Generation' of Blacks Expresses Most Distrust of Whites." Washington *Post,* March 25, 1981.

——. "Lingering Racial Stereotypes Damage Blacks." Washington *Post,* March 26, 1981.

Doudna, Christina. "Women at the Top." The New York *Times* Magazine, November 30, 1980.

DeWitt, Karen. "Black Women in Business." *Black Enterprise,* August 1974.

Dreyfuss, Joel. "Civil Rights and the Women's Movement." *Black Enterprise,* September 1977.

England, George W. "American Managers." *Academy of Management Journal,* March 1973.

Epstein, Edwin M. "Dimensions of Corporate Power, Pt. 1." *California Management Review,* Winter 1973.

——. "Dimensions of Corporate Power, Pt. 2." *California Management Review,* Summer 1974.

——. "Every Man for Himself." *Time,* September 7, 1981.

Faltermayer, Edmund K. "More Dollars and More Diplomas." *Fortune,* January 1968.

Farney, Dennis, and Jaroslovsky, Rich. "Reagan Revolution Enters a Critical Phase for President, Party." *The Wall Street Journal,* January 13, 1982.

Fogelson, Robert M. "Violence and Grievances: Reflections on the 1960s Riots." *Journal of Social Issues,* 1970.

Foy, Nancy, and Gadon, Herman. "Worker Participation: contrasts in three countries." *Harvard Business Review,* May–June 1976.

Ford, David L. "The Black Adult and the World of Work," in *Mental Health: A Challenge to the Black Community.* Lawrence E. Gary, ed. Philadelphia: Dorrance & Co., 1978.

——. "Cultural Influences on Organizational Behavior." *Social Change,* 1978.

Gallese, Liz Roman. "Women and the Race Up the Corporate Ladder." *The Wall Street Journal,* November 3, 1980.

Goodman, Richard Alan. "A Hidden Issue in Minority Employment." *California Management Review,* Summer 1969.

Greenberger, Robert S. "Many Black Managers Hope to Enter Ranks of Top Management." *The Wall Street Journal,* June 15, 1981.

Gumpert, David E. "Seeking Minority-Owned Businesses As Suppliers." *Harvard Business Review,* January–February 1979.

Hayes, Thomas C. "High Bendix Executive Quits Post Amid Controversy Over Favoritism." The New York *Times,* October 10, 1980.

——. "Chief Personnel Executives Look at Blacks in Business." Heidrick and Struggles, Inc., 1979.

——. "Profile of a Black Executive." Heidrick and Struggles, Inc., 1979.

Henderson, J. W. "A White Employer Tells It Like It Is." *Administrative Management Society Report,* September 1969.

Herbert, Adam. "The Minority Administrator: Problems, Prospects, and Challenges." *Public Administration,* November 1974.

Hoard, Bruce. "Informal Poll Finds Racism Felt by Black DPers." *Computerworld,* October 6, 1980.

Holsendolph, Ernest. "Black Executives in a Nearly All-White World." *Fortune,* September 1972.

Jackson, G. G. "Cultural Feedbacks of the Black Backlash in Mental Health." *Journal of Afro-American Issues,* Winter 1976.

Jackson, Raymond J. "Black Women in Administration (From the Point of View of a Black Man)." *The Crisis,* December 1976.

Johnson, Harold L. "Can the Businessman Apply Christianity?" *Harvard Business Review,* September–October 1957.

Johnson, Thomas A. "A Debate Over Affirmative Action: Will Blacks Lose to Other Groups?" The New York *Times,* August 12, 1980.

——. "The Job-Bias Juggernaut." *Newsweek,* June 17, 1974.

Jones, Edward. "What It's Like to be a Black Manager." *Harvard Business Review,* July–August 1973.

Kanter, Rosabeth Moss. "Corporate Success: You Don't Have to Play by Their Rules." *Ms.,* October 1979.

Kerp, Charles, *et al.* "Industrialism and World Society." *Harvard Business Review,* January–February 1961.

Kerr, N. "The Black Community's Challenge to Psychology," in R. Pugh, *Psychology and the Black Experience.* Monterey, California: Brooks & Cole, 1976.

Kirk, Alton R. "Suicide: A Stress Component in Black Males." *Urban Health,* September 1977.

Lindsey, Karen. "Sexual Harassment on the Job." *Ms.,* November 1977.

Loomis, Carol J. "AT&T in the Throes of 'Equal Employment.'" *Fortune,* January 15, 1979.

Mackay-Smith, Anne. "Recruiting Top MBAs Can Begin with a Dry Martini on the Rocks." *The Wall Street Journal,* February 12, 1981.

Markham, William T., *et al.* "Self-Expression at Work: A Theory-Based Questionnaire Instrument." *Journal of Applied Behavioral Science,* 1980.

Maslach, Christina. "Burned-Out." *Human Behavior,* September 1976.

McLean, A. A. "Job Stress and Psychosocial Pressures of Change." *Personnel Psychology,* 1976.

McMurry, Robert N. "Conflicts in Human Values." *Harvard Business Review,* May–June 1963.

——. "The 'Me Generation' in the Executive Suite." *U.S. News & World Report,* March 9, 1981.

Meyer, Herbert E. "Remodeling the Executive for the Corporate Climb." *Fortune,* July 16, 1979.

Miner, John B. "Motivational Potential for Upgrading Among Minority and Female Managers." *Journal of Applied Psychology,* 1977.

Morrison, D. E. "Stress and the Public Administrator." *Public Administrative Review,* July 1977.

Morrow, J. J. "American Negroes—A Wasted Resource." *Harvard Business Review,* January–February 1957.

Murphy, Richard T., and Baldwin, William Lee. "Business Moves to the Industrial Park." *Harvard Business Review,* May–June 1959.

——. "Negro Executives." *Ebony,* February 1961.

——. "A New Boss Breathes Life Into Affirmative Action." *Business Week,* May 10, 1976.

——. "Now 'Men's Lib' Is the Trend." *U.S. News & World Report,* March 18, 1974.

O'Reilly, C., and Roberts, K. H. "Job Satisfaction among Whites and Non-Whites: A Cross-sectional Approach." *Journal of Applied Psychology,* 1963.

——. "Our New Elite." *U.S. News & World Report,* February 25, 1980.

Pell, Eve, and Dowie, Mark. "Mission Improbable." *Mother Jones,* February–March 1980.

Perry, John. "Business—Next Target for Integration." *Harvard Business Review,* March–April 1963.

Podhoretz, Norman. "My Negro Problem—And Ours." *Dissent,* February 1963.

——. "'Reverse Discrimination'—Has It Gone Too Far?" *U.S. News & World Report,* March 29, 1976.

Rice, Berkeley. "Can Companies Kill?" *Psychology Today,* June 1981.

Rogers, R. E. "Executive Stress." *Human Resource Management,* 1975.

——. "Room at the Top." *Black Enterprise,* September 1971.

Sarachek, Bernard. "Career Concerns of Black Managers." *Management Review,* October 1974.

——. "Slaying the Corporate Dragon." *Mother Jones,* February–March 1980.

Slocum, J., and Strawser, R. "Racial Differences in Job Attitudes." *Journal of Applied Psychology,* 1972.

Starr, Jerold M. "The Peace and Love Generation: Changing Attitudes toward Sex and Violence among College Youth." *Journal of Social Issues,* November 2, 1974.

Steiner, Jerome. "What Price Success?" *Harvard Business Review,* March–April 1972.

Stevens, George, and Marquette, Penny. "Black MBAs: Room at the Top?" *MBA,* August–September 1978.

Summer, Jr., Charles E. "The Managerial Mind." *Harvard Business Review,* January–February 1968.

Swinyard, Alfred W., and Bond, Floyd A. "Who Gets Promoted?" *Harvard Business Review,* September–October 1980.

Taylor, S. A. "The Black Executive and the Corporation—A Difficult Fit." *MBA,* March–April 1972.

Thompson, Jacqueline A. "Corporate Survival: Make the Right Connection." *Essence,* August 1978.

Watson, John, and Williams, John. "Relationship Between Managerial Values and Managerial Success of Black and White Managers." *Journal of Applied Psychology,* 1977.

Watson, John G., and Barone, Sam. "The Self-Concept, Personal Values, and Motivational Orientations of Black and White Managers." *Academy of Management Journal,* March 1976.

Westin, Alan F. "Manager's Journal." *The Wall Street Journal,* November 10, 1980.

———. "What Helps or Harms Promotability?" *Harvard Business Review,* January–February 1964.

———. "What Negroes Think." *Fortune,* January 1968.

Weathers, Diane. "The Working Woman and the Men in Her Life." *Black Enterprise,* August 1977.

Yorks, Lyle. "What Mother Never Told You About Life in the Corporation." *Management Review,* April 1976.

Zaleznik, Abraham. "The Dynamics of Subordination." *Harvard Business Review,* May–June 1965.

BIBLIOGRAPHY AND REFERENCES

Suppes, et al. In Б. В. Гнеденко. Курс теории вероятностей.
Изд. Государственное, 1969.

Swinyard, Alfred W., and Floyd A. Bond. "How Constructive Are Boards?" *Harvard Business Review*, 1980.

Terkel, Studs. *Working*. New York: Pantheon, 1972.

Thompson, Victor A. *Modern Organization*. New York: Knopf, 1961.

Walton, John, and Geoffrey Duncan. *Methods and Issues in Social Research*. New York: Wiley, 1975.

Webber, Ross A. *Management*. Homewood, Ill.: Irwin, 1975.

Wren, Daniel A. *The Evolution of Management Thought*. New York: Ronald Press, 1972.

INDEX

Sounds like playing

Music and the early years curriculum

Marjorie Ouvry

EARLY EDUCATION

The British Association for Early Childhood Education
136 Cavell Street
London E1 2JA
tel 020 7539 5400
fax 020 7539 5409
email office@early-education.org.uk
website www.early-education.org.uk

Designed by Susan Clarke for Expression, IP23 8HH

Cover picture of George by Marjorie Ouvry

ISBN 0 904187 31 4

Contents

Foreword

This book is a gem. It is evidence based and builds on theory, but it does so in very practical ways. The spirit is inclusive. Some people are music specialists. Some are not. But, whichever you are, you will come away from reading this book knowing more.

For those who are expert musicians, the book will help you to think about how children develop and learn, so that you can share your enjoyment with them in ways which are appropriate. For those who do not see themselves as confident musicians, the book will give many practical ways forward, which will take away the feeling that only music specialists have anything to offer.

The title, *Sounds like playing*, encourages us all to enjoy ourselves and join with the children in developing a love of music and song.

Tina Bruce
Visiting Professor, Early Childhood Studies
University of Surrey Roehampton

Notes on this publication

Accompanying CD

This icon indicates that the text is supported by explanation or music on the accompanying CD. The track number is shown.

New songs on the CD have been written by **Soo Beer** – an accomplished professional trumpeter and qualified music teacher who combines playing and teaching commitments with extensive work as a music consultant. She has published several music books and songs for primary children, and was recently appointed Merton's first advanced skills teacher for primary music.

The CD is attached to the back cover of the book. A list of the CD contents and printed song lyrics can be found on pages 109–12.

The early years curriculum

Sounds like playing can be used by all practitioners working with young children wherever they may be – whether in pre-school settings or reception and infant classes. The book does not focus on or work towards any specific early years curriculum (for example, the Foundation Stage in England or the Curriculum Framework for Children 3 to 5 in Scotland), as the principles and practical ideas it contains can be applied within any good early years curriculum framework.

Although the book concentrates on the education of three- to five-year-olds, it should underpin children's experiences from birth to eight years.

Using references

References to publications are shown in rounded brackets as the author followed by the date of publication, *eg* (Bruce 1997). The relevant book or article can be found in the 'References' section on pages 104–06 by searching for the author's name and then for the correct date reference.

Anything contained in a square bracket, *eg* [see page 45], is a reference to another page, section or chapter in *Sounds like playing*.

Acknowledgements

It was not until my college years that I was supported as a singer, and began to recognise myself as one. At that time, teacher training was more appropriately named teacher education, because it enabled students to follow interests at their own level and with teaching in view. Had it not been for that excellent experience, my life would have been creatively impoverished and my ability to communicate through music absent. So, my thanks go to all the music staff at Aberdeen College of Education from 1966 to 1969 and, in particular, to Elizabeth Izaat. The motivation for writing this book comes from the sadness I feel about the number of people who tell me that they feel musically unfulfilled, as I would have been. Is their musical potential frustrated because of the way we teach music, even to the youngest pupils?

I began to gather evidence about how children experience music in group settings and realised that the holistic approach of weaving music through the whole curriculum, which I had used, was not widespread. However, I did also find examples of where music and sound-making were gloriously encouraged, and I would like to thank many people for their generosity in allowing me to use examples of their good practice; in particular early years educators Lucy Vallejo and Emma Herzberg, both of whom really inspired me in the way they skilfully and respectfully released children's musicality.

Others inspired me and contributed to this book. Inevitably, not all of their photos and observations have been included, but I would like to thank them all the same: Marian Funnell at Brunswick Nursery in Cambridge for her wonderful observations of musical children, and for photos; Barbara Morrison of South Normanton Nursery School in Derbyshire; Joy Potter at Legh Vale Early Years and Childcare Centre for the Sound Factory contribution; Olivia Travers for her help with Kodaly information and songs; Sue Bainbridge, Frances Davidson, Maureen Brookson, Linda Caroe and Sue Wadhams, who had helpful discussions with me about children's musical play; and to Lewisham LEARN team.

Thanks to George at Rowland Hill Family Centre in Haringey for the cover photo.

Thanks to teachers and other practitioners on courses up and down the country who were willing to take part in surveys about how they taught music, particularly those in Derby City and Devon.

A huge thank you to Steve Grocott, music specialist teacher at Clyde Early Years Nursery Centre, for the interest and help he took over an early draft, and to Celia Burgess-Macey for her invaluable help in discussing aspects of cultural diversity and contributing examples.

Thanks to Soo Beer for writing songs and Dave Cook for arranging songs and directing the work for the accompanying CD. Also to Pat Gordon Smith, my ever-encouraging and ever-patient editor, and to Diane Rich for suggesting I publish through Early Education.

Finally, thank you to Jonathan, whose help and encouragement is never failing.

1 Music in the world of children

The care and education of young children – those in pre-school settings, and reception and infant classes – is a highly complex process. Practitioners engaged in it know that they have been disadvantaged by society's view that it is easy work which anyone can do. This attitude means that early years work is likely to be under-funded, under-qualified, under-confident and, most significantly, prey to inappropriate practices foisted on practitioners by those who only understand approaches which are suited to older children. This is particularly true for the teaching of music in the early years.

Many practitioners working with young children would like to know more about how to give their children stimulating and appropriate musical experiences. Practitioners know that making music can be a joyful and meaningful form of expression for children. They want to increase their awareness of the opportunities for children to learn about music and through it, but many say that they don't know how:

- 'I feel that I lack background knowledge in music, and so music sessions become repetitive for the children and for me.'
- '[My problem is] not being confident enough and therefore not having full control.'
- '[I'm not sure] how to organise for small-group, pair and individual work with music. Consequently, it always seems to be with the whole group.'
- 'I am concerned about progression, and keeping records of children's progress in music. I really don't know what I am looking for.'

Clearly, a lot of practitioners lack confidence with music. But there is a key to help release them from this worry. Instead of concentrating on 'music', practitioners should simply keep their focus on children and childhood – the very things that they already know and are confident about. By observing children learning through all the experiences offered to them, practitioners will see how musically active children are in their play, and this provides all the information and confidence needed to help children progress in their learning.

Children love music and musical activities. The vast majority of practitioners know that music brings great benefits for the children they care for and educate, even though most will not have thought consciously about what those benefits are. When I asked a number of practitioners working in early years settings and in reception classes for their reasons why music should be taught, the vast majority of replies concentrated on the children's pleasure. Typical responses included the following.

- 'It's a release for some children from the formal way we have to run our reception class.'
- 'All the children come together and enjoy the music.'
- 'Music opens up children with special needs.'
- 'I love singing with the children and teaching them new songs. I think my enthusiasm is infectious.'
- 'I enjoy seeing children's obvious delight and enthusiasm.'
- 'It creates a very nice atmosphere in the classroom when we play music to the children.'
- 'There is noise and creativity; fun, relaxation and freedom.'
- 'I like how they use their imagination when they are using instruments.'
- 'The spontaneity of responses surprises me sometimes.'
- 'It's interesting to see the way some children respond naturally to the beat yet others don't.'
- 'It's wonderful to see the children's faces reacting with delight at playing instruments "loudly" and to see the concentration when playing "quietly" and clapping syllables.'
- 'I am astonished at the confidence of some children when asked to sing in front of others.'
- 'It's marvellous when music reaches the shy, introverted children and their faces light up.'

While every one of these comments is positive and very encouraging, they are also rather superficial. To give music its proper place in the curriculum, it is important to provide better arguments than these, and to show how music can be incorporated in all areas of children's early experiences.

Sounds like playing offers a practical approach to the teaching of music to young children by helping practitioners find ways to extend children's observed musicality throughout the playful environment which they provide.

Why music is so important

There is a vast diversity in the ways that people come from a state of not knowing and not understanding to a state where they *do* know and understand. Sometimes understanding comes in a sudden flash and other times it gradually dawns on us. Some things are learned in childhood; others much later on. Some people learn some things better through listening, some visually, others through their bodies and through movement, alone or with others, and so on. Offering to children only a few ways of accessing knowledge limits the connections they can make with their existing knowledge.

Children need to experience the world in lots of different ways in order to make sense of it and draw from it what they like best. Because sound-making and rhythm is such a source of enjoyment to children, music is an excellent pathway into areas of the curriculum which they might otherwise see as difficult or irrelevant.

This is very important for all children, whatever their ability or special learning needs, and the practitioners working with them. This book provides examples of how the entire curriculum in the early years can be supported through music.

Giving children confidence in themselves as learners

There is no reason to assume that simply because children are 'taught' something they will learn it. Nobody really knows the full extent of what children are learning at a particular time. Even so, children may be learning about friendship at the same time as learning the skill of throwing a ball; they may learn that the strongest always gets the trike while seeming to wait their turn. But the more that practitioners know about children and their development, the more they are likely to see what children *are* learning – especially if practitioners use the principles of early childhood education to inform their practice. They will use professional judgement.

However, it is quite easy to know *when* children are learning, because they behave like learners and display the following characteristics:

- enjoyment
- concentration
- listening
- perseverance
- self-confidence
- willingness to take risks

- commitment to the task
- exploration
- problem-solving
- questioning.

When children behave in these ways they are sufficiently motivated to be learning something which matters to them. The practitioner can then investigate what that something might be. This detective work makes the job interesting and creative.

One of the themes throughout this book is to demonstrate how music, singing and musical discovery can support all these characteristics of a learner and give children the feeling, self-knowledge, fulfilment and satisfaction that meaningful learning can bring. These feelings give children tremendous confidence in themselves as active learners and not just passive receivers. In one setting, Jolene spent 20 minutes at the water tray outside, dipping a leaf into the water, raising it up, looking at it closely and then putting it slowly down into the water again, all the time singing to herself 'Down, down, down', which was the end of a song about autumn leaves that the children had learned ('Leaves are falling gently', from Wood & Scott 1962). [For more on confident, happy learners, see 'Music learning through play', pages 32–7.]

Learning about culture and the past

Music, like language, is a 'way of life' (Whitehead 1997, page 7). It is a powerful means for passing on cultural heritage without the need for reading and writing. Very young children can learn their own history and culture, and that of others, from songs and music. Playground songs such as 'Ring-a-ring-o-roses', 'London Bridge is falling down' and 'Pop goes the weasel' are steeped in history. Not only have they been sung by generations of children, they help keep the past alive – in these cases by remembering the bubonic plague, the great fire of London and commercial life in 18th-century London.

Music has been said to act like a 'memory bank' (Bruce Chatwin, cited in Pound & Harrison 2003, page 120). As a Scot, traditional songs tell my history. The Skye Boat Song romantically recalls for me far more of the feeling of Bonnie Prince Charlie's escape after the battle of Culloden than any history lesson could. This is true of many cultures around the world and songs can be a fine way of sharing with parents the setting's interest in the cultures of the children.

All children know songs from their family's history and culture, and in their home language; they will have heard them since infancy and they form part of any child's identity. Different musical instruments and the sounds they make are also intrinsic to different cultures: the tabla and sitar in India, the pipa in China, the pan pipes in Peru, the bagpipes in Scotland, the electric guitar across Western pop music.

Shared cultures

- Jazmin's Spanish grandmother knows that an important aspect of her own culture can be specially communicated to her granddaughter through the music, song and dance of Spain. They regularly attend a community music and dance session together, which creates a close and unique bond between them. They are very proud to share this very distinctive aspect of their relationship with the children in Jazmin's class. Not only is this an important recognition of Jazmin's dual heritage but the children in her class and the staff are enriched by the experience.
- At Diwali, the children in one setting listened to a parent singing a song about Diwali. Some of them wanted to learn it, so the parent spent time singing it with them. At going-home time, these children enjoyed singing the song to their parents.
- Reception teacher Melinda noticed some children pretending to be marching soldiers after they had watched some of the Queen's Golden Jubilee parades on television in 2002. She found a tape of military band marching music and played it outside for them to join in and march to.
- Songs and music from the home culture of children new to the UK, such as asylum seekers and refugees, can help them feel more accepted (Pound & Harrison 2003). Parents in a community nursery were enabled by skilled staff to tape-record lullabies from their own culture which had been sung to them when they were babies. These songs were put on the tape machine in the home corner and the children could play them to the dolls (and each other) to get them off to sleep.

Importance of music in people's lives

Beyond its usefulness as a way of learning about the world, music is a unique means of expression and of conveying emotion. Where would the Golden Jubilee celebrations have been without music, singing and movement? It is unlikely that anyone would have turned out to see a lorry load of children working on maths problems and worksheets.

Some things can only be said in and through music, and the wasted potential for those who have never been able to 'find their voice' because they have been put off at the earliest of ages is a tragedy.

The musician Bob Geldof (2001) said of a recent period of utter despair in his life that 'some things are literally unsayable and remain so. Why music becomes important is that you can articulate the unsayable through a heightened language'.

As a teacher I used music to catch children's attention. One day I wanted Justin to come in from the garden to wash his hands before lunch. I chanted, 'Justin Finn, will you come in?' and was very amused when he replied from a distance on the same pitch and rhythm, 'No, I won't!'

In spite of its importance, music education has become marginalised for many children, especially the fostering of musical imagination. As educator Robert Walker (1988, page 208) says: 'Researchers have paid far more attention to children's drawings and storytelling than to their exploration and expression using sound. Children's drawings are accepted and taken seriously on their merit as important sources of information about children's view of the world. Yet our young musicians are only taken seriously if they play or sing other people's music to a high performance level.'

② Why music is marginalised

Lack of training

In 1970 Alice Yardley, principal lecturer in education at Nottingham College of Education wrote: 'Fortunately, most colleges now expect all students training as primary teachers to take music as a professional course, and very often each student must learn to play an instrument. They are given definite help in selecting and introducing music to children, and many [who thought they were] "non-musical" discover unexpected talents and pleasure in music as a result of these courses.'(Yardley 1970)

Sadly, things have changed. These days, when practitioners train to become pre-school supervisors or nursery nurses and early childhood educators or teachers, there may be very little emphasis given to child development, how children think and learn or even the importance of supporting play, let alone music education. Trainees may not be told about the amazing recent research into how babies hear and listen to music from birth and before (Papousek 1996), or to the place of music and movement in making connections between both hemispheres of the brain (Odam 1995).

By 1988, despite recommendations that all intending primary school teachers should have a compulsory music element in their course, music remained optional in most teacher-training colleges. Later, students could only take music as an option if they had an A level in the subject. Opportunities were further eroded by the concentration in training on the core subjects of literacy and maths. Teacher training tutors lacking early years expertise or experience were unable to make links from subjects taught in the primary school to the joined-up early years curriculum. They were not capable of demonstrating how music was an essential integrating element in young children's learning.

Now that schools are more directly involved in teacher training through school-based mentors and work-based training, it is a lottery for students as to whether they work within schools where music has any impact at all (Pugh & Pugh 1998, page 110). Although music is included as a module in teacher training, the difference between an early years approach to teaching music and the approach more suitable for older children may not be made clear to them.

Here are the main problems created by limited training in techniques for supporting music in the early years setting.

- **The cycle of music deprivation is not broken.** Few people who train as teachers are given the second chance to find out that they themselves *are* musical or learn to sing with enjoyment and confidence.
- **Practitioners have little knowledge of songs and singing.** In a few settings there is the very limited repertoire of 'Wind the bobbin up', 'Baa, baa, black sheep', 'Twinkle, twinkle little star', 'The wheels on the bus' – and not much else.
- **Practitioners know little about the appropriate use of instruments.** Surveys of practitioners carried out by the National Association for Music Education reveal that most settings do not have a music corner and practitioners do not know how to organise one. Practitioners regret that they don't know what to look for as signs of children's musical progress in instruments or how to plan for their musical progression.
- **Music is used as a management tool.** Whole-group music sessions sometimes become a way of keeping children occupied while staff get on with other things rather than helping the children to learn. In this situation, music is not being valued in its own right and there are likely to be lots of unplanned circle times where children sing a very limited repertoire of songs. Meaningful small-group planned music sessions or planned musical interactions with individuals are rare, especially in reception and infant classes. It is while children are still learning to hear that adults can help them to make their hearing grow into listening. Being listened to is part of learning to listen, and the adult who listens to children as they chatter or sing or explore sound and music is starting to plan progression from what the child knows and is interested in. For this reason it is important to plan for small-group music sessions as it is impossible to listen or respond to the enthusiastic expressions of 30 children.

Lack of practitioner confidence

The lack of training means that practitioners often fall back on the unconscious positive or negative feelings about music which may stem from their own experiences of music education.

When asked how they felt about the way in which they were 'taught music' (during surveys that I undertook with practitioners up and down the country), practitioners' reactions ranged from the very positive:

- 'I learned to play the recorder'
- 'BBC radio music programmes were good fun'
- 'brilliant, especially my first school where the deputy head was an actress and musician first and then a teacher'

... to the very negative:

- 'scary, terrifying, humiliating – the worst part of school life'
- 'can't remember primary but secondary was very structured and formal'
- 'boring, just singing hymns'
- 'full of dread as I was unable to carry a tune and was forced to participate and be exposed'.

Practitioners often express a lack of confidence in musical knowledge:

- 'I can't sing or play an instrument. I'm afraid that I am a bad example.'
- 'How do I introduce musical concepts when I don't know them myself?'
- 'I need to move on from "banging" and "shaking".'
- 'I am concerned about my limited knowledge and the few resources I have.'
- [On using instruments] 'I feel I become repetitive and miss the point a lot of the time.'
- 'I would like a wider repertoire of songs but don't know how to learn them.'

Following on from this, practitioners often feel inadequate when asked about their approaches to teaching music:

- [On children using percussion freely in the music area] 'It gets really noisy and the instruments get broken.'
- 'I'm reluctant to have a free-play sound corner because of the noise level.'
- 'I want to provide a balance between singing, instrument work, composing and improvisation with much more participation, but I don't have time. There's too much else to cover.'
- 'The music session is a time-filler, really.'
- 'I always feel that the children might get out of control when I am using instruments with them.'
- 'Our music sessions are more like crowd control.'

This lack of confidence with music and the teaching of music have some significant knock-on effects, the most obvious being that many practitioners allow literacy and maths to dominate the curriculum. Practitioners often say that there is no time for music except as a relaxing pastime or pleasurable addition to the programme. And this seems to be confirmed in early years curriculums across the UK, in which guidance dedicated to music is massively outweighed by ideas for learning through other aspects of the curriculum. In England, for example, the *Curriculum guidance for the Foundation Stage* has a single page dedicated to music with 19 suggestions of what practitioners can do, compared with 10 pages on communication, language and literacy providing 142 things that practitioners can do. Of these 142 ideas, only eight are to do with music and rhyme (DfEE/QCA 2000).

Music as a separate subject

'There is as rich a heritage and tradition of music as there is of literature. Yet the teacher who can give a child access to this store of material need be neither a musician nor an expert musical critic.

Unfortunately, however, in many schools music tends to be regarded as a pleasurable addition to the programme rather than as an integral part of the child's education. Teachers feel inadequate, and while, as non-specialists, they will tackle most other aspects of education with confidence, they have the mistaken idea that only the gifted musician can teach music. Even in schools which run an otherwise integrated programme, a musically talented member of staff or even a visiting specialist teaches music as a separate subject.

If she has developed her own enjoyment of music and has taken the trouble to acquaint herself with the material available she is perfectly capable of helping the child to become appreciative of good music and to become musically literate.'

Alice Yardley (1970)

With a focus on 'core' curriculum subjects, music is increasingly seen as a specialist area, and many settings are now using specialist music teachers rather than their own staff for music education. The introduction of such teachers is not necessarily a new or bad thing. I have seen some excellent music specialists working with children and practitioners to increase their competence, knowledge and confidence in music-making as a natural part of their everyday learning, and this relationship between specialist and practitioner is explored later in the book [see pages 97–8].

However, some practitioners simply step out of the picture when the music teacher arrives: 'When she comes in we just leave her alone. I don't know what she does but the children love it', was how the owner of a private nursery described how she employed a music specialist. This kind of weekly session goes on in some schools too, and is likely to involve the whole group being taken to the hall with some instruments but without meaningful follow up. Seen as a separate event, these sessions do not encourage the development of music exploration areas where children can explore for themselves, and they often mean a lot of sitting for the children instead of music being linked to gross movement.

The use of a music specialist can actively contribute to the practitioners' lack of confidence. One practitioner said to me that 'only a musician is really competent to teach music'. This can only reinforce the sense that music should be handled separately from all the other wonderful experiences offered to children – something that is in direct opposition to one of the abiding principles of early years education, that 'everything connects'.

The consequence of seeing music as a specialist subject is that the people who write books about teaching music tend to be musicians and music specialists, not the early childhood practitioners who have worked with young children on a daily basis. Their experience has been in settings where the children are gathered together for the special weekly input. Often, they add to the perception of separateness in their books by advocating teaching approaches more suitable for older children where subjects are taught separately.

Conversely, while those who work and write about child development and the early years

Children's own confidence with music can be inspirational.

curriculum do acknowledge the importance of music in the curriculum, they tend largely to steer clear of detailing how music could play an integrating role.

One of the aims of this book is to share ideas that appropriately link the special nature of music with learning across the early years curriculum. The next chapter shows how children already have all the knowledge and potential they need to become musicians, composers and performers. Given the right environment, they explore sound and musical ideas just as fully as they do science or language. The practitioner's job is to set up the environment and interact with the children to add to their observed existing knowledge.

Practitioners need not be unconfident about teaching music to young children because they and the children know so much about music already.

3 Learning and teaching arising from what children know already

'We only learn what we know already.' (Katz 1995)

In this quotation from Lilian Katz lies the heart of an appropriate approach to the early years curriculum and the reason why children should not be rushed through the first-hand experiences offered to them. The skill for practitioners is in finding out what children know and when to offer help towards their next line of inquiry and learning.

Children's learning must be based in their own life experience. This means that practitioners need to add to and complement the stimulating experiences that children are receiving in their home and community. If practitioners are to help children progress in their learning, they must be aware of what the children know already and make *them* conscious of that knowledge. How to make children conscious of their own knowledge, skills, attitudes and ability is the basis of good early years teaching in all areas, including music.

What children already know about music

Here is an introduction to the musical foundations that children build on from birth and before.

The research of Colwyn Trevarthen (1998) focuses on how musicality starts in the relationships between infants and adults. Trevarthen finds that adults and babies are predisposed to speak to and coo at each other in rhythms and melodies right from birth, and that this interaction affects emotional and cognitive growth.

Music is powerful in its relationship to physical and mental processes. Adults and babies play vocal games with each other such as 'round and round the garden like a teddy bear'. These, coupled with movement activities, contribute to babies' and young children's sense of belonging to their family, community and culture.

Pre-school and reception children already know a great deal about singing and songs, learned at home, with their extended family, in their community and places of worship, and from films or television – there aren't many children these days who haven't picked up something from advertising jingles, *The Tweenies* or *Teletubbies*.

'Our nursery is right in the middle of a large city. But we take children out to buy things or post letters nearly every day. One of our children had English as an additional language and had not yet spoken to adults. One day he went out with me to buy something for the nursery. I spoke to him but got no response until we began to pass the shops and banks and he began to sing the jingles from the adverts (the bank that says 'yes').

I taped some of these jingles and cut out pictures from magazines to make a book with him. He was so pleased with the book when it was finished, and he used it and the tape a lot to communicate with others. His confidence in speaking English increased from that time.'

The 5 ways of producing sounds

Children already know how to:

1 **Bang, hit and tap.** From the earliest weeks and months of life a baby is able to grasp a spoon and bring it down against a surface producing a 'bang' sound. A wooden spoon and some metal saucepans are a source of sound exploration to many babies, as parents and carers can testify.

2 **Shake.** A rattle has been a favourite gift for babies throughout the ages. The movement of the arms combined with the ability to grasp produces the 'shake' sound and, from the earliest days of life, the child responds to the sound.

3 **Scrape.** The tiny nails of a baby often scratch their faces, but when these same nails scratch a hard surface they produce a 'scraping' sound. Give a child a stick and they will take it along the railings and do the same.

4 **Blow.** Children's active experiences of blowing start with the wonderful 'raspberries' of their early infancy. But even simpler than that, the very breath of life produces a unique sound when it passes over the vocal folds; it makes an individual voice. Children are delighted when they realise that they carry their own instrument around with them.

5 **Twang and pluck.** What opportunities do babies and children have for realising that they can produce a sound by twanging and

plucking? The elastic band or tight string is at first pulled and then let go, and a twanging sound is discovered.

The elements of music

The elements of music refer to how sound can be varied. They are the building blocks of music and musical compositions. Children know about these elements already but need the practitioner to point them out. When children begin to explore musical sounds, practitioners can use the following musical words when talking to children about their explorations, improvisations and compositions, introducing them spontaneously in play situations.

Here is what one childminder did.

'One of my children picked up a "fairy wand" and began to sing and conduct the other children. It was easy for me to sing along, being conducted by him and showing him that I was following his lead. I found a picture of the conductor of an orchestra and said that was what he was doing to keep everyone singing together – *keeping the beat.*'

Loud/quiet sounds

Do children know about loud and quiet? Of course they do. They will probably also know the word 'volume' because they use a button to control the television.

Babies are often frightened by a loud noise and yet the same sound will excite young children, making them jump or run. They have a physical and emotional response to sound.

To babies and children, the knowledge that they can make loud sounds is powerful, at times provoking strong reactions in them and others. Young children enjoy being able to produce a loud sound and seem to be highly motivated to sing songs where they have to shout at some point.

It takes much more control to produce a quiet sound. Our knowledge of how children learn informs us that the more play opportunities children are given the more self-control they can muster. In many places throughout this book, there are strategies for enabling children to explore loud sounds without annoying others.

The musical word for loud and quiet is the **dynamic**.

Fast/slow sounds

Children know about fast and slow movements. They know about running fast and about the emotional state of excitement that this can create. This knowledge is available to them when they come to explore sounds.

The musical word for fast and slow is the **pace** or **tempo**.

High/low sounds

Do children know about high and low? They know about screaming and they know that men's voices are at a deeper pitch than women's. When toddlers flop down from a wobbly standing position onto their nappies, adults who notice them will often make a descending sound from a high pitch to a low. (Never the other way around.) The children themselves will often make the same sound. They might also be aware of environmental sounds such as the vacuum cleaner or spin cycle on the washing machine going up and down in pitch as it turns on and off.

The musical word for high and low sounds is **pitch**.

Hard/soft sounds

Making a hard sound mostly requires hard surfaces coming together, while making a soft sound requires a padded surface coming into contact with either a soft or a hard surface. Experience of textures when crawling gives babies the knowledge of the meaning of the words 'hard' and 'soft', and they can be used when children come to choose beaters which have wooden or felt heads. As children become more experienced, their vocabulary for describing the quality of sounds burgeons and becomes more creative and poetic. 'It sounds witchy!' was one child's description of a piece of orchestral music.

The musical word for the quality of the sound is **timbre**.

Thick/thin sounds

What children know about the texture of sound is the experience of one child singing or playing an instrument compared to all the children singing or playing together at the same time.

The musical word for one sound or lots of sounds layered together is **texture**.

Pulse, rhythm and pattern [see box, right]

Children know the words 'long' and 'short' from a multitude of experiences, and have little difficulty in hearing sounds in these terms.

The musical word for how long sounds last is **duration**.

Current learning and teaching approaches to music

The way in which individual practitioners organise the teaching of music will be consistent with the approach they take and the beliefs they hold about how children learn generally. Here are four examples of beliefs that practitioners hold about how children learn best. (Continues on page 26.)

Pulse, rhythm and pattern in 'Polly put the kettle on'

Pulse

Pulse and beat are the musical terms used when clapping, marching or even waltzing along with a tune. Some bits of the tune are accented more than other bits.

For example, 'Polly put the kettle on' can be clapped to the pulse 1, 2, 3, 4, like this: '**Pol**-ly **put** the **ket**-tle **on**'. The bold words or parts of words show where the four claps of the pulse appear.

Rhythm

This is made by accenting each note of the tune or syllable of the word, and noting whether the sound is short or long. Here is Polly again, written out in syllables with the rhythm given underneath:

Pol-	ly	put	the	ket-	tle	on
Short	**short**	**short**	**short**	**short**	**short**	**long**

Pol-	ly	put	the	ket-	tle	on
Short	**short**	**short**	**short**	**short**	**short**	**long**

Pol-	ly	put	the	ket-	tle	on,	we'll
Short	**short**	**short**	**short**	**short**	**short**	**short**	**short**

All	have	tea
long	**long**	**long**

Pattern or structure

The pattern shows how the whole tune is constructed: how sections of rhythm are repeated or adapted, and when a new section comes in. Polly uses repetition and a little adaptation.

Pol-ly put the ket-tle on **[rhythm 1]**
Pol-ly put the ket-tle on **[rhythm 1, repeated]**
Pol-ly put the ket-tle on, we'll **[rhythm 1, adapted]**
All have tea **[rhythm 2]**

When rhythm 1 is adapted in the third line, the two short words 'on' & 'we'll' take up the same amount of time in the rhythm as the long 'on' in the first two lines.

Belief 1 *Children learn by exploring and discovering*

'We have a big box of instruments of all types and children can fish about in this box to find the instrument that they want. We do not intervene because we think that the children are learning by using the instruments by themselves. Sometimes the noise gets too great and the box is put out of bounds.'

But that is not good enough. The adult needs to observe and cannot just leave children to explore on their own because they will get stuck. They need an adult or a more experienced child to take their learning forward.

Belief 2 *Children learn in whole group or class music sessions*

'One member of staff sings songs or gives out instruments to the whole group, as this keeps the children together while the rest of the staff get on with setting up or tidying away.'

But that is not good enough. Practitioners who only give children the opportunity to engage in singing and musical instruments while sitting with the whole group miss all the ways in which individual children demonstrate their musicality. In some settings the music session is unfortunately used to keep children together and controlled.

Belief 3 *Children learn when the practitioner decides what and when the child is to learn*

'We only have music at circle time as a whole group. All the children take part and one of the staff leads the session. We have percussion instruments out once a week.

But that is not good enough. What about observing what children know already or supporting children's own music-making while they play?

Belief 4 *Children learn when practitioners use their observation as a basis for their teaching plans*

'We have areas (music corners) inside and out, set up so that children can explore music and sound-making on their own or with friends and adults. So we create an environment for music investigation. Our planning is based on what we observe are the children's interests in general and that has to include the way they respond musically. We can then have planned music-teaching sessions based on how the child or group of children is developing musically. Some children seem to respond to music most effectively only when they can move to the music. These target-planned sessions are more likely to be outside, in the home corner or other play area and in small groups than at together time when the session would have more general appeal. We also make time in the day to talk about children's progress in all areas of their development and that must include music.'

That *is* good. There are three clear steps in this example to helping children learn more by using what they already know:

- first the adult *observes* what the child is interested in, playing at and bringing to the setting
- then the adult *supports* the child's learning
- finally the adult *extends* the child's learning.

Practitioners provide the music-rich environment, then they observe how children react within it, then they support and extend the children's learning.

Starting from the child, or group of children – from what they know already and their interests – is the teaching approach encouraged in all other areas of children's learning. It is the integrated approach to learning which enables children to make connections. They have an essential input into how the curriculum is planned and through this approach they are more likely to develop a positive attitude towards music.

(4) Learning music through play

This chapter deals with how the general principles of early learning need to be compatible with the principles of early music learning, and looks at how children weave their knowledge of music into their play themes if we provide an interesting learning environment

Principles of early childhood education

More than at any other stage of education, practitioners in early childhood education need to match up their practice against a set of thought-out principles. This is necessary for three main reasons.

1 People who work with young children, give advice on their education, inspect their settings and make policies about them have diverse beliefs about how children learn best – probably more diverse than at other stages of the educational process. The beliefs of some influential people are based on experiences of work with older children in a different stage of development. A set of early childhood education principles enables practitioners to articulate their beliefs and hold out against any pressure to carry out unsuitable practice.

2 Principles are necessary because children in the early years are vulnerable and more willing to please adults, and will comply with inappropriate experiences. Adults are stronger and will always 'win'. Although children's uncooperative behaviour tells us that the practice is inappropriate, the children themselves are often seen as being at fault and the inappropriate practice remains unchanged.

3 How practitioners behave towards children and their families is heavily influenced by their personal beliefs. For example, where a setting has lots of adult-dominated tasks and lots of sitting in large groups with an adult doing most of the talking, the practitioners' underlying belief is that children learn best when they are sitting listening to an adult – whether or not they articulate that belief.

Practitioners and parents have to take time to share their beliefs and come to a common agreement about the principles upon which their practice is based. If there are conflicting practitioner beliefs within a setting, the children will receive confusing messages. One practitioner may play with a group of children, sustaining and valuing their play. Another may interrupt the play by calling children away from it to do an adult chosen 'activity', thereby giving the play little status.

The table 'Applying the principles of early childhood education to music', on pages 30–31, draws together 16 fundamental principles of early childhood education from a range of respected sources

Principles of music education in early childhood settings

Having established the ways in which some principles of early childhood education impact on the teaching of music, it is important to establish a series of principles for music education in early childhood settings (Pound & Harrison 2003). Again, these are fundamentals to bear in mind at all times, and which should help direct any approach to the way in which children learn through music. The principles are that:

- all children are natural musicians and singers
- music can be integrated into every experience
- children's natural curiosity and sense of wonder flourishes through a wide range of sound and musical experiences, including a wide repertoire of songs
- children become more musically aware and learn best from adults and practitioners who:
  - recognise and build on their musical ability and their developing ideas about the nature of music
  - plan, through skilful observation, using children's existing knowledge of music
  - make sure children know that the music they bring to the setting and the music that they make matters to the adults and is worthwhile
  - value the music of children's cultural background
  - share music-making with parents and carers
  - sing enthusiastically with children
  - give children time and opportunities to explore sound individually and as a small group
  - ensure that in together time the musical activity is enjoyable for *all* the children in the group.

Applying the principles of early childhood education to music

The 16 principles in this table have been adapted from Bruce (1997), which pulls together the principles of the UK early childhood tradition which has developed from the philosophies of Robert Owen, Friedrich Froebel, the McMillan sisters, Rudolf Steiner, Maria Montessori, Susan Isaacs and Jan Vygotsky.

Principles of early childhood education	Implications for music teaching
1 Childhood is not merely a means of preparing for future stages of life, it is a unique time to be experienced and valued for itself.	Music should not be viewed simply as a way to make other aspects of the curriculum accessible; it is valid in its own right.
2 How children feel about what they are doing or are told to do significantly affects their learning.	Music teaching must be enjoyable for all the children and taught in a way that will not 'turn them off'.
3 Learning is not compartmentalised into separate subjects or developmental areas in the mind of the young child; everything links.	Music learning must not be a separate subject but integrated into the whole curriculum planning.
4 Children need to be given responsibility and feel safe enough to take risks.	Experimenting with sound and independent music-making should be on hand at all times and given approval.
5 There are times when any child is particularly interested, receptive and able to learn quickly, and practitioners must look out for these opportunities.	Some musical experiences should happen in early childhood in order to catch individual receptive moments.
6 Children learn best where practitioners value their culture, gender and language, and challenge their own and children's stereotypes.	Practitioners must be aware of how the words of songs and their choices of music and music-making can challenge or confirm stereotypical behaviour.
7 Children learn best where practitioners respect parents as being the people from whom the child learns most significantly.	Enabling parents to become involved and to contribute to music-making in the setting is vital.
8 Children learn best in an environment which encourages them to pretend, play and talk.	Practitioners must be conscious of how the environment they establish for children will support and promote play with sounds, singing and music-making.

9	Children learn best when practitioners plan from what they have observed to engage children's interest.	Children's musical knowledge and experiences need to be recognised through planned observation, and included in the planning and assessment.
10	Children learn best from first-hand experience. They need real and meaningful situations in which they can move about and handle, smell, taste, look at, hear and listen to things that are worthwhile to them.	The music-rich interactive play-based environment of the setting is complemented by frequent visits to people and places of musical interest and visits from musicians.
11	Children learn in a variety of ways and at different rates.	Children need opportunities to re-present their experiences in a variety of musical ways [see 'The creative curriculum', page 41].
12	Children learn best in an interesting environment which gives them personal and physical space, especially outside.	Movement and music need to be offered both indoors and out throughout the session and throughout the year.
13	Children learn best where practitioners teach children indirectly for most of the day and do not give tasks and tell them what to do all the time.	Music and singing should not be confined to circle or all-together times.
14	Children learn best where there are interesting and interested people to be with them.	It is important for practitioners to learn more about music and to invite interesting musicians into the setting to interact with the children.
15	Children learn best where practitioners evaluate their practice honestly, putting children's and family's interests first.	The approach to music education that practitioners adopt needs to be systematically reviewed and evaluated.
16	Children learn best where practitioners want to learn more about how children learn best!	Practitioners need to improve their own skills in music and learn more about its importance in children's development.

Music learning through play

It takes time to establish play and learning that is satisfying to children. It is of little use to children to be given a few minutes of free play as a time-filler after the adult-directed task is completed. When children are playing we know that they are learning because they behave like learners and display particular characteristics [see pages 11–12]. But good-quality play does not happen by magic. Practitioners have to:

- **think about a routine** that allows lots of time for play and hands-on experiences for children, and time to observe and get involved for practitioners
- **plan and set out a playful environment**, be aware of the learning opportunities within it and write them down
- **observe children** who are behaving like learners, and find out what they know already
- **get involved** and support the learning that they have initiated by participating in some way
- **evaluate** the child's present understanding and **record** it in the individual's profile, suggesting possible lines of progression
- **plan to further the children's ideas**, perhaps by offering information that they can only find out from the more experienced (child or adult).

If learning about music is integrated throughout the curriculum, then what is good practice for one area of learning applies to all. The box 'Planning for Amy's music play' [pages 34–5] shows how the staff in one nursery dealt with all these aspects of planning.

Identifying music play

Early years practitioners need to look out for signs of children's music-making in their play just as much as they look out for signs of emerging interest in other areas of the curriculum, such as reading and writing. Once practitioners get into the habit of listening to children's play as well as observing it for signs of music-making, they begin to remark on how much is going on which they hadn't noticed before. From the observation comes the excitement for practitioner and children of planning from this observation. Here are some signs of music that can be spotted as children play, and some examples of how these have been observed in early years settings. All these observations would be worthwhile for the practitioners to follow up in some way.

- **Real-life experiences of music are used in play.** Jody imitated the flautist she saw busking in the underground. She and her mother had stopped to listen and to give the musician some money. Jody held a pencil across her mouth and hummed a tune.

- **Items which have been made or found are used as play props in musical play.** Jamal filled a bottle with buttons. He went around the garden shaking it and calling out in a chanting voice 'Who wants some ice-cream?' Children stopped him and he pretended to give them an ice-cream.
- **Sounds and singing are incorporating into play.** Bobby zooms round the outside area making the noise of a fire-engine, with sounds going up and down in a siren-like wail.
- **Music is used as part of role play.** Pia sings a lullaby to a doll in the home corner (she has a new baby brother at home).
- **Articles are transformed from one thing and used as something else in pretend play.** Ben uses a bat as a guitar while Reanne sings into her spoon 'microphone'.
- **Children play an instrument, explore sound or sing alone or with others, spontaneously and cooperatively.** A group of children have made a boat with crates and, once they have all climbed in, start singing 'Row, row, row your boat' together.
- **Recently acquired skills and competencies are tried out as play, allowing the children to be in control and go at their own pace.** Daniel, Suky and Cash are rolling a ball to each other, and each time one of them rolls it, they all sing a two-note chant, 'roll the ball'.

Musical play is everywhere

In any of the provision areas at any time, children may be exploring how sound is made by tapping, scraping, blowing, shaking or twanging. They may be experiencing some element of music, such as making sounds which are fast/slow, high/low or loud/quiet. They may be singing as they play or creating rhythms and new songs. Here are some practitioners' observations and an example of how one led on to exciting developments.

Observation 1: in the home corner

Matthew loved drumming, and used the home corner saucepans as drums and the chopsticks as drumsticks. [Observations continue on page 36.]

Planning for Amy's music play

Routine

Jane is three-year-old Amy's key person at nursery. She plans to make time to observe, support and extend Amy's play in the in the home corner.

All the staff at the nursery know what they will be doing during the day, and the staff role of 'playing with children' is written in the daily staff task rota.

Environment

In the home corner there is a bed that is big enough for a child to get into and three little beds or cradles for a big doll, little doll and very little doll – all with clothes that fit the relevant doll. There are also storybooks and songbooks to read stories and sing from.

When the children play in the home corner they get to know what is available to meet their learning needs.

Observation

Practitioners know that the home corner fulfils Amy's learning needs. She often plays there alone and sometimes alongside others. She acts like a learner while she is there [see pages 11–12]. She sometimes 'irons', sometimes 'cooks' and so on.

Getting involved

Amy is tucking her 'baby' into bed for the night. Jane does not know how she will extend Amy's play; it depends on what the play that she observes is about.

'She doesn't want to go to sleep,' says Amy.

Jane says, 'Do you think a story or a song would help or shall we tip-toe away?'

(Jane is putting Amy into the role of knowledgeable expert and giving Amy the chance to go ahead with this idea or to opt out it if she would prefer.)

Amy says, 'Sing.'

Jane uses humour to engage Amy's understanding of what is appropriate for the situation. 'We can sing a very loud song to get her to sleep.'

'No! Shhhh,' says Amy, putting her hands up to her mouth in glee.

'Oh, yes, you're right,' says Jane. 'We have to sing it quietly. What song would your baby like us to sing?'

'Rock-a-bye baby.'

They begin to sing, but Jane begins to get louder and louder.

'No!' says Amy, laughing, 'you've got to do it quiet.'

'Oh, yes, I forgot,' says Jane.

They continue this play for some time, with Jane getting it wrong from time to time, until they are satisfied that the baby is asleep.

Evaluation and recording

Jane is pleased that Amy has used the word 'quiet' in the right context and makes a note that she will add this information to Amy's music assessment profile. Amy learned this concept and word very quickly because it was totally meaningful and embedded in the situation.

Some other children join them around the bed and enjoy the joke of getting louder.

Future planning

This turned out to be a 'lesson' about louder and quieter.

At group time the rest of the group was told about Amy's baby going to sleep and waking up 'when we sang too loud', and everyone sang some songs loudly and quietly. For example, when they sang 'The dingle, dangle scarecrow', the children shouted very loudly when they came to the line 'up jumped the scarecrow and shouted very loud'.

Jane and the staff team planned some activities for the coming week based on voices and instruments being loud and quiet [see 'Can you use your shouting voice?', page 70].

The staff decided to carry out an activity using three beaters (one made of metal, one wood and one padded rubber) with a small group. They stuck notices to the music table which prompted ways of using the beaters: 'Which beater makes the loudest sound?', 'Can you play the chime bar loudly and then quietly?'

Lullabies were collected from songbooks and some parents contributed.

[See page 88 for how to make beaters.]

Observation 2: during maths games

A group of children were investigating magnetic shapes. Martin asked Jonathan to pass the diamond. Jonathan laughed and said, 'Ha! Like a diamond in the sky.' All of the children playing with the shapes joined in as Jonathan sang, 'Twinkle, twinkle little star'.

Observation 3: outside on the bread crates

Three children outside were jumping from crate to crate, being very active as they played a follow-my-leader game. Quite soon, their jumping became rhythmical so that they were jumping in time with each other: three bounces on each crate, a pause, then three more jumps.

Nursery teacher Emma observed what they are doing but, as the children were playing and clearly behaving like learners, she took a digital photo of what they were doing rather than getting involved.

At together time, Emma showed the digital image, and the children involved described to everyone else what they had been doing. Emma clapped out the rhythm of the children's bouncing and the whole group stood up to bounce three times, pause then bounce three times again. Emma asked the children if there is any way that the rhythm could be recorded on a flip chart so as to help everyone remember it (she had imagined some form of mathematical tallying).

Katie said she could, and she came and wrote music notes in sets of three.

The others were very impressed, saying it was real music and Jade went to get some music books from the piano to compare. Katie said it was 'lines and dots, it's not really music yet – you have to play the piano to get it, you have to put it on the thingy and play it'. Katie then pointed to the notes as the group clapped along.

There is so much potential for meaningful learning in this child-initiated but practitioner-supported line of inquiry. Emma and a group of interested children in this setting followed up the session by:

- writing a letter to a sister of one of the children, inviting her to come and play the trumpet at nursery and to show everyone how to read music
- putting some writing materials on the table in the music area, alongside some music books; the written music was then put out beside the crates for children to 'read' and jump to the written rhythm
- observing who was interested in writing music
- sharing the new knowledge with the parents and adding to Katie's profile (and those of other children) their present knowledge of and interest in musical notation.

Observation 4: outside

Some children were engrossed in chalking and pattern-making on an old tractor tyre in the garden.

Matilda said to Henry, 'We must whistle while we do this work' ('must' meaning – you whistle when things are fun and you're feeling in a good mood).

She had a good go at whistling!

Did Matilda know about the song 'Whistle while you work' from the Disney version of *Snow White*? Could learning that song be a possible future plan?

5 Music across the curriculum

'What other school activity enhances our general feeling of wellbeing, develops physical coordination, improves verbal memory, helps us learn languages, generates strong community spirit, increases our capacity for mathematical and scientific reasoning and puts us in touch with our heritage?' (Kendall 2001)

In each of the four UK countries, the curriculum for young children has been split up into separate areas, and practitioners identify children's learning in terms of these areas for planning purposes. Yet the children themselves do not separate the curriculum into different areas. Learning is not compartmentalised in their minds; everything is linked. If children can't make connections from one idea to another, the experience is often discarded and forgotten. What *is* retained, however, are feelings of enjoyment or boredom, fulfilment or injustice.

While the curriculum for early learning has been compartmentalised into areas across the UK, they have been prioritised differently in different jurisdictions. In Scotland, for example, there is no separate curriculum area for maths. Mathematical development is so much part of the child's experience of the world that it is subsumed under 'emotional learning' and 'knowledge and understanding of the world'. Everyone can remember complaining when they were little if their friend got the bigger biscuit or more sweets. Maths is learned in early childhood through experiences which touch the emotions or are significant in other ways. Any emphasis on the formal teaching of number names and the names of shapes is largely a waste of time, as most children will learn such things easily in meaningful play and real-life situations (see Skinner 2001).

Around the world, practitioners are offered guidance into ways of thinking about children's learning which is holistic and connected. In New Zealand, for example, the curriculum for young children, Te Whariki, does not mention subjects at all, but divides what the adults need to offer to children into the following strands:
- wellbeing
- belonging

- contribution
- communication
- exploration.

In the UK, the Quality in Diversity framework helps practitioners to evaluate the curriculum they offer young children. It regards a good-quality early years curriculum as one which enables children to:
- be and become [see 'The creative curriculum', page 41]
- belong and make connections
- participate and contribute
- be active and expressive
- think, imagine and develop understanding of themselves and the world in which they live (Early Childhood Forum 2003).

Children learn by making connections. The implication for practitioners is that there is a great responsibility to give children experiences where links are sensible and satisfying. If a curriculum is fulfilling, children will persevere and are more willing to try and try again, and to achieve the outcome they have set themselves.

Music is a useful 'connector' because its powerful and enjoyable influence helps children make sense of 'non-sense'. Sounds are among the first things that children experience. Babies can hear in the womb, and neurological research tells us that music (and movement) bridges the two hemispheres of the brain, with language and conscious thought on one side, and intuitive and emotional thought on the other (Odam 1995). So when practitioners use children's natural delight in and knowledge about music, they are supporting the development of the whole child.

Although music is such an important area of learning, it has been subsumed under the umbrella of creative or expressive development in early years curriculums across the UK, and this makes it possible to omit music during planning. When asked why music doesn't feature in their written plan, practitioners often say that they do music, but don't write down what they do. It is often looked on as 'a useful fill-in where there are unplanned gaps in the timetable' (Goddard 2002).

In the following sections, there are examples of how practitioners have found that music can link all areas of the curriculum for young children. Practitioners have listened to children's interest in music and sound-making, and have been able to support children's learning. The learning areas in all the UK early years curriculums cover:
- aesthetic/creative development
- personal, social and emotional development

- physical development and movement
- language, literacy and communication
- mathematical development (though not, of course, as a separate subject in Scotland)
- knowledge and understanding of the world around us.

The rest of this chapter provides some simple principles, ideas and examples to show how children use and experience music in all of these areas.

Aesthetic/creative development

The aesthetic/creative curriculum stems from children's sensory experiences. They have unique aesthetic experiences through all their senses, experiencing the world by hearing, tasting, moving, touching, smelling and seeing. Significant emotions, both happy and unhappy, are bound up in these aesthetic experiences, for example the taste of candy floss may revive a childhood seaside holiday memory [see 'The creative curriculum', opposite].

Children's responses to experience are personal. One child may want to exhibit delight at seeing the tadpoles wriggling about in the tank by wriggling his body in a dance-like way; another may enjoy helping to make up a story or poem about tadpoles full of 'wriggly' words; another may want to paint black tails and heads all over a large piece of paper.

Skilful practitioners look out for children's preferred way of expressing what they know and what they feel. They may like to represent their experience and how they feel about it through dance, imaginative or fantasy play, art, story-making, poetry or *music*. Each must be available. A rich environment, where children can benefit from all sorts of creative opportunities, offers children the best opportunity to express their sensory and emotional experiences.

The UK early years curriculums for creative and expressive development are concerned with:
- exploring materials and media
- responding to experiences
- expressing and communicating ideas
- imagination and role play
- music.

See page 42 for examples of how elements of this curriculum have been fostered through sound and music.

The creative curriculum
helping children to make sense of the world in which they live

Aesthetic experiences
Experiences are bound up with emotions (sadness, happiness, etc).
That makes each experience unique to one child.

The creative curriculum helps children to hold on to and *re*-present their
experiences and provides a learning environment where children can choose
the way in which they can best reflect upon their experiences.

Music is one of the means of expression. Children need opportunities to:

be a dancer

be dramatic and imaginative in play

be musical

be a poet

be a story-teller

be artistic

Exploring materials and media
Responding to experiences
Expressing and communicating ideas

At the workshop art and craft area, Adama fills a brown paper bag with metal bottle tops. As she shakes it and sings loudly, some bottle tops come out. She gets Sellotape and wraps it round and round at the neck of the bag, stopping to cut some wool and incorporate that into the wrapping. She then puts the whole thing round her neck and goes to the role play space rocket. One of the children won't let her in, so Adama stands and watches until another child approaches and goes in. She then disappears and returns with a handful of 'train tickets'. Then, standing outside, she shakes her rattling bag and calls, 'Tickets! Tickets!' The children inside the rocket come dutifully out to buy a ticket and then they and Adama go into the rocket together.

Imagination and role play

Adama is holding the mop at the end of lunch time, waiting for Amina to sweep the floor before she can mop it. As she waits, she uses the mop handle as a microphone and sings loudly, swaying and moving the mop from side to side.

Music

This book is full of examples of children being creative and expressive, and ideas to help them do so. The next three chapters contain more creative activities through singing, making and using instruments, and making and using music areas.

Personal, social and emotional development

Although the terminology differs slightly across the UK early years curriculums, each one is keen, in this learning area, to foster children's:

- self-confidence and self-esteem
- respect for and sensitivity towards others
- understanding of other cultural backgrounds
- positive relationships – among children, and between children and adults
- positive behaviour and self-control
- self-care
- sense of community.

Here are some examples of how music has linked into these aspects of children's development through play through skilled adult intervention in play and activities which have been planned by adults.

Self-confidence and self-esteem
Respect for and sensitivity towards others
Understanding of other cultural backgrounds

At together time, the children talked about the weather. They walked around doing cold-weather actions – slapping their arms and stamping their pretend cold feet. The teacher sang a song about weather which the children had only just learned:

> *A cold and frosty morning – good morning, good morning*
> *A cold and frosty morning – good morning to you.*

At the appropriate time in the song the children stopped and shook hands, and sang 'good morning'.

Anna, a five-year-old Turkish girl, had been very reluctant to take part in group activities and did not want to join in. The teacher had asked Anna's mum how to say 'good morning' in Turkish, and had told her she was going to introduce this into their song. She told the children that people all over the world say 'good morning' in their home or community language, and that when Anna does this, she says 'merhaba'. She asked them to sing this instead of 'good morning', and they changed it to:

> *A warm and sunny morning* – merhaba, merhaba
> *A warm and sunny morning* – merhaba *to you.*

Anna was clearly delighted when she heard all the children singing a word that was familiar to her and she immediately joined in.

Other children told the teacher what 'good morning' was in their language, and everyone sang the song using the 'good morning' words for each language.

Positive relationships
Positive behaviour and self-control

Adam (3 years, 3 months), and Serena (3 years, 6 months) were observed working together at the music area.

Serena held a book of rhymes and songs and showed Adam the pictures. Adam then picked up a shaker and was instructed by Serena to keep shaking in time to her singing. They sang four songs without any adult intervention before Serena walked off to another activity (adapted from Northumberland County Council 1995).

Self-care

The children were interested in wind instruments and had a recorder, a mouth organ and a kazoo to explore on the music table. The practitioner had told them that they should wipe the mouthpiece of each with the tissue on the table when they have finished playing. She has a photo and a notice to remind them.

Sense of community

Songs and dances are inherent in every culture. If the songs which the children sing reflect the diversity of the local community and of society in general, children will experience a strong sense that their own community is accepted and respected.

In many settings, parents are regularly asked if they know performers from different countries for children to see in a group visit, or who might come to the setting itself. In one setting, the children listened to and saw Morris Dancers, an Indian dancer, steel pans from the local secondary school, and bagpipes in one year alone.

Physical development

The UK early years curriculums for physical development are concerned with:

- movement
- sense of space
- health and bodily awareness
- using equipment
- tools and materials.

There is no reason why children should be still when listening to music, nor is it a desirable response. It is only in Western, classical music where being still is an expected response to music, and this is quite out of step with the vast majority of music listening in the world, where people are actually expected to join in and be physically active.

It is true that when some children listen to music they will sit still and concentrate, that their breathing becomes slower and shallower and at the end of a piece they might give a deep sigh (Moog 1976, page 109). But other children (or the same quiet children on a different day or with different music) naturally want to move when they hear and take part in musical experiences. As a result, it is no surprise that the words 'music and movement' have traditionally been teamed up in the early years curriculum. Long may the tradition continue!

Other aspects of this curriculum area are fostered through sound and music in very simple ways:

- children's spontaneous vocalisations as they zoom about relate to their **sense of space**, and these can be given more direction if practitioners teach them playground games
- made-up songs can help create **health and bodily awareness** if they deal with things like washing hands after going to the toilet, getting hot after exercise, dressing appropriately or eating healthy food (*eg* 'This is the way we wash our hands, wash our hands, wash our hands. This is the way we wash our hands when we've used the toilet')
- playing and making instruments help children to **use equipment, tools and materials** [see Chapter 7].

Language, literacy and communication

The UK early years curriculums for language, literacy and communication are concerned with:

- language and communication
- language for thinking
- linking sounds and letters (emphasised strongly in the English curriculum guidance: DfEE/QCA 2000)
- reading and writing (also emphasised strongly in the English curriculum guidance).

Language and communication

The spoken word should precede the written word by years. Without opportunities for lots of talk and lots of opportunities to communicate to interested and interesting friends, learning how to write and read will be meaningless for many children. They will simply not have lived long enough to experience all they need to know about language before starting to write it down formally (Rich 2002).

At present, there is a strongly perceived pressure on early years practitioners (especially in England) to hurry children on to the written word before they have exploited the rhythms, rhymes, syllables, jingles and alliterations of the spoken word.

Singing songs, learning rhymes, echoing or inventing rhythms, and moving to music help 'focus attention on contrasting elements in words, while avoiding the distortions of analysing the sounds in words letter by letter' (Bullock 1975).

Because children enjoy singing and are natural and successful explorers of rhythm, music has an obvious and essential place in the language and literacy curriculum. Practitioners and parents must exploit and celebrate it frequently, laying aside the sterile and often sedentary pencil and paper activities concerned with 'vexing children with letters before they can barely talk' (McMillan 1920).

Support for children with English as an additional language

Songs are also invaluable for supporting children with English as an additional language, because they introduce words, phrases and syntax in ways that are easy to remember, reproduce and apply to different situations. Here is an example from one setting.

Vinod uses English as an additional language and came to nursery with virtually no English. He hums frequently and his key worker usually finds that his humming relates to what he is doing. Here are three ways in which he has shown that his understanding of songs taught in the nursery helped him with English words and meaning.

- Vinod hummed 'Row, row, row the boat' and, when asked what he was building, he replied, 'A boat'.
- Vinod was humming 'Chick, chick, chick, chick, chicken, lay a little egg for me' as he looked at an information book about the egg/chicken life cycle.
- Vinod hummed 'Five little dinosaurs' as he played with the toy dinosaurs.

Language for thinking

Traditional songs and nursery rhymes from all cultures are permeated with nonsensical ideas. Think, for example, of 'the dish ran away with the spoon', 'four and twenty blackbirds baked in a pie' or 'bananas in pyjamas' or 'Tinga Layo' from the Caribbean. Nonsense songs and rhymes are to be encouraged because they can feed the imagination by giving children permission to 'turn the world upside down' (Meek 1982, page 33). Moreover, far from confusing children, they ground them more in reality, confirming for them what is real and what is fantasy – which is the basic power of humour. Silly songs encourage the sense of humour necessary in building warm and caring relationships between child and adult and child and child, thereby dovetailing into the curriculum for personal, social and emotional development.

Using instruments to enhance stories

So many well-loved stories can be extended by the introduction of instruments. Lots of them are potentially 'noisy'. Here are some examples.

- *Peace at last*, **by Jill Murphy.** When the children know the story well and they know the available instruments well, they can decide what a good sound would be for snoring, toy aeroplane, the tick-tock of the clock, and so on. When the story is retold the children can come in at the appropriate time with the 'noise' of their instrument.
- *We're going on a bear hunt*, **by Michael Rosen (illus. Helen Oxenbury).** Children can decide what instrumental sound would make a good 'swishy swashy sound', and so on.
- *The whales' song*, **by Dyan Sheldon (illus. Gary Blythe).** While a practitioner in one setting was reading this story to a small group, one of the children stamped her feet at the point when 'Uncle Fredrick had stomped off'. Afterwards, the practitioner asked the children if they would like to go to the music area to see what other sounds they could make. Together, they decided which instruments would be good to represent different bits of the story and the practitioner suggested bottles filled with water would make good ocean sounds. She re-read the story and the children supported each other with their cues for when to play. They used drums, chime bars, water in bottles, piano, feet and voices. *The whales' song* was left in the music area afterwards rather than put back in the book corner, and small groups of children returned day after day for more than three weeks to retell the story by themselves with the instruments.
- *So much*, **by Trish Cooke (illus. Helen Oxenbury).** As each person comes to the door, in the story, the text of the book says 'DING-DONG'. This is a perfect opportunity for a child to use two chime bars with a beater. After having introduced the idea at story time or with a small group, put the book and the chime bars on the music table or in the book corner. As an extension, put the chime bars outside the home corner, where the children can 'ring the bell' before entering.

- **'*Ahhh!' said Stork*, by Gerald Rose.** '"Ahhh!" said Stork, "I will eat this egg," and she pecked it. But it did not break.' Discuss with the small group of children what sounds or instruments could sound like a bird's beak pecking at an egg, or the zebra kicking at the egg, or the elephant stamping on the egg, etc.

Similar fun can be had with any number of books which the children enjoy. When looking to introduce music into the reading stories, plan out how many 'instrumental' sounds might be included and then involve that number of children. This is not an activity for a large group as it takes a lot of discussion and problem-solving. However, when the story is next retold the instrumentalists can 'perform' to the whole group.

[Full publication details for the books used in this section are available on page 108.]

Linking sounds and letters
Reading and writing

Practitioners are often lulled into thinking that young children learn the alphabet sequence through a rather contrived song about it. Rote learning perhaps has its place for older children later in the school system, but not at this stage. Sound games and made-up songs are much more useful to children who have started to show an understanding of the connections between letters and sounds. Not until the very end of the early years is it necessary or appropriate to formalise writing, that is not before Year 1 in England – around age five to six.

This is how I linked sounds and letters for children in one setting. On the music table we made shakers and put **p**eas in a **p**ot and **p**asta in another **p**ot. Then we got bottles and wondered what we should put in the **b-b-b-b**ottles. Some children in the small group didn't understand the connection we were making, and for them the fun was to be found simply in making the shakers. But other children picked it up straight away and suggested that **b**eans, **b**eads or **b**uttons could go in the **b**ottle. That helped me to know that those children were starting to be interested in how letters made sounds and I was able to note this progress in their profiles and begin to play more challenging games with them.

Rhymes that children begin to recognise in song are also invaluable. The rhyme in songs like 'Little Bo P**eep** has lost her sh**eep**' not only help the children remember the song, they provide some key information for future spelling.

Mathematics

The UK early years curriculums for maths are concerned with:
- patterns and calculating
- numbers and counting
- shape, space and measures.

Mathematics, like music, is another area of the curriculum where many practitioners lack confidence. They fail to recognise how much maths they know already and how much they use in everyday life, such as:
- the mathematical vocabulary of positions like up and down, along and beside, over and under, or in and out
- numbers, estimations and calculations needed to shop, drive or cross a busy road
- knowledge of time needed to plan an appointment
- estimations of capacity and volume used to transfer left-overs into a bowl which is the right size to put into the fridge.

The many mathematical concepts that children are capable of exploring are undervalued if practitioners see maths only as numbers and shapes which children will learn very quickly in situations that are meaningful to them (after all, they soon learn to count if they think their big brother has got more Smarties in the share-out). Most of all, maths is about patterns, sequencing and recognising similarities and differences, and everyday maths such as this is the key to successful teaching of maths to young children, as it enables practitioners to recreate the circumstances of first-hand experience for the children.

Patterns and calculating

Mathematics and music are closely linked in many ways. When children learn rhythm they are well on their way to learning ratios, fractions and proportions. A musician must be able to count beats and bars in a piece of music, to add up the number of notes in a bar and to discern patterns.

For example, on one occasion, Charlie came up to me and said that she liked my beads. I pointed out that they were in a pattern which went: red, blue, red, blue, red, red, blue, red, red, blue. She joined in the pattern calling. Then I said that I could sing my beads and on two notes I sang them. 'Can I make some beads to sing?' Charlie asked. So a group of children started threading beads and sang them to each other, adding new colours and new notes. I said, 'You are reading your music'. This was a starting point for musical notation – and graphic scores. Mathematically speaking, Charlie and her friends needed to be counting successfully in order to maintain the correct pattern.

Children easily recall stories and songs arranged in sequences and patterns. All parents and practitioners know that children can detect the slightest deviations from the original (a source of much laughter and fun as adults try to trick children by their alterations). It is most important to try to vary the sequence and it is a good indication of something well learnt that the child notices and scolds the adult. 'Heads, shoulders, knees and toes' is a good song for this.

When children are playing, especially outside, they can use the full range of their voices. The musical element of 'loud' and 'quiet' can arise naturally from voice sounds and draw children's attention to ordering, a mathematical concept that is often dealt with only by visual means [see box, 'Ordering game'].

Ordering game

Four children stand in a row. Ask the first child to say or chant her name, ask the second child to say it more loudly than the first child, the third to say it louder than the second child, and the fourth to say it louder than the third:

Susan   Susan   Susan   Susan

When the children get the idea, they will start to play around and make it funny by starting off very loud or, if it is to get quieter, by starting off very quietly. Loud and quiet, loudest and quietest; long and short, longest and shortest; high and low, highest and lowest – these are all are musical terms with possibilities for sound games.

Numbers and counting

There are so many songs which help children to remember numbers, count, add and take away. This is one of the areas that is best resourced, and practitioners usually have lots of songs at their fingertips to teach to the children: firefighters, astronauts, frogs, elephants, green bottles, rolling people in bed and a few currant buns or chapatis can all be acted out with great enjoyment.

Practitioners need to have a wide repertoire of maths singing games and songs which use movement. Children use counting songs such as 'What's the time, Mr Wolf?' a great deal in their outdoor play. (There are more ideas for outdoor maths games and songs in Ouvry 2000, pages 77–80.)

Here is an example from my own experience of another way to foster counting (and also to help language development). My reception classroom assistant and I had fun listing words to do with a theme of 'transport' and noting the number of syllables in each word. We wanted to be prepared before we asked the children to think up transport words and then to clap or stamp to each syllable in each word. Most of the single words or groups of words had one, two or three syllables and so would have only one, two or three claps, but some more complicated phrases had more, for example:

- car, train – 1 syllable, so 1 clap or stamp
- lorry, traffic – 2 claps or stamps
- aeroplane, taxi rank, motorway – 3 claps or stamps
- petrol station, traffic police – 4 claps or stamps
- articulated lorry – 7 claps or stamps.

The small group of children hit their instruments while silently 'saying' the word in their heads, and then the adult or another child hit their instrument and guessed which word they were thinking of. Sometimes we said, 'I'm thinking of a word beginning with C', and then clapped once. We put up pictures at the music table and the numbers and we watched how the children used the pictures as prompts to the number of times they hit the instruments.

Shape

This is an excellent example of a song being used to incorporate shape in action. Baillie is in the outside area moving bread crates round purposefully and humming a song. The practitioner recognises the tune but doesn't realise its significance until Baillie stands back to look at how he has arranged the bread crates in a square shape. He then climbs on them and walks round and round the top of the crates singing in a loud voice the song he had been humming. It was 'Square' by Helen MacGregor (1998).

Find four corners, find four corners,

Sides the same, sides the same,

Put them all together, put them all together,

Square's my name, square's my name.

Knowledge and understanding of the world around us

The UK early years curriculums for knowledge and understanding of the world are concerned with:
- exploration and investigation
- design and making skills
- information and communication technology
- sense of time
- sense of place
- culture and beliefs.

Exploration and investigation

In one setting, the children had been very involved over a period of time waiting for and watching chicks hatch in an incubator. The home corner had been transformed into a 'chicken run', with play hats, straw, food bowls and a large cardboard egg. The children could climb into this egg, close the 'lid' and wait to 'hatch'. A child was heard singing inside the 'egg' (to the tune of Frère Jacques):

Can you hear me?
Can you hear me?
Tap, tap, tap.
Tap, tap, tap.
I am hatching out now.
I am hatching out now.
Cheep, cheep, cheep!
Cheep, cheep, cheep!

Design and making skills

After a visit to the local technology museum, some children did a machine-type movement session to some music. This was followed by a suggestion from an adult to make their own machine using their voices.

A group of 12 children were involved. One child started the 'engine' and others added their sounds until the whole group was involved, while the adult conducted the machine parts, making the engine go faster and faster and louder and louder, and then gradually fade out and stop in sequence until it was quiet again.

Following on from this, the children made a group musical instrument from materials discovered when dismantling a lot of old household equipment – hairdryers, radios, clocks and vacuum cleaners – to see what was inside.

Information and communication technology

Children quickly learn to use the tape recorder and the computer.

Amina looked at the computer screen which was showing a bedroom and asked an adult what it was. The adult explained the game called 'Find the teddy' – but look as they might, the teddy was nowhere to be seen. Amina then walked off singing to herself, 'Teddy bear, teddy bear where are you?' to the tune of 'Tommy Thumb'.

Sense of time

Recalling past events is not about just remembering dates in history. For young children, it is a recalling of significant things they did when they were a baby, yesterday or even this morning. At together time, sharing these can be turned into songs and everyone can join in. For example, children in one nursery come together at the end of the morning and sometimes sing about what they have been doing …

Sam went to the garden and dug up the ground, dug up the ground,
* dug up the ground*
Sam went to the garden and dug up the ground, on Monday in the
* morning*

or

Sue played in the sand tray and filled all the pails, filled all the pails,
* filled all the pails …*
Adam went to the sofa and read all the books, read all the books,
* read all the books …*
Joe played with the water and got very wet …

(Adapted from Beer 1999).

Sense of place

Songs and sound exploration reinforce children's knowledge of people who help us (Thank you song), transport, places, picking up litter, road signs. Children in a Year 1 class who visited a restaurant decided that, to make their own restaurant back at school, their role play area would need Chinese music and authentic kitchen tools to make the right clanging sounds.

Culture and beliefs

Listen to music, learn songs and dances from different cultures with the help of parents. One class had a supply of tapes with many different musical styles. Alex chose to dance to reggae songs which his parents played at home, and which he had heard on his holiday to Jamaica.

The Sound Factory

A music project which spanned all areas of the early years curriculum

Joy Potter, Foundation Stage coordinator at Legh Vale Early Years and Child-care Centre in St Helens, describes the project and how they made it work.

'The idea to have a sound theme play area, with opportunities to make a lot of noise, first occurred to me after I had seen a dance company called Stomp at The Lowry Centre in Salford. It was such fun, so energetic. All the sounds were made using everyday household items like bins, brushes, pans, sticks, chairs and tables – all of various sizes and materials. The show was too long for early years children, but as a school we have close links with St Helens Primary Dance Company, so we invited them in to do a show based on sound with a similar theme for the children.

This was the perfect springboard for setting up our own Sound Factory. The children knew that different sounds could be made in different ways, and were given experiences which showed them that sound travels in waves.

We discussed with the children what they had seen and what they knew about sounds already, and invited them to bring in things from home to contribute to the Sound Factory. This was done via our weekly home–school news sheet and led to a lot of discussion at home as to what was going on.

Some children just wanted to use the item they brought, which needed some careful explaining.

Once we had made a collection, we discussed what we had and how we could use it all to make sounds. Lots of noise followed! The children soon found out that they did not like uncontrolled noise, and soon began to discuss who should play when, how they would know when to play and when to stop – and the whole idea of the need for a conductor was born. We very quickly found out the children who loved to be in control and had to hold the baton.

We used focus activity times to reinforce the different ways to use the factory. These were semi-spontaneous, often picking up on what we had noticed the children doing. For example, we saw the children rolling things down the sound pipes we had made from the insides of carpet rolls – one child rolled while another listened to the sound at one end. This led to an activity where we experimented with a variety of objects, listening to the different sounds made.

We noticed that a number of children were only able to use one hand at a time and had very little control over the sounds they were making when hitting things, so we invited a real live drummer in to school to give them some inspiration and to teach the children some skills. This was a huge success! The children loved the drummer's short performance and had the opportunity to work with him in small groups. By the end of the time most children were able to use both hands, copy a rhythm, and stop and start in turn. There were several children who were able to keep a separate rhythm with each hand over a sustained period, which amazed us.

We had a multicultural theme running at the same time, so introduced tapes of music from around the world for the children to play along to at various stages. This included some original singing recorded by one of the staff in a village in Tanzania, which sparked a lot of discussion.

Most of the time, the factory was used outside. This was so that the children could have the space to spread out and enjoy all they were doing without fear of disturbing others.

The cost of the whole project was minimal. Our only significant expense was the hire of St Helens Primary Dance Company for one show and two follow-up workshops – and we included Key Stage 1 children for the show to make it really worthwhile. We also needed to buy lots of rice, lentils, pasta and cous cous for shakers.

Lots of things were donated, including a packet of chopsticks, a load of old pans, yoghurt pots, wooden and metal spoons, tins, ice cream cartons and even elastic 'spiders' to keep the sound pipes still on an old water tray frame. The sound pipes themselves were donated from a carpet warehouse and decorated by the children, with the help of a 14-year-old student.

The Sound Factory ran and sustained interest over a period of about five weeks. The quality of play in terms of group interaction, use of language, turn-taking, taking on a role, negotiating a role, practising and refining skills was wonderful. The children have loved it and we will do this type of music-based project again.

Planning for music across the curriculum

A well-planned play-based environment is a major arena of opportunity. What practitioners need to predict and plan for are the possible lines of inquiry which children will be likely to take and which will lead effortlessly to their development in each of the areas of the curriculum. Practitioners need to be creative and flexible, and to change their strategies to suit the child's interest. Through regular observation, playing with the children and communicating with their families, practitioners are able to direct their

The building site planning sheet showing the opportunities for music exploration

Initial observation

There is excitement over the school extension which the children can see being built through the fence.

Individuals and groups of children are observed (seen and heard) being interested in:

- machinery
- dressing up in hard hats, *etc.*
- noises (making and hearing)
- physicality
- building
- what is being made
- what the men have for their lunch
- quantities of sand, bricks, piping, *etc.*

Curriculum areas

- Aesthetic/creative development:

- Personal, social and emotional development:

- Physical development and movement:

- Language, literacy and communication:

- Mathematical development:

- Knowledge and understanding of the world around us:

Music and sound exploration

Activities following the children's interests will aim to help children explore and find appropriate ways to consolidate their musical knowledge. In the course of the project, the children will probably experience:

- new ways to produce sound and elements of music
- ways of making sounds and composing
- listening and responding to recorded and live music
- learning new songs.

– role-play being builders – sing 'Put a brick on a brick on a brick on a brick, and we'll build up our house so high' (Charlton 1973) or 'Put a crate on a crate'.
– Bob the Builder songs
– trikes become machines to go fast and slow, *etc.*

– singing together
– singing mobile phones – chant game: 'What do we need on the building site?' One child chants (into a pretend mobile phone), 'What do you need?' Another chants back the answer (into another pretend mobile), 'I need some pipes / bricks / tiles / cement'. [See Chapter 6 for lots more on chanting.]

– moving fast or slow, high or low in response to music or songs and tape recorder outside
– dance in response to mechanical/electronic music
– 'Anvil chorus' from Verdi's *Il Trovatore* – move and then 'hammer' in time to the music.

– rhythm clapping games in connection with syllables and words [see page 51]: dig-ger, J-C-B, ca-ter-pi-llar-wheels, hard-hats, and so on can progress to a rap, or a said or written poem
– read the story of 'The three little pigs' and adapt songs such as 'blow the man down' to 'blow the house down'.

– sing counting songs, such as 'Peter hammers with one hammer'
– shape songs, such as the song 'Little boxes on the hill side, little boxes made of ticky tacky' can become: 'Little windows on the building, little windows that are made of glass, Little windows on the building and they all have a shape; there's a square one and a round one, at the corner there's an oblong one and they're all made by the builders and they're all made out of glass'.

– people who help us: songs about builders, plumbers, electricians, architects (all can be women)
– construction noises – metal, wood, can be explored on the sound exploration and music area and made into instrument sounds – making up songs and making instruments from off-cuts procured from the building site
– song: 'Gonna knock that fence down' adapted into 'Gonna build that house now' (saw that wood now; hammer that nail in; put a roof on) (Bird & Bennett 1988, page 47)
– technology of designing and making musical instruments individually or as a group to produce a noisy machine, harsh sounds and soft sounds
– our need for mobile phones – using long lengths of piping (scrounged from the builders) to set up speaking and listening areas.

planning so that children will encounter experiences and activities that are relevant to them.

Medium-term planning in many nurseries and reception classes is topic-based. There is a brainstormed planning sheet on pages 56–7, based on the topic of a building site showing the many possible lines of enquiry that music offers. It is not a full planning sheet as such, but shows ideas of how music and movement are not limited to the creative area but can be woven through all the curriculum areas.

Assessing musical progress

Children in the early years generally have a portfolio in which evidence of their achievements is kept and usually arranged in the curriculum areas. When children have made progress in one area, their key worker notes down significant events in appropriate sections.

High-quality experiences always contain information which overlaps into many curriculum areas, and musical experiences are no exception. For example, when a child chooses a tape, puts it in a tape recorder, listens to the music with a friend, accompanies it on instruments and puts the tape back at the end, personal, social and emotional goals are being met in abundance and there is evidence of mathematical ordering as well as the musical development itself.

Reading, writing and mathematical development are some of the elements of communication but they are increasingly being treated as isolated subjects, as if they are ends in themselves. By focusing planning on activities and an environment which supports music and movement, the rest of the curriculum will more easily fall into place for children and practitioner planners.

Charting children's progress – on tape

In one setting, the practitioner took a 'snapshot' of children's singing development by asking them to sing their favourite song or nursery rhyme and record it on to a tape. She introduced the song, eg 'Number 1 – here is Aaron singing Eensy Weensy spider', then he sang. The practitioner suggested to the children that they could make a book to accompany the tape. They all drew a picture of their song and the practitioner put a photo of each child alongside the picture. Six months later she did the same and was able to compare with children and parents the singing progress made. These tapes were very popular and were often listened to.

6 Singing

All children can sing, unless there is specific damage to the vocal mechanism.

Children are able to develop as singers if the way they accompany their actions with sounds and singing is noticed and valued by practitioners. Even children with hearing impairment can 'feel' the good vibrations of a voice or an instrument and need not feel excluded from learning new songs or other musical and sound-making activities.

Children often speak and chant in rhythm, and make noises as they ride the trikes or move like a lorry or aeroplane. Just as a child puts on a hard hat and in his imagination becomes a builder, so he makes the noise of a train or dog to nourish his pretend play. This vocal dressing up needs to be noticed and supported. When practitioners echo or repeat the sounds the children are making it encourages children to use their voices, make up songs and 'find their own voice'.

Researcher Helmut Moog (1976, page 113) found that 'between the ages of three and four ... girls and boys who are taught songs and games by their parents, brothers and sisters, or in nursery schools, have a clear cognitive advantage over other children'. The trouble is that, while children of this age love to sing and show a readiness and willingness to do so, fewer parents are teaching games and songs to their children – and it has been that way for a long time. The knock-on effect is that practitioners themselves know fewer songs as time goes by.

But practitioners working in pre-school settings, and reception and infant classes need a large repertoire of songs on the tips of their tongues, ready to use when the occasion arises. They need to know lots of songs in each of the following categories:

- finger songs and number games
- action rhymes, songs and games which need space
- clapping/stamping songs
- rocking/lullaby songs, and songs for babies
- songs using children's names
- nursery rhymes
- songs from a variety of cultures

- songs in languages reflected in the homes and communities of children in the setting
- songs about animals/birds/mini-beasts/farms/machines
- songs about people who help us
- songs that tell a story
- songs to help children tidy up and remember routines
- songs about plants and planting
- songs about the weather
- songs about the seaside.

It is worthwhile taking an audit of all the songs known by the children and practitioners in a setting. In one, the staff team did this in the period of one month, during which time they wrote down all they songs they knew. Song lists were put on the wall as an aide-memoire.

Singing is natural to children. They often vocalise and sing to themselves frequently in a low pitch as they play, and they learn new songs easily if the adults sing with joy and enthusiasm. Vivian Gussin Paley has shown early years practitioners that 'you can't say you can't play' (Paley 1992). It is just as true that 'you can't say you can't sing'.

Techniques to get everyone singing

Teaching and learning new songs

In watching an episode of *The Tweenies*, viewers can quickly become aware of how the characters teach the watching children new songs:

- they always sing the song with enthusiasm and energy
- they don't sing too high or too low
- they sing about subjects that are relevant to and fun for children
- they rarely sit down to sing, and instead usually move in time to what they are singing.

These are very good techniques to adopt in any setting. Practitioners have also come up with good ideas:

- 'I can't sing so I put the song I want the children to learn on a tape and I mime (like mad) with the singer on the tape. I think it is important to look at the children while you're singing.'
- 'I love singing and I try to learn the new song first off by heart. I sing the song to the children and then the next time I sing it, I miss out a word and they have to fill it in.'
- 'I use song props. For example, there is a song about five little kites (Wood & Scott 1961). It goes:

One two three four five
Five little kites flying up in the sky (fingers all spread out and up in
  the air)
Say 'Hi' to the clouds as they go by (hand makes a 'Hi' gesture)
Say 'Hi' to the bird (gesture again)
Say 'Hi' to the sun
Say 'Hi' to the aeroplane
Oh what fun!
Then 'whoosh' goes the wind
And they all take a dive (hand swoops downward)
One, two, three, four, five.

'I drew and cut out five little kites, putting Velcro on the back so that
they could stick on to a woolly glove. Then I made pictures (song props)
for the clouds, bird, sun, aeroplane and the five kites, cut them out and
laminated them, putting magnetic tape on the back so that they stuck on
to a magnetic board. It's easy (for me too!) to remember the order that the
kites meet the different things in the sky. Once everything is ready I put
the props on the music table and the children sing the song, moving the
props accordingly by themselves.'

Getting better at being singers

'I sing in an adult choir. Before the rehearsal proper we "warm up" our
voices. I thought of doing some of the exercises with the children, so that
our voices are ready for singing. We take big deep breaths and let the air
out slowly, hissing like snakes; we make "stretchy faces"; we pretend we
are going down the slide from the top to the bottom with our voices; we
pretend we are babies saying bbbbb-mmmmmm; and we swing our arms
and stamp our feet. The children (and adults) are more energised by the
exercises and the singing is definitely better.'

How practitioners learn new songs when they don't read music
Most song books and nursery rhyme books are sold with CDs and tapes
[see 'Resources', page 107]. Some practitioners transfer a selection of songs
to a smaller tape so that children can find the songs when they want and
sing them while they listen to the tape.

The following BBC radio programmes are particularly good: *The song
tree*, *Playtime* and *The music box*. Order only the teachers' notes and CD or

cassette for each term [see resource list]. These are intended to be a tutorial for practitioners, as the programme is quite advanced and requires the children to be at a stage where they can sit for a length of time. Listen to the songs and learn the ones that will be relevant and then teach them to the children. *The music box* teachers' notes contain good ideas for keeping the music corner dynamic and relevant, and also things to say and do with children (be selective, though, as some ideas are too advanced). The songs in the teachers' notes are generally themed – for example, songs about holidays or mini-beasts – and over time build into an excellent resource library which practitioners can draw on when the need arises.

Using songs and singing everywhere

This section shows how songs can be used in any situation at any time and in any place.

Songs to include children's names

Use songs and singing to mention children by name, and change songs to include a child's name – a particularly good way of contributing to children's feeling of being special. For example:

> *Down by the river where the green grass grows*
> *There sits **Anoushka** washing her toes ...*

Children make up their own songs

The more children sing songs and increase their song repertoire, the more they have a base on which to make up their own songs. This is one reason why it is important to teach children lots and lots of songs.

Gina, a practitioner in a nursery centre, was operating a glove puppet who was playing a little drum. Some children came to see and asked the puppet its name and what it was doing. The puppet said it was drumming and wanted the children to teach it a song with its name in it that it could play. One child started the chant of, 'Pippa is banging the drum', and so Pippa the Puppet banged in time to the rhythm.

Gina had hoped this would happen but the other staff were surprised at how this planned episode subsequently gave rise to the children making up lots of songs to do with what they were doing.

Songs in all the activity areas

It is worthwhile thinking about building up a collection of songs which can be sung in connection with what children are doing. It is also a good idea to make up songs to a chant (two or three notes) or to the tune of a song everyone knows. There are songs for most provision areas on the CD, which are in italics below. Also listed are a few well-known song titles:

- **In the block corner.** *'The block song'*; *'The crate song'*; 'Put a brick on a brick on a brick on a brick and I'll build up my house so high' (Charlton 1973).
- **In the digging area.** *'I'm off'*; 'One potato, two potato' (traditional).
- **In the home corner.** *'Lots of jobs'*; 'If I knew you were coming, I'd've baked a cake' (Anon).
- **In the workshop area.** *'This and that'*; 'Little boxes on the hillside, little boxes made of ticky-tacky' (Malvina Reynolds).
- **In the painting area.** *'Colours all around me'*; 'I can sing a rainbow' (Arthur Hamilton).
- **In the water area.** *'Splish, splosh'*; 'The big ship sails on the ally-ally-oh' (Anon)
- **In the sand area.** *'The sand tray song'*; 'Digging up sand from the bottom of the sea' (Anon).

Songs for special occasions

Find and learn songs which can be sung on, for example, Pancake Tuesday, Diwali, Hanukkah, Christmas and birthdays. Songbooks might include ideas, the children may know celebratory songs, and the internet is also a good source. For example, enter the words 'early years hanukka songs' into Google (a particularly good search engine: www.google.com), and it finds a page on the Early Years Experience website (www.bigeyedowl.co.uk) with lots of songs about festivals and food, one of which is:

> *Hanukkah, Hanukkah, festival of light*
> *Candles burn, tops spin round, time of delight.*
> *Hanukkah, Hanukkah*
> *Let us dance and sing,*
> *Candles burn, guests come in*
> *Presents they will bring.*

(This same website has pages of songs on all sorts of subjects, as well as other useful resources.)

Work songs and chants

Children often sing while they work, sweeping leaves, cleaning paint-pots and so on.

Children and adults were working on a papier mâché covering for a large collaborative dinosaur model. The adults showed the children how to dip the strips into the paste (which was very runny), let the paste drip back into the bowl then smooth it on to the model. This soon developed into a chant and all the children joined in: 'dip ... drip ... and smoooooth it on, dip ... drip ... and smoooooth it on'.

The adults then decided to show the children that songs can help people to work together. One practitioner found some Hebridean songs and some sea shanties with a strong pulse to keep the workers together for collaborative work [see page 25 for a definition of 'pulse']. She put them on a tape to play to the children. Six children sat at a table pulling a cloth from side to side while the tape was playing; others hauled on a rope outside while the sea shanty played. The songs were available on the tape for the children to play and very soon they had learned the songs and sang them linked to the movements.

Singing to learn and reinforce the rhythms of the language
See the section 'Group singing – making it work' [pages 68–73] for lots of examples of how children can use songs to get the rhythm and syllabic pulse of language as a stage in increasing their confidence and their vocabulary.

Singing to help remember routines
Singing is very useful for helping children to remember routines. Music along with movement helps link the two sides of the brain and has significance in the functioning of memory – so that's why children and adults remember better when the message is made into a song. Advertisers know this all too well.

Sing made-up tidy-up songs (for this to work there has to be a place for all the equipment to go that is obvious and well labelled). For example, to the tune of 'Here we go round the mulberry bush', sing:

I wonder where the skittles go, the skittles go, the skittles go
I wonder where the skittles go
When it's time to tidy up?

Leon knows where the skittles go, the skittles go, the skittles go
Leon knows where the skittles go
When it's time to tidy up.

They go in the trolley drawer, the trolley drawer, the trolley drawer
They go in the trolley drawer
When it's time to tidy up.

In this example, Leon would sing the last verse. The second verse could be 'Who knows where the skittles go?', with the third verse sung by everyone who knows.

Singing to defuse a situation

Children often feel ashamed when they lose their temper, and song can help them restore their dignity and sense of humour. For example, in one setting Jamie threw down the crayons in a temper. To the tune (again) of 'Here we go round the Mulberry bush', the practitioner sang:

I'll pick up the blue ones, the red ones and yellow ones,
I'll pick up all the other ones, if you pick up the green.

It worked and his anger dissipated as he helped to put things back as they were.

Singing to challenge stereotypes

Gender

Staff are often worried when children reveal very gender-stereotyped views of what men and women can do and how they should feel. Some nursery rhymes, songs and fairy stories belong to an earlier time when roles for men and women were more clearly defined: girls make cups of tea for us all, farmers need wives, princesses are rescued by gallant princes, witches are horrid old women, Peter does the hammering and mummies chatter on buses. These views can limit aspirations if not challenged.

Most practitioners now are very aware of these problems and, for instance, change the gender of the doctor to a female who comes to see 'Mr Holly' and 'his' dolly. However, it is not enough to rely on one strategy of changing 'firemen' into 'firefighters' or the Grand Old Duke of York having ten thousand 'friends' to counter children's views. Other methods are needed in the images and photographs children see, the toys they play with, the provision they attend and in the skill of practitioners to question and support children's growing belief systems.

To do this well, it is important to plan as a team to be aware and to look out for evidence of children working and playing at non-stereotyped activities, and then find ways of sharing those observations with others [see box, 'Henry goes shopping'].

Singing can also help to reinforce the concepts of number and other mathematical ideas, such as classification and pattern – and this is especially good for girls, who are often stereotyped away from maths. Playing 'Ten in the bed' or jumping off logs like the 'Five little speckled frogs' can introduce children to adding, taking away and counting backwards. Doing it outside and in connection with movement is the most effective combination.

Henry goes shopping

In small groups the children talked about what they are going to do during the day, making up songs. For example, when Henry told the group that he was going to buy things in the play shop everyone sang (to the tune of 'Skip to my loo')

Henry's going shopping, what will he buy?
Henry's going shopping, what will he buy?
Henry's going shopping, what will he buy?
Skip to my loo my darling

Once he had told the group what he wanted to buy, everyone sang:

He'll buy apples, that's what he'll buy
He'll buy apples, that's what he'll buy
He'll buy apples, that's what he'll buy
Skip to my loo my darling.

Disability

Practitioners are likely to work with children with a range of disabilities and additional needs. How children who have visual or hearing impairment, autism and mobility or behavioural difficulties react to music and sound exploration will be interesting for the practitioner to observe and respond to on an individual basis. The important message throughout this book is that developmentally appropriate nursery and infant practice is based on observing how children are acting and reacting; what they are interested in is the starting point for planning the next step for all our young children.

For example, an adult who had observed Lynne, a child with visual impairment, standing listening to some lively taped music being played outside began describing to her the fast movements that some children were making in response. Lynne was asked if she wanted to move to the music now. 'No,' she said. 'What if I held your hand?', asked the practitioner. 'No,' said Lynne again. Soon, the music changed to a slower tune. 'Hold my hand now,' Lynne said. 'I [can] move to this music.' She also enjoyed it when the practitioner let her feel her mouth as she sang.

Many nursery, reception and infant-class practitioners teach songs in sign language to all the children – and it is equally valuable and enjoyable to do this in settings where there are no children with hearing impairment. Songs can also be adapted to include children with mobility difficulties. For example, 'The wheels on the bus' can just as easily be 'The wheelchair wheels go round and round', and the song can then include other verses adapted along that theme.

Culture (CD track 16)

15 It is easy to change the words of songs to take account of children's experiences in their home backgrounds. For example, instead of 'Five currant buns in a baker's shop', sing:

> *Five* (four, three, two, one, no) *chapatis in a baker's shop,*
> *Small and round with seeds on the top*
> *Along came a boy/girl with a penny one day,*
> *Saw the chapati and took it away.*
> (Last line for last verse: *The baker said, 'No chapatis today'.*)

or

> *Five samosas in a baker's shop*
> *Tri-ang-les with a crispy top*

or

> *Five baklava in a baker's shop*
> *Small oblongs with honey on the top*

Song props of currant buns, chapatis, samosas and baklava will help the children remember the variations and the maths as well as the taste. This is an example of how good early years practice is relevant to all children. Similarly, traditional songs from a variety of cultures can also be used with new words too – it is not necessary always to start with English traditions. By planning for inclusion in the example above, a creative approach to mathematical understanding has also been discovered.

Group singing – making it work

If music is to be given its rightful and valued place in the curriculum, then it has to be planned for. In a fully planned, well-run music session, the children will:

- learn new songs and rehearse old ones with joy and enthusiasm
- have something to practise at the music area that they have experienced at the group session
- build up positive ideas about their own ability in music and ability as part of a group.

Whenever a group comes together to sing or play instruments, practitioners must ask themselves the following questions:

- **Is the session planned or improvised?** Is it just a holding exercise to keep children 'controlled' while other staff get on with jobs?
- **How are the children experiencing this session?** It is important to observe the children in a group music session. They will generally make it quite clear by their behaviour and body language whether it is interesting to them or not. Generally, when a session is planned, all the children will be enthralled, willing to cooperate, willing to listen to others and purposefully active. In an unplanned session, many children are likely to be fidgety and bored, clamouring for a 'turn' and perhaps even being disruptive.
- **Does the session follow up an observed interest or need of an individual child or group of children?** For example, earlier in the day a practitioner noticed that Kabir put on the ankle bells and danced to a tape he had chosen. It was not possible to support this at the time, but when the group was gathered together, she asked him to show everyone what he did and he was pleased to do so – as the practitioner knew he would be. She had also looked out a picture of an Indian dancer to show the children.
- **Can children just watch?** Some children will not want to come to the small- or whole-group music sessions. They often need to watch from the safety of the sidelines before they are ready and confident enough to commit themselves to a new experience. This is an important learning process for some children, and practitioners need to be alert to children who learn by observing. I remember a child who came to very few of the music sessions on offer and yet his mother told me that he knew all the songs, as he sang them to her at home.

Guidelines for running successful music group sessions

One of the messages of this book is that 'music teaching' is planned in response to what individual children are observed to be interested in. Here are some guidelines to help practitioners respond in this way. Note that a together-time music session, where the whole group or class is involved will consist of a different content than a targeted small-group session.

1 Plan a daily music activity with not more than 1:8 for four- and five-year-olds; fewer for children who are three and under. A good ratio guide is the group should be no bigger than double the age of the child to one adult.

2 At whole-class or pre-school group together times all the other adults need to join in and model listening and joining-in behaviour, and support the practitioner leader. It is not a time to leave one member of staff with all the children. Adults act as model listeners, helping the children to see that music is highly valued.

3 Have enough space for all the children to be able to move during action songs (this is why music and movement sessions are more successful outside).

4 Plan the session carefully, pacing it to include times when children are physically active as well as when they are sitting.

5 Keep the sessions short. Don't congratulate yourself because you can keep a group of children on the carpet for 30 minutes or longer.

6 Relate the songs to what children have been doing and are interested in.

7 Use song props, puppets and other real items to involve children, and make the session relevant and active.

8 Respond to the children's level of concentration – stop *before* they've had enough.

9 Give positive and specific praise to children who respond. If necessary let those with shorter concentration spans leave the group to do something else.

10 Have a permanent music area available for the children to explore and extend the ideas shared at the together and group sessions in their own time and at their pace.

11 Value listening and watching as well as taking part. Children do not always want to sing, but take pleasure in and learn a lot from watching. It also helps them build up the confidence to take part.

These same guidelines should be followed when running sessions with instruments, as well as for group singing.

Games and other ideas for group singing sessions

Rhythm

This is a game to help the children's sense of rhythm while using the voice in different ways.

A small group of children (each of whom has chosen to come and is free to go) kneel sitting back on their heels in a small circle. The practitioner asks the children to start by patting their hands on the front of their thighs, and then to copy a rhythm of 1-2-3-4, 1-2-3-4, 1-2-3-4. Once that is going well, the practitioner says phrases in time to the rhythm, patting knees on the beat for each word or part of the word. Here are some examples, with the word or syllable where thighs are patted given in bold.

Adult   **Can** you **use** your **spea**-king **voice?**

Children   **Yes** I **can** and **yes** I **can**.

This is repeated using as many types of voices possible, with the adult part and children's response said or sung in the kind of voice identified. The four-beat rhythm should be maintained relentlessly.

- **Can** you **use** your **sing**-ing **voice?** (two-note chant)
- **Can** you **use** your **witch**-y **voice?** (scratchy voice)
- **Can** you **use** your **whisp-'**ring **voice?** (whisper)
- **Can** you **use** your **think**-ing **voice?** (no sound in response; just pat your forehead in rhythm: 1-2-3-4)
- **Can** you **use** your **shout**-ing **voice?** (this is a great favourite).

It is easier to write a list of the types of voices as a crib sheet to have beside you.

Pitch, using chanting songs

Having the 'right' pitch is about being in tune, so it is useful to have a member of staff who can sing in tune to lead a pitch-oriented session.

Everyone can sing in tune if they practise, and listening and 'echoing' games are a good way to start. Don't leave one person to sing with the children. If it is a whole-group session, two or more members of staff can sit in among the children and model how to behave in a group: any adults who think they can't sing will also be learning to sing in tune by joining in. Many people think they can't sing because they don't give their voice enough air energy and their sound comes out rather lack-lustre. Model enthusiasm by listening carefully, straightening your body, and taking good breaths before singing, and the sound will become better and better.

It is sometimes helpful to children if they just have to sing two or three notes as a chant. The two notes in a fire engine's siren work well as a starting point, and good notes to use for this are middle G and middle E (because they are not too high or too low for the children – or the adults). These notes can be identified using chime bars or can be played on an instrument.

There are lots of rhymes that can be adapted and sung to a chant. The following are a few suggestions, but it is even better to make them up with the children as themes and interests arise. The more singing there is of this kind, the more the children themselves will start to make up songs. Children make up songs much more readily if they have had 'permission' and encouragement from the way adults behave. When practitioners become creators and composers, the children do so too.

Hey! hey! look at me (slow, slow, quick, quick, slow)

18

Hey!	Hey!	Look	at	me
G	E	G	G	E

I	am	tap-	ping,	can	you	see?
G	G	E	E	G	G	E

The children tap as they chant this, and practitioners can vary the children's actions by chanting 'clapping', 'jumping' or 'hopping' in place of 'tapping'. The notes in this chant can also be changed, perhaps by going up to an A on the word 'tapping' and coming down to middle C on the last word.

What's in my magic box?

19 Find a small box or make a sack out of sparkly material. Put into it a few items with different numbers of syllables: a pink purse, a doll with black hair, a spiky shell.

What's	in	my	ma-	gic	box,	ma-	gic	box,	ma-	gic	box?
G	E	A	G	G	E	G	G	E	G	G	E

What's	in	my	ma-	gic	box?
G	E	A	G	G	E

Please	tell	me
G	E	G

After singing this, give the items out to the children. Make sure that the group is small enough for all the children to have something from the box (around six items is enough otherwise children lose interest in the game as they have to wait so long for their turn). When everyone has something, sing the following, using a rhythm that is long-short-short-long-long. (Either a practitioner or all the children can sing the first line; the child with the relevant item sings the second.)

Who's got	the	pink	purse?
G	E	A	G	E

Who's got	the	pink	purse?
G	E	A	G	E

I've	got	the	pink	purse
G	E	A	G	E

Who's got	the	mir-	ror?
G	E	A	G	E

I've	got	the	mir-	ror
G	E	A	G	E

Listen to the children and begin to assess who is singing in tune and who is hearing and reproducing the rhythm. Add a comment to the child's profile under music development. Parents love to know how their children are developing, and although some will be aware of their child's musical ability it is good to give them details of how the child is progressing.

Doggy, doggy where's your bone

20 Ask the children to sit in a small circle. One child goes into the middle and kneels right down with her head on her knees to hide her eyes. In front of her head is a bone (plastic bones are available from pet shops). One of the children 'steals' the bone while the one in the middle is hiding her eyes. Then all the children sing the following using a rhythm of short-short-short-short-short-short-long:

Dog-	gy,	dog-	gy,	where's	your	bone?
G	G	E	E	G	G	E

The child in the middle sings:

Some-	one	stole	it	from	my	home
G	G	E	E	G	G	E

All the children sing (rhythm: long-short-short-long-long – with the last two notes on 'bone'):

Who	stole	the	bo-	ne?
G	E	A	G	E

The child who stole the bone then answers:

I	stole	the	bo-	ne
G	E	A	G	E

Then the child in the middle (who still can't see) has to guess who sang 'I stole the bone'. That child then becomes the 'doggy'.

Apple tree, apple tree

21 Ask a small group of children to sit in a circle. Give one child an apple and, as the children sing the song, the apple is passed around the circle. The tune is the same chant as above, but goes down to a C on 'out' at the end:

Ap-	ple	tree,	ap-	ple	tree	
G	G	E	G	G	E	

Will	your	ap-	ples	fall	on	me?
G	G	E	E	G	G	E

I	won't	cry	and	I	won't	shout
G	G	E	E	G	G	E

If	your	ap-	ple	knocks	me	out
G	G	E	E	G	G	C

The person left holding the apple at the word 'out' has to leave the circle, but gets to play an instrument in time to the song – that is, keeping to the beat. Keeping to the beat or pulse is something that children need a lot of experience with before they understand it. Of course, it is important to notice which children are able to keep to the beat because their expertise can be used and extended. The way to do this is by making them aware of what they know, that is making learners aware of their ability, or 'consciously competent'. For example:

'Gemma, I can hear that you are keeping to the beat in "Polly put the kettle on". It's 1-and-2-and-3-and-4, isn't it? And you're tapping only on where I've just said a number, not where I was saying 'and'. If you were just tapping the rhythm, you would be tapping every sound: 1-2-3-4-5-6-7-8.'

It is much more effective if you point out individual children's progress to them when you have noticed it.

Action rhymes

Here are a few rhymes where children have to be active as well as saying the rhyme. To do both is something to watch out for, as it is tricky for some children doing both actions and words. However, it's important to remember that they are still joining in if they do one and not the other.

Touch your shoulders

22 This can be said or chanted. There are four beats in each line, which are indicated on page 74.

Touch	*your*	*shoul-*	*ders*
Touch	*your*	*kne-*	*es*
Raise	*your*	*arms*	*and*
Drop	*them*	*plea-*	*se*
Touch	*your*	*an-*	*kles*
Touch	*your*	*toe-*	*s*
Pull	*your*	*ears*	*and*
Blow	*your*	*no-*	*se*

Children will touch their right shoulders with their right hand and so on. More difficult is to touch your left shoulder with your right hand and so on. Few children under five can cross over in this way. When children display this physical maturity it is one sign of mental readiness for reading and writing. Some even say that children should not be taught how to read and write formally until they show this cross-lateral maturity (Goddard-Blythe 2000, page 18).

Where is Michael playing today?

23 Question and answer chant:

Where is Michael playing today?
There he is, there he is?
Where is Michael playing today?
There he is, there he is?

Where is Michael playing today?
Here I am, here I am.
Where is Michael playing today?
Here I am, here I am.

⑦ Instruments

What are instruments called?

There are often a lot of percussion instruments in an early years setting, reception and infant class, but even those practitioners who use them frequently don't know their names or how to hold or play them to get the best out of them. An excellent book, called *Agogo bells to xylophone*, lists the names of all percussion instruments and how to play them (Cotton 1996).

Before deciding to buy or make instruments, take an audit of the instruments already in the setting in order to help identify what is needed. Include in the audit details of what instruments are made of, *eg* wood, metal, cane or skin. Throw out any broken instruments and give away or sell any that are not appropriate for this age group or for group settings. See the table on the next page for an idea of how to categorise instruments into the five ways of producing sound: strike, shake, scrape, pluck and blow. Tuned percussion is the sixth category for sorting your instruments; each category has one example of an instrument which might be entered there.

Buying instruments

This section provides a list of core instruments which are the best to have as a base for any collection, and are the first instruments to acquire if the setting has nothing at all. Buy two of some instruments so that a practitioner can play with a child, or two children can play together.

- Buy instruments made of natural materials like wood, cane, metal or skin; avoid plastic on the whole.
- Buy a very few good instruments rather than many cheap ones.
- Buy instruments that satisfy the five ways of producing sound categories [see table and text on pages 76–79].
- Don't fall for gimmicky instruments such as 'boomwhackers' to *start* your collection; they can come later (with added string holders).

Audit of instruments

Type of musical experience	Instrument	Made of	Condition	Fate
striking, hitting and tapping	drum	plastic	'skin' broken	throw out
shaking	shaker	cane	good	store
	tambourine	wooden	good enough	store
	rain stick	bamboo	cracked but still interesting	use for now, but keep an eye on quality
scraping and rubbing	guiro	wood	cracked	throw out
plucking	home-made double bass	5-litre plastic bottle, broom handle & string	good enough	keep until interest wanes, then give to child to take home
blowing	3 kazoos	plastic	good	store
	recorder	plastic	tuning poor, but good enough	use for now; replace next year
tuned percussion	chime bars	metal	good	store
	xylophone	wood	one bar missing	replace

- Build up the collection in response to observations of the children's use and exploration.
- Keep a list of what you have bought, where and how much. Share information about your purchases with the parents.
- Take care of the instruments; store and display them wisely.

Instruments to bang, hit or tap

The **tambour** or **hand drum** is a very simple drum that is particularly useful for giving a beat for movement and other activities which practitioners can initiate with children. It looks like a tambourine without the cymbals. It is also an instrument which children can play easily. Some tambours have useful stretchers which children can hold on to as they play.

There are several ways to use a tambour. First of all, hold the wooden part with one hand and play on the skin side of the drum with the other hand. Use fingers to tap the skin or a hand to smack it. Bouncing fingers or a hand on the drum will make a good sound, and modelling this to the children will make it easier for them to copy the technique. The skin side can also be struck using a beater. Put drums out sometimes without beaters to encourage playing with fingers and hands.

Lentils, rice or beans can also be put inside the drum to create sound effects. The beans are kept in by layers of cling film covering the drum and secured by adhesive tape (though be prepared for children to test the strength of the cling film).

A **tambourine** is the same as a tambour, but with little cymbals set into the wooden part so it jingles when shaken and struck. Headless tambourines have cymbals but no skin.

There are lots of types of **drum**, but one of the best for young children is a small African drum which is placed between the sitting child's outstretched legs and which therefore leaves both hands free to play.

A **wood block** is played with a wooden or a rubber beater. Children hold it in one hand and strike it using the beater with the other. If this is difficult, put the wood block on the table or the floor with a mat underneath to prevent it from slipping and rattling.

A **cow bell** is made of metal and is struck with a beater. If it is held loosely, it makes a ringing sound; held tightly, it makes a duller sound (or changes the timbre).

Claves or **rhythm sticks** make good sound effects, as do **tone blocks**. They are easily held with their handle and struck with a wooden beater. One side gives a higher sound than the other.

Instruments for shaking

Cane rattles are wonderful instruments for using with children. They are satisfying to hold and to play. They can be incorporated into children's imaginative play as they are easily portable and almost indestructible. They are available from Acorn Percussion [see 'Resources, page 106].

Maracas can suffer very badly in the children's hands, as they get banged together and can crack. For this reason, it is often best to use just one maraca at first.

Children can put on sets of **ankle bells** and **wrist bells** to dance. It is important to buy the ones with Velcro fastenings (not a buckle) so that children can put them on by themselves, and take them off quickly if they tire of them. The bells heighten children's awareness of their own movements.

Instruments for plucking

It is very difficult to get instruments for plucking for little fingers. Most commercial instruments like the thumb piano make their fingers sore and require a stronger muscle power that young children can summon.

Instruments like **guitars** can be brought into the setting to show the children how sound is produced by plucking.

The **pentatonic harp** is a simple instrument for children to play (though it is a little costly). Because its five notes all harmonise with one another, it has the advantage that, by plucking it, children will always make a pleasant and harmonious combination. The notes are C, D, E, G, A or C#, D#, F#, G#, A# (these are the black notes on the piano, and the symbol after the note name is called a 'sharp').

Home-made instruments can be very satisfying [see 'Instruments for plucking', page 85].

Instruments for scraping

The **guiro** is a good instrument for giving a scratchy sound. Scrape the wooden stick end of a beater along the guiro away from the body.

Instruments for blowing

Blowing instruments are also pitched instruments because they can make high and low sounds.

Remind children that they carry an instrument for blowing around with them all the time in their throats. The **voice** is an instrument they can make sounds and music with any time they like.

The **kazoo** reminds people of the sound they made when they wound a piece of wax paper round a comb and hummed or sang into it. Children find the idea of using their voice to toot-toot into the kazoo odd as they expect to make a sound when they blow rather than when they speak or sing. Once they cotton-on, there is no stopping them.

The **mouth organ** is a good instrument for blowing. It makes a satisfying chord-like sound and, even better, works with both blowing *and* sucking.

Tuned percussion

Chime bars are made of metal and, if bought individually, are the most versatile as they can build up into the pentatonic scale or into an octave. You can buy little glockenspiels (metal bars) with stands which make the higher notes literally higher than the lower ones. When it comes to wooden sets of tuned bars, called xylophones, it becomes more expensive but very satisfactory to play.

Making instruments

One of the things that I had to learn as a new teacher was that children experiment. The nature of childhood is to test everything to the limit. When I displayed a set of expensive drums on the music table after having introduced them at a together session, they soon had holes through them. I felt very guilty; clearly I hadn't shown the children effectively how to use them 'properly'.

'What a pity that someone has spoilt our instruments,' I said to the children with genuine reproach.

Yet, what were the mixed messages I was giving to these children about the environment that I was trying to create? On the one hand I was trying to create a 'yes' environment, in which the messages are that:

- children can do things
- they can have a go and test things out (emotions, friendships, anything) in safety
- it's OK to be noisy or quiet, alone, just watching or needing a cuddle
- adults will give children time and space to learn, both with and without our support
- adults are there to help, but they won't unless needed
- adults will keep children safe
- adults will help children to learn
- adults will help children to be adventurous and curious (adapted from Bruce & Meggitt 2002).

On the other hand, the children met with my disapproval if they:

- tested the drum out (how strong am I? how strong is the skin of the drum?) and broke it
- were noisy with it (how loud and fast can I hit it?) and broke it
- were adventurous and curious (I wonder what will happen if...?) and broke it.

How were the children to differentiate between what was an appropriate use of instruments and what would be classed as naughty and destructive? Was it fair of me to expect them to cotton-on immediately to quite a fine distinction? Eventually, of course, I *would* have that high expectation of them, but in the intervening 'learning' period, it is reasonable and sensible to employ another strategy: to make a home-made instrument with the children and help them work out the level of care involved in useful exploration using that.

The benefits of making instruments

- Children can explore sounds and musical elements just as effectively with home-made or familiar objects as with expensive and fragile instruments.
- It becomes unnecessary to keep expensive instruments for the exclusive use of adults or use by children only under supervision.
- Everyone is sad at the breakage of the instruments, but when it is home-made, the perpetrator who might even have made it in the first place or had seen his friends making it, is more likely to understand what happened.
- Even very young children can be involved in the restitution and restoration of their inappropriate explorations if they have made their own instruments. So, when a child puts the beater through the home-made instrument or breaks it in some other way he can be the one who leads some others in making a new one.
- Children who have had access to home-made instruments are far less likely to damage expensive instruments when they are eventually offered. By this time, the children have built up their confidence and coordination in using an instrument.
- The more time and opportunities that children have to play and experiment with instruments, the more physically coordinated and self-controlled they become.
- It is quite easy to classify the learning that children gain from making instruments under many of the curriculum areas concerned with technology, language and communication, fine motor skills, mathematics and social skills [see the example of Dana on page 100].

Recipes for home-made instruments

Here are just a few ideas for making different kinds of instruments. More can be found in *The I can't sing book* (Silberg 1998).

Instruments to bang, hit or tap

Drum A

This can be made with lots of help from the children.

Ingredients
- a round tin or firm carton (catering tins for baked beans or instant coffee are ideal)
- 6 large sheets of greaseproof paper
- flour made into a paste with water to a consistency of yoghurt
- a large elastic band
- string
- paint or other material for decoration.

Tools
- scissors
- pasting brushes
- a gluing brush.

Method

Remove the lid from the tin. Make sure that the greaseproof paper is large enough to cover the top of the tin with at least 10cm over. Lay out one sheet of greaseproof paper and slosh the flour-and-water paste onto it. Put the next sheet of greaseproof paper on top, and paint that with paste. Repeat this until all the paper is used up. The wet and heavy greaseproof paper can now be put carefully on top of the tin. Put the elastic band around the tin and the greaseproof paper to hold it together while you secure the top with the string tied as tightly as possible. Leave to dry in a warm dry place. Each day, pull the paper tighter around the top of the tin below the string. When it is dry (after about a week), decorate the tin, trim the greaseproof paper around the top of the tin and play the drum.

Drum B

This should be made by an adult, with a group of children watching and helping.

twine

brace

curtain ring

(from Block Ridge 1951)

Ingredients
- a round tin or firm carton (catering tins for baked beans or instant coffee are ideal)
- a piece of rubber sheeting – *eg* from an old hot water bottle (ask parents for an old leaky one)
- cloth loose-leaf hole reinforcers
- one metal curtain ring
- string
- paint or other material for decoration.

Tools
- scissors
- Sellotape
- large-eyed needle or crochet hook.

Method
Remove the lid and decorate the outside of the tin. Cut a piece of rubber to cover the open end of the tin, with an overlap of about 5cm. Using the point of the scissors, pierce small holes around the circumference of the rubber, about 2.5cm from the outer edge. (Make sure to mark where the holes are, as they close up again.) Stick the cloth loose-leaf reinforcers behind the holes to strengthen them and prevent them from tearing.

The next bit can be tricky, so get the children to help. Fix the rubber temporarily on to the top of the tin with strips of Sellotape. Begin to thread the string through the holes and through the curtain ring on the base of the tin. Weave a length of string round the string spokes on the base for strengthening (as in the picture above). Make drums from different sizes of tins.

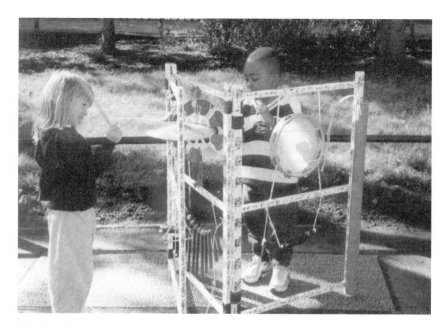

Hanging frames

Ingredients (for outdoor frame)
- a wooden frame – *eg* an old clothes' horse
- metal hooks with screw ends.

Method
Screw the hooks into the frame, leaving enough space between them for each hanging object.

curtain hooks
metal bracket
metal lid
metal saucepan
metal bracket

cup hooks
plastic mug
wooden spoon
offcut of wood

Indoor frame [see page 84]

Ingredients (for indoor frame)
- 1 50cm × 30cm × 3cm piece of wood for the base
- 3 lengths of wood, each about 50cm
- 4 metal brackets
- screws
- metal hooks with screw ends.

Equipment
- screwdriver.

Method
Join the wood together using the brackets and screws, so that the finished item looks like the one in the illustration. Screw in the hooks, as for the outdoor frame.

Using music hanging frames
There are great advantages in using the hanging frame for objects which can be hit. Young children find it hard to hold an instrument with one hand and to hit it with the other. This is one of the reasons why triangles are such a bad buy; as they spin around they become almost impossible to hit. With a hanging frame, the children can concentrate on listening to and comparing sounds – and they don't need to worry about their coordination, or lack of it.

The items hung on the hanging frame can be linked to themes, topics or centres of interest which are happening in the setting. For example, if a group of children is exploring 'holes' as a topic, it might be a good idea to hang a piece of metal tubing, a plastic colander and a terracotta flowerpot.

The hanging frame can also be used as a 'theatre'. Make a curtain and hang it up in front of the frame. Then, from behind the curtain, make sounds on the frame which the children, who are on the other side of the curtain, can't see but can try to identify – an excellent game for encouraging listening skills [see Chapter 5, for how this can be used within the early years curriculum].

Instruments to rattle or shake
This is about putting things into containers: a few things, no things, or lots of things. A few hard things like buttons, beads or dried beans will make a loud harsh sound. Many smaller things, like lentils and rice, will make a gentler 'shushing' sound.

Rain stick

Ingredients
- a cardboard cylinder
- a piece of strong, but flexible plastic
- tough duck tape
- one or two handfuls of dried beans (or peas or coffee beans)
- a quantity of thin nails, shorter than the diameter of the cylinder.

Tools
- hammer or something that will bang nails into cardboard.

Method
Seal up one end of the cylinder with a piece of plastic, covered and secured down with duck tape. Put the beans into the cylinder. Seal up the other end of the cylinder. Tap nails into the side of the cardboard systematically around and down the sides, at 4cm intervals, until the cylinder is covered with nails embedded in the side of the cylinder. Cover the whole cylinder (and therefore all the nail heads) with duck tape, and decorate the outside of the cylinder. Invert the rainstick, and hear the beans trickle down as they are caught by the horizontal nails. This is what makes this sound L-O-N-G.

Instrument for plucking
Polystyrene has very good resonating qualities, and this recipe makes good use of it.

Elastic band guitar

Ingredients
- a block of polystyrene packing, such as that used to protect computer hardware
- elastic bands of different sizes and widths
- paint or other material for decoration (optional).

Method
Stretch the elastic bands around and over the area of polystyrene with a shape cut out of it (*ie* where the computer or other part was originally housed). Experiment with the sounds they make when twanged – high and low. Stretch them further, and hear how the pitch rises. (Elastic bands can be frightening if they break suddenly, so make sure the elastic bands are fresh and not too tight.) If the children wish, they can decorate the polystyrene. (Always discard polystyrene when it starts to disintegrate.)

Instruments for scraping

When exploring scraping, it is good to start with beaters, as children will scrape the beater along any surface outdoors and in. Children particularly like corrugated surfaces. Have available metal and wooden sticks in a container for children to use in their sound exploration play outside as well as in.

Sand-block scrapers

Ingredients
- sand paper
- 2 small blocks of wood for little hands to grasp
- good strong PVA glue.

Method
Cover the blocks of wood with the sand paper, and stick it down.

Instruments for blowing

Straw trumpet

Ingredients
- A4 sheet of card or paper
- a round plate
- duck tape
- plastic straw.

Tools
- pen
- scissors.

Method
Put the plate on the card, draw it and cut out the circle. Find the middle of the circle by folding first in half and then in half again, to make a quarter segment. Keeping it folded, snip off the point to make a very small hole in the pointed end. Open out the circle and cut out one quadrant, folding over the remaining three to make a cone. Secure this with duck tape. Cut a straw in half and push half its length through the hole in the pointed end of the cone. Secure the straw with duck tape. Pinch the top of the straw together and cut an upside down V shape (Λ) in the top of the straw about 1cm deep on either side of the cut.

Playing the straw trumpet

To play a straw trumpet, lips need to be pulled inside the mouth as far as possible so that only a small amount of air will escape when blowing out. (It will make a noise like a trumpeting elephant, and those lips will tingle like anything.) Wet the straw and blow, and the instrument should make a big sound. It takes a bit of practising, but some children will get it and those who don't will just make a trumpet sound with their voices.

Kazoo

Ingredients
- a 1 pint plastic milk carton with a handle and a screw top
- greaseproof paper or wax paper
- elastic band.

Method
Remove the screw top. Cut the bottom off the milk carton just below the handle. Attach the greaseproof paper to the cut end with the elastic band. Hum a tune into the mouth of the other end. Feel the greaseproof paper vibrating. This is an effective instrument for focusing the attention of children with hearing and sight impairment on the nature of sound.

Musical installations

A sound collage (for inside)

To offer a large piece of card or paper for children to stick various textured materials on is in itself an interesting process. But when the end product is something that you can not only see but also hear, it becomes really stimulating. This collage offers children the opportunity to experiment with sounds to stick on to the collage and then to 'play' their collage. Paper and foil can be scrunched and flicked; corrugated card and sandpaper can be scraped; fabric of different textures can provoke vocabulary which helps musical and movement ideas (smooth, sharp, bright, *etc*); while bubble wrap, containers and cylinders (filled or empty) are perfect for bashing and popping.

Ingredients
- a selection of materials, such as:
  - paper of different textures (greaseproof, tin foil, corrugated, sandpaper)
  - fabric of different textures (velvet, cotton, upholstery, silk)
  - plastic and tin containers

- 2 paper cups
- string
- bubble wrap

Method
Stick the materials and paper on to a large sheet of strong paper or card. Attach the beaters [see ingredients below] to the collage with string. Hang the collage on the wall. Now play the collage. Tins can be tapped or struck; bubble wrap can be popped; paper can be scrunched; and corrugated paper can be scraped – and perhaps the sounds made can even be recorded.

Making beaters

Ingredients
- wooden cooking spoons
- metal spoons of different sizes
- broom handles
- padding
- duck tape
- string
- strong glue
- strong tape.

Method
Make beaters for the 'drums': cut down the broom handles into 60cm lengths, pad the top to make a very soft ball, cover the pad with duck tape to secure it to the broom handle. (Other examples of how to make beaters can be found in Bird & Bennett 1988.)

8 Music areas – indoors and out

Children can do with sound what they do with two-dimensional space in drawing and painting or with words in creating their stories. Adults have a timorous attitude toward children's activities with sound, particularly those that do not result in recognisable rhythms or melodies (Walker 1988, page 216).

When asked why they do not have a music area in their pre-school setting, reception or infant class, practitioners generally say that they have difficulty with the noise aspect. Studies in child development have revealed that children explore and learn through all their senses, yet teachers seem to be saying 'but we can't let them learn through sound because it disturbs the others'.

It is certainly true that random pounding can be wearing. Everyone working in early years has experienced children who bang blocks together or bash a spoon on a tin can in the home corner, getting progressively louder, faster and more intrusive. Without the means to progress in their exploration of sound they will get into a rut, with repetitive behaviours which really do drive everyone mad.

But why are practitioners so wary of letting children experiment with sounds?

Perhaps there still remains a little of the idea that a quiet class or pre-school room is a sign of good practice. But that is surely not the real reason. Evidence of good planning, with clear aims and the ability to explain the purpose of noisy activities can always deal with that sort of narrow-mindedness. No, the underlying reason is that a lot of practitioners feel that they don't have the skills to help children move on from this seemingly random noise-making, and so they become afraid that the children will get out of control.

A key to this problem is to have a well-organised music area which enables the children to progress in what they want to discover. Children explore sound from a very young age and when they have access to places where making sound is approved of, the exploration becomes much more purposeful. They can try out ideas on their own, in pairs and small groups, or copy and extend ideas from planned group activities directed by adults.

Music areas provide opportunities and time for children to learn to handle instruments confidently and with respect. They can practise and play with the songs they have been learning if there are reminders like 'song props' to help them [see 'Songbooks and song props', page 93]. At the music area they can find new, exciting things to do with musical ideas which they have.

Lots of time to explore sound

Here is an observation from a practitioner in North London.

'A boy in my class, Obiu, was using the blocks as drums in the block area. On and on he went … bang, bang, bang! I felt it was very intrusive but I saw that he was really interested otherwise he wouldn't have spent so much time doing it, though after a while he seemed stuck for more to do.

I scavenged round for some tins, set them up in the music area and pointed out to him that I had noticed his interest in drumming and that there were some drums and beaters now in the music corner. He immediately went there and spent time with a friend singing and drumming on all the tins. I continued to observe his interest which led to some really worthwhile discoveries.

In our garden we have set up a drumming area where there are drums of different kinds on three sides. Obiu was there on Friday for 15 minutes with a beater in each hand, drumming this way and that, using alternate arms sometimes to beat a drum strongly. I was amazed at his energy to keep going actively for so long. His perseverance and commitment to this activity indicated that he was deriving great satisfaction from it. We videoed some of his drumming and showed it to his parents.'

An indoor music area

The music area shown on page 91 has a purpose. Instruments have been selected so that children can shake, tap and scrape.

Create a sectioned-off area where children can move as they explore. It is important that children can hear what they are playing. If they are competing too much with the rest of the sounds in the room, they will have to become louder. If space is limited, use the setting's outdoor space or local park for the movement and dance aspect of music play and keep the indoor area for less active and more focused exploration. A small selection of instruments in the music area is better than a big box or plastic chest of random and ill-assorted instruments. If the setting has a lot of

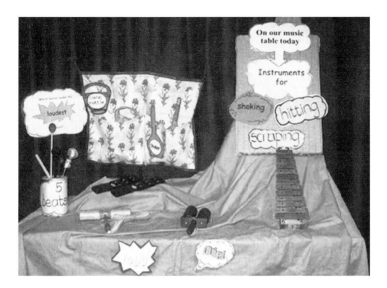

instruments, it is better to select a few according to the current interest than to have them all out at once. In this case, it is important to decide where the instruments that are not in use will be stored. Instruments can be displayed in transparent wall pockets if there is not enough space to have a music table.

The music table can also reflect some aspect of current learning. For example, in the autumn children may bring into the setting lots of conkers, sycamore spinners, beech nuts or crunchy leaves. All of these are capable of making wonderful noises and so the music area can become a place where shakers are made into an autumn noises display.

A note on instruments

One good-quality instrument is far more beneficial that many poor-quality, plastic ones which are really not instruments but toys.

See Chapter 7 for ideas on making instruments [pages 80–81]. Home-made instruments are often more practical, especially with younger children and babies.

Signs and silhouettes

The instruments that are available to children need to be well organised. Identify their storage position using silhouettes cut out of coloured paper and laminated so that children know where to put them when they have finished with them. In the music area there may be photographs of instruments or pictures of children using the area displayed to give children new to the area an idea of what is expected of them.

Good signs help the children learn by themselves, or with support, using the instruments on display. For example, a drum in the music area might be accompanied by three beaters made of different materials. The children can find out which will make the loudest sound, and the following sign will help them to do this by themselves and to pass the activity on to others:

Which beater makes the **l o u d e s t** sound?

With a selection of instruments, put up a sign like this:

On our music table we have instruments to strike and shake. Can you shake one very slowly and strike one very fast?

Computer design can be used for some special display signs for words relating to the elements of music. Cut them out and laminate them, string them up into a mobile to hang over the music area. So, 'loud', 'slow', 'fast' and 'quiet' can become:

loud s l o w *fast* quiet

Although not all children will be able to read notices on the music area, adults will, and the signs will give practitioners and parents ideas to pick up on when they see children working with the instruments. Even better, if signs are distinctive enough, they still act as prompts once the children know what they say.

Tapes and a tape recorder

There is a wide selection of really good song tapes specially recorded for children. What practitioners find time-consuming is sifting through them to find the ones that are suitable or sufficiently challenging for particular children.

Use a staff meeting to listen to tapes, learn new songs and transfer preferred selections to compilation tapes for easy access. Parents might be able to help out with this [see 'Resources' page 107 for sources of good song tapes].

One setting turned a small cupboard into a comfy place where children could listen to tapes and take musical instruments and accompany recordings of music. They called it the Music Box. Children often use the pretend microphone to mimic pop singers and perform in a karaoke style. Some children create and improvise dance movements to accompany their songs.

Songbooks and song props

When children have learned a new song, they need reminders so that they can sing the song by themselves. At the music area, have a *few* songbooks with the words, pictures and notation of new and familiar songs. Point out to the children that the black dots with tails on the lines and in the spaces tell people what to sing. Very often, children become interested in this and some will start to pretend that they are reading the music.

Song props and puppets on the music table remind children of the songs they know and they will want to practise them.

Each song prop picture is laminated and has a piece of Velcro on the back, which children can stick on to a board with felt on it. Alternatively, use magnetic tape on a magnetic board [see the example under 'Teaching and learning new songs', page 61].

Writing music

Children play at writing by acting in the same way and doing the same thing as they observe more experienced writers doing: they might 'write' forthcoming events on a 'calendar' if this is what they have seen their parents do, or make lists before going to the shops. Early experience with writing music can be similar, and it is a wonderful skill to foster with young children. Music writing must be introduced carefully. On only some occasions and with just some children, explain that:

- some songs are made up using new words to the tune of a familiar song, for example the tidy-up song is to the tune of 'Here we go round the mulberry bush' [see pages 64–5].
- some songs are in our memory, for example many of the nursery rhymes and songs sung in nursery, reception or infant classes
- but some songs are quite new to us and are learned by reading the words and 'notes' from a book – show the children the notes and words of a new song.

By being shown the written music for the songs that the children know already or are currently learning, it is possible that some children will become interested in writing music and in singing what they have written. In this way, they are acting like music readers. There are different ways we can draw children's attention to traditional notation. Having paper, including manuscript paper, available at the music area encourages this interest and reminds staff that it is something to look out for and support. Children can also create their own manuscript paper using special printing sets – including stamps that make the five lines of a stave – from music shops.

A collection of sticky dots and shapes to stick on to manuscript paper in the music area will encourage children to 'write' music and can encourage the idea of reading long and short notes.

Outdoor music areas

Music outdoors can be much more active than indoors. Children are much freer to make lots of noise outside. Not only that, but outdoors is where many children want to be, especially boys – so having music experiences outdoors means that the curriculum is being taken to them. Music can also be more easily linked to movement and dance outside.

A sound area (for outside)

Areas for sound exploration outside have already been exemplified throughout the book. Outside, children need similar experiences with the five ways of producing sound:

- something to scrape, eg a length or two of miniature Corolux clear plastic flashing (available from DIY stores)
- something to hit, *eg* big catering tins, old pots and pans
- something to blow, *eg* a tube, cardboard cylinders from carpet warehouses
- something to shake, *eg* large bottles filled with noisy 'stuff'
- wooden and metal cooking spoons can be used as beaters and larger beaters can be made out of broom handles, padding the head and securing it with duck tape and string.

  Make beaters for the drums [see 'A sound collage', pages 87–8].

  Attach the Corolux to the wall with nails or screws, so that children can scrape the ridges. These will be played with the spoons, which are attached to the wall with long pieces of string (so they are not taken away).

Find a way in your outdoor area to hang up the old pots and pans, and other sound-making things; use cardboard cylinders filled with pebbles and covered at each end with duck tape as long rain sticks. Large powder paint buckets can be used as drums or, if filled with conkers, can be giant shakers. Once you have set this up, observe what the children are doing and interact with them in a musical way. Copy what they are doing and reflecting their experimentation and compositions.

Young children often create performance areas out of bread crates and use pretend microphones to imitate pop singers or dancers. Here is an example of that from the Scottish early years curriculum (Scottish CCC 1999, page 33):

'Four children were observed making a 'stage' with large blocks and playing at being dancers.

Some children continued to build bigger and better stages to use during role play. Others were provided with dressing-up clothes, skirts and waistcoats, and an adult read and discussed some books about dancing with them. A group of children was taken to the library to find more books. Music was played on the cassette recorder for the children to listen and dance to. Several other children began to get involved, either as watchers or as dancers. Some colourful fabrics were provided and children began to use them as scarves to move about when they were dancing. Music with different paces and moods was played for children to respond to in their dancing.

A parent who taught a local dancing class was invited to come to the nursery and show the children some dance steps. Children looked at photographs of a dance display and talked about the costumes. They were invited with their parents to watch a dancing class. Some parents organised a visit for all the children and accompanied them. The children had a very enjoyable and informative session watching and talking to the dancers.

The visit continued the interest in dance and the nursery staff planned over the ensuing weeks to introduce music and dance from a variety of cultures.'

 ### *Tapes and cassettes*

24 Tapes and a tape recorder (just a cheap one, used with batteries) for playing outside triggers the children into dance and other imaginative responses to music. From time to time introduce a complementary activity such as bubble blowing kits to accompany the 'Aquarium' section from 'Carnival

of the Animals' by Saint-Saens. (You can also use the 'Bubbles song' from the CD.)

Songs and games

Writing out and printing the songs and games that are suitable for singing outside, laminating the paper and posting the information outside for all to see reminds staff what a good place outside is for singing and playing musical games (see Ouvry 2000, page 78). Stages, microphones and dress-ups give children support towards making music and using their musical imagination.

Writing outside

Having an easel or white board outside encourages writing, especially when the adult gets involved in what the children are 'performing'. The practitioner can ask the children: 'How can we tell others what and when you are going to be performing?' So the adult can write up the information and the children can see the relevance of the written word. Fliers and programmes can be made by older children, and some may also become interested in set design.

9 Working with music teachers, visitors and parents

There are three sorts of music specialist:

- a regular visiting music specialist (weekly, fortnightly, monthly)
- a special visitor, perhaps from a community outreach musical programme or education music project
- parent, carer, other family member or other musician who comes to share their music – to show and play an instrument or to sing to the children.

Using and learning from the skills of a specialist is as relevant to childminders who take young ones to the local library for a music session as it is to the many early years settings who employ a music teacher.

Visiting music specialist

The most significant advantage to using specialists is that they generally have a deeper knowledge of music than any of the setting's practitioners. This means that they will have access to a vast repertoire of songs, tapes and sources of music of all types. They will know about instruments, their names and how to play them, and have information about potential musician visitors. And they will have the confidence to command the children's musical attention – something which non-specialists can find particularly difficult. (There is help out there in terms of giving staff that confidence. For example, Voices Foundation – www.voices.org.uk – works with staff to raise the profile and confidence of staff in singing.)

The disadvantages are that specialists may not know about child development or how to work with young children. This means they may not tune in quickly to what children will be interested in. As teachers of older children, they may not understand that very young children need different teaching strategies or that young children's reactions differ wildly from those of older children. They may even try to introduce instruments which are unsuitable for young children to use on their own.

But these are all difficulties which can be overcome through close support from practitioners, who can provide specialists with knowledge of the children in their care and of child development. The following guidelines will help get the most from a visiting specialist.

- Keep the specialist abreast of themes the children are working on and the progress in musical development made by individual children. Ask for help on learning new songs, music to listen to and instrument work associated with the theme.
- Always participate in the specialist's session so that ideas can be followed up throughout the week or between sessions.
- Discuss suitable strategies, such as working with or making connections with what the children have been and are interested in.
- Teaching strategies employed by a visiting musician may not work with regular staff. Sometimes, children are very interested in a new person doing new musical things and will sit in rapt attention for this musician who has planned the session well with pace and novelty value. But what works with a visitor may not be as riveting when practitioners try to duplicate it.
- Help the specialist to understand and incorporate the following elements of teaching young children:
  – young children are active learners, so they need to move to learn
  – make connections between the music and first-hand experiences all the children have had in and out of the setting
  – children need a lot of experience before they can understand the symbolic nature of music – it is not easy to understand why a composer decided to depict some experiences with particular sounds, or to pick out the solo instrument from the other orchestral sounds
  – children are taught best in small groups, sometimes with the option to go when they've had enough; it is not a reflection on the competence of the specialist if some children do not want to come for the session
  – children need to use their imagination and creative ability, so a store of song props and puppets will help children to remember, concentrate and make connections.

One-off visitor or educational 'entertainer'

As with any special event, whatever the experience, it is important to recognise such a visit as a trigger for follow-up activities or to deepen an interest. Joy Potter's use of the Dance Company as a trigger and shared source of inspiration for her Sound Factory shows the marvellous impact that a one-off visit can have [see pages 54–5]. It is worth finding out from your local music college or in large cities from concert halls, orchestras, opera houses or schools of music if they have an education department and outreach programme. You can then ask if there is a programme of visits from performers suitable for our youngest children.

Specialist teaching designed for young children

At one setting, the staff told the visiting specialist that some children were very interested in transport and traffic and had been doing lots of things, such as making stop signs and traffic lights and a route for the wheeled toys outside.

Together, they agreed that the children's lollypop signs for 'stop', 'go', and 'slow down' could also be used for the music session, to tell the children when to stop playing their instruments or moving to music, when to start and when to slow down. If the children pretended to be cars to fast music, they could use the stop signs when the music was to stop.

The visiting specialist discussed with practitioners the fact that she wanted to help the children with listening to orchestral music. Because she knew about some of the children's interest in transport, she was able to choose some orchestral music which depicted traffic (Gershwin's 'An American in Paris'), and to which the children could move. The specialist did not plan in isolation. She and the staff were able to make a link and connection with what the children knew already. The staff stayed for the short movement session and joined in with the children to point out that even the tooting of car horns can be heard in the music.

As the children moved to the music they were motivated to listen out for the sound of the horns. Some even stopped moving and listened by the tape recorder and were delighted to hear the horns.

At the workshop area, some of the children wanted to make horns to put on their 'cars' outside. Working out how to do that was a problem they were highly motivated to solve.

Additionally, the visiting specialist was able to suggest some new traffic songs such as 'Big red bus goes slowly, slowly' and 'Busy little motor car goes hurry, hurry, hurry, hurry', emphasising fast and slow musical elements. She taught them to the staff.

The music area was developed to highlight the speed and tempo elements of composing, and that was the focus for staff when they played with the children who chose to come to the area to play and explore.

When a visiting musical group was invited to come into four-year-old Marvin's school as part of the annual school carnival celebrations, he was fascinated by the African drummer playing in the outdoor area, and came closer and closer to the drums. Sensing his interest, the drummer stood to one side. He allowed Marvin to take the lead on the African drums and accompanied him on a Talking drum.

The staff were astonished at Marvin's musical proficiency and were able to look to him as the drum expert in subsequent small-group music sessions. It is important that children are enabled to make connections with their musical roots.

Visit from parent or other musician

Dana and the guitar

In four-year-old Dana's setting, a guitar-playing mum was invited into the setting to play her guitar. The children listened from wherever they happened to be; practitioners did not insist that they all come to sit down by the guitarist, though some of the children did so. When the mum had finished, she placed the guitar on a special mat and invited the children to pluck the strings. Dana was particularly interested, asking questions about the hole in the sounding box and what it was for.

The next day, Dana found a Kleenex box in the workshop area and began to make a guitar for herself, with an adult supporting her ideas. Dana chose her materials with care, experimenting with various pieces to make the neck – finally deciding on the cardboard tube from a kitchen roll. She needed to think of a way to attach it to the tissue box, and the adult helped her with this task. Dana selected an elastic band as the string for her instrument. One with sufficient stretch was required, and this took some time (and courage) to find.

When she had finished, Dana decorated her instrument. Then she pretended to be a guitarist and sang, delighting her audience. She, in turn, was delighted when her friends asked her about how she made her guitar and wanted to make one too.

Encountering 'live' musicians and 'live' music is a magical experience for many children, and subsequent listening to recorded music becomes meaningful as the children pick out the sound of the instrument they have heard recently 'in the flesh'.

'Dana and the guitar' is a perfect example of how a visit from a parent musician can inspire children to new discovery. By analysing this case study, it is possible to see how having the setting's workshop approach encouraged Dana's exploration of her ideas about instruments.

She was able to choose and select from a wide range of recyclable materials, and was helped in this by the fact that the junk was already sorted into groups of shapes: boxes or cuboids (*eg* cereal packets); cylinders (*eg* kitchen roll middle); prisms (*eg* Toblerone box); other shapes (*eg* bottles, bottletops, buttons). Each section was labelled.

Dana was discovering far more than an adult-directed task would have provided. She was in control of what she was doing and independent. Nobody was making her express what she knew about her experience in a way that was not relevant to her (what good would colouring in a picture of a guitar be to Dana?).

The freedom to explore her own interests brought about a range of incidental learning for Dana, all of which can be expressed in terms of the early years curriculum:

- **Knowledge and understanding of the world around us.** The guitar involved technology in its making and science in the tension of the elastic bands.
- **Mathematics.** Dana had to decide which 3D shapes (the boxes and cylinders) would work best.
- **Physical development.** Good hand–eye coordination was needed for cutting, gluing and making of the guitar.
- **Aesthetic/creative development**. Dana used her musical imagination and sang to her guitar.
- **Personal, social and emotional development.** There was a great deal of experimenting and problem-solving to be done, especially in the tuning of the elastic bands, all requiring concentration. Having made the guitar, Dana enjoyed a sense of personal achievement. She also took responsibility for clearing up after herself.

The practitioner working alongside Dana also benefited from this activity. She spent time with Dana, supporting her interest without dominating, and this was valuable helping to plan effectively for her future learning. The practitioner wrote about this creative episode in Dana's profile and demonstrated Dana's progress through the early years curriculum. It was also noted that her interest in the guitar, her technological skill and her growing musical awareness were shared with her parent.

Involving parents

Parents have a right to be involved as partners in the learning process we offer. The relationship that practitioners have with parents means they can act as a bridge and interpreter between home and setting. Since home life is the major source of children's experiences, it is vitally important to find out about the musical life of children when they are at home. Moog (1976, page 113) has pointed out how children with a musical home life are advantaged in many ways over their less musically supported peers.

What strategies can be used to involve parents and inform them of the importance of the musical experiences they and we offer children? Pound and Harrison (2003, page 134) provide a list of ideas, some of which have been illustrated throughout the book:

- encourage children to sing songs that they know from home
- encourage parents and carers to perform for children
- encourage children and parents to bring in recorded music from home which can be played to other children
- encourage parents to join in music-making at school or nursery, either in designated sessions or more informally
- make tapes of songs sung at school or nursery for children to take away and sing at home
- make books of favourite songs so they may be sung at home
- invite parents in when live performances are planned, or to accompany children to live performances held elsewhere
- ask parents to recommend people who would be willing to come in and perform for children.

And finally ...

At the beginning of this book I suggested that the training of early years practitioners is woefully inadequate in breaking the cycle of music deprivation in adults who consider themselves unmusical and therefore not up to the task of teaching music appropriately to young children. There is an urgent need for the teacher-training agency, pre-school and NVQ courses to address this deficit in their training.

To unlock the musician in the adults themselves must be an aim for all early years care and education training. Then every practitioner will enjoy singing and learning lots of songs to share with the children, take pleasure in exploring instruments, making sound patterns alongside children as they offer them ways of progressing and above all stem the practice of marginalising music as separate or being used as a means of group control.

I hope that this book and the small but growing number of books which seek to show how music is integrated into all areas of the play-based early years curriculum will go some way in raising the profile of music, giving confidence to practitioners in their minute-by-minute interaction with the children they seek to educate.

References

Beer, S. (1999) *Play-a-round recipe book: a musical feast for pre-school and reception classes*, Stowmarket: Kevin Mayhew.

Bird, W. & Bennett, E. (1988) *Music all the time*, Teachers' Book 1, London: Chester Music/Wilhelm Hansen.

Block Ridge, K. (1951) *Making musical apparatus and instruments*, London: Nursery Schools Association.

Bruce, T. (1997) *Early childhood education* (2nd ed.), London: Hodder & Stoughton.

Bruce, T. & Meggitt, C. (2002) *Child care and education* (3rd ed.), London: Hodder & Stoughton.

Bullock, A. (1975) *A language for life*, The Bullock Report, London: HMSO.

Cartwright, P., Scott, K. & Stevens, J. (2002) *A place to learn: developing a stimulating learning environment*, London: LEARN.

Charlton, P. (1973) 'Building up my house', in *Bang on a drum*, London: BBC/Keith Prowse Music Publishing Co.

Cotton, M. (1996) *Agogo bells to xylophone: a friendly guide to classroom percussion*, London: A&C Black.

DfEE/QCA (2000) *Curriculum guidance for the Foundation Stage*, London: Department for Education and Employment/Qualifications and Curriculum Authority.

Early Childhood Forum (2003) *Quality in diversity in early learning: a framework for early childhood practitioners* (2nd ed.), London: National Children's Bureau.

Geldof, B. (2001) quoted in C. Sullivan, 'Songs in the key of death', *The Guardian*, 'Friday Review', 28 September.

Goddard, L. (2002) 'Music in the early years curriculum', University of North London, unpublished BEd. dissertation.

Goddard-Blythe, S. (2000) in Ouvry, *Exercising muscles and minds*.

Katz, L. (1995) *Talks with teachers of young children*, New York: Ablex Publishing.

Kendall, P. (2001) 'The keys to a quick mind', *The Daily Telegraph*, 28 February.

MacGregor, H. (1998) *Tom Thumb's musical maths: developing maths skills with simple songs*, London: A&C Black.

McMillan, M. (1920) *The nursery school*, London: Dent.

Meek, M. (1982) *Learning to read*, London: The Bodley Head.

Moog, H. (1976) *The musical experience of the pre-school child*, London: Schott & Co.

Northumberland County Council (1995) *Early years curriculum guidelines*, Morpeth: Northumberland County Council.

Odam, G. (1995) *The sounding symbol: music education in action*, Cheltenham: Stanley Thornes.

Ouvry, M. (2000) *Exercising muscles and minds: outdoor play and the early years curriculum*, London: National Early Years Network (2003 reprint available from the National Children's Bureau).

Paley, V. G. (1992) *You can't say you can't play*, Cambridge, MA: Harvard University Press.

Papousek, M. (1996) 'Intuitive parenting: a hidden source of musical stimulation in infancy', in I. Deliege & J. Sloboda (eds) *Musical beginnings: origins and development of musical competence*, New York: Oxford.

Pound, L. & Harrison C. (2003) *Supporting musical development in the early years*, Milton Keynes: Open University Press.

Pugh, A. & Pugh, L. (1998) *Music in the early years*, London: Routledge.

Rich, D. (2002) *More than words: children developing communication, language and literacy*, London: British Association for Early Childhood Education.

Scottish CCC (1999) *A curriculum framework for children 3 to 5*, Dundee: Scottish Consultative Council on the Curriculum.

Skinner, C. (2001) *More than numbers: children developing mathematical thinking*, London: British Association for Early Childhood Education.

Silberg, J. (1998) *The I can't sing book: for grownups who can't carry a tune in a paperbag but want to do music with children*, Beltsville, MD: Griffon House.

Trevarthen, C. (1998) 'The child's need to learn a culture', in M. Woodhead, D. Faulkner & K. Littleton (eds) *Cultural worlds of early childhood*, London: Routledge/Open University.

Walker, R. (1988) 'In search of a child's musical imagination', in K. Egan & D. Nadaner (eds) *Imagination and education*, Milton Keynes: Open University Press.

Whitehead, M. (1997) *The development of language and literacy*, London: Hodder & Stoughton.

Wood, L. & Scott, L. (1961) *More singing fun*, New York: McGraw-Hill.

Wood, L. & Scott, L. (1962) *Singing fun*, London: George Harrap & Co.

Yardley, A. (1970) *Senses and sensitivity*, London: Evans Brothers Ltd.

Resources

Music shops
(catalogues available on request)

Acorn Percussion
Unit 33
Abbey Business Centre
London SW8 3NS
tel 020 7720 2243
Very wide range of instruments – mail order.

Bina Musicals
31–33 The Green
Southall
Middlesex UB2 4AN
tel 020 8843 1411
Instruments for playing Asian music.

Fox's Music
Outlets in Doncaster, Hull, Nottingham, Leeds, Lincoln, Sheffield
tel 01302 811811 (HQ)

Knock on Wood
13 Eastgate
Leeds LS2 7LY
tel 0113 242 9146
Multicultural instruments.

Music Education Supplies Ltd
101 Banstead Road
South Sutton
Surrey SM2 5LH
tel 020 8770 3866

Song books

A&C Black

Phone 020 7758 0200 for A&C Black's catalogue or visit their website, www.acblack.com. All books now come with CD or cassette or a CD-ROM. Here are some from the catalogue that I particularly recommend:

- *Music express Foundation Stage* (really good help for practitioners on the CD-ROM)
- *Okki-tokki-unga* (action songs)
- *Apusskidu* (for 5–11-year-olds but with some songs that are suitable for younger children)
- *Mango spice* (Caribbean songs; also for 5–11-year-olds but with some songs suitable for younger children)
- *Tom Thumb's musical maths* (number and shape words to familiar tunes)
- *Sonsense nogs* (silly songs for 5–11-year-olds but with some songs that are suitable for younger children
- *Bobby Shaftoe clap your hands* (new words to familiar traditional songs)
- *Agogo bells to xylophone* (tells you all you need to know about instruments).

BBC publications

Phone the BBC for their catalogue on 0870 830 8000 or order online at www.bbcshop.com/education. The Teletubbies and Tweenies websites are excellent for songs and ideas: www.bbc.co.uk/teletubbies, and www.bbc.co.uk/tweenies.

The teacher's notes and cassette for the following programmes are particularly worthwhile. Listen to the tape and learn the songs to teach to the children, but don't simply play the tape to the whole group of children as it is much better to customise it for the children in a particular setting. The programmes are often themed (transport, mini-beasts, *etc*) and so help you to build up a repertoire of songs and movement ideas to be used as interests arise.

- *Playtime and EAL playtime*
- *Music box*
- *The song tree* (some good songs to stretch the most experienced musicians in the group)
- *The song catcher video* (order the video and watch it to learn some good songs and teaching techniques but don't show it to the children, and be careful to adapt what you see to the level of very young children).

Children's books

Incorporating instruments or other sounds can extend the enjoyment of just about any children's fiction book. For example the 'ding dong' for a door bell on the chime bars, the wind sound on a swanee whistle, all the noises that keep father bear awake and so on can be produced by different instruments. Here are a few that I have used:

Cooke, T. & Oxenbury, H. (1994) *So much*, London: Walker Books.

Hewitt, A. & Broomfield, R. (1999) *Mrs Mopple's washing line*, London: Red Fox.

Martin Jr., B. & Carle, E. (1994) *Polar bear polar bear what do your hear?*, London: Puffin.

McNaughton, C. (1992) *Who's that banging on the ceiling?*, London: Walker Books.

Murphy, J. (1980) *Peace at last*, London: Macmillan Children's Books.

Rose, G. (2001) *'Ahhh!', said Stork*, London: Macmillan Children's Books.

Rosen, M. & Oxenbury, H. (1989) *We're going on a bear hunt*, London: Walker Books.

Sharratt, N. (2000) *The animal orchestra*, London: Walker Books.

Sheldon, D. (1993) *The whales' song*, London: Red Fox.

Stanley, M. (2001) *What's that noise? Ring! Ring! (Look and talk)*, London: Ladybird Books.

Waddell, M. & Barton, J. (1993) *The happy hedgehog band*, London: Walker Books.

Further reading

Bayley, R. & Broadbent, L. (2003) *Helping young children with steady beat*, Walsall: Lawrence Educational Publications.

Geoghegan, L. (2002) *Singing games and rhymes for early years*, Glasgow: National Youth Choir of Scotland.

Geoghegan, L. (2002) *Singing games and rhymes for tiny tots*, Glasgow: National Youth Choir of Scotland.

Matterson, E. (1969) *This little puffin*, London: Puffin.

McNicol, R. (2000) *Music explorer for infants*, London: London Symphony Orchestra Ltd (includes CD).

Young, S. (2003) *Music with the under-fours*, London: RoutledgeFalmer.

Young, S. & Willis, M. (2001) *Guide to choosing and using musical instruments*, London: National Association of Toy and Leisure Libraries.

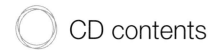

CD contents

Notes on the CD contents

- New songs and words by Soo Beer, with additional songs and words by Marjorie Ouvry and, in tracks 17–22, traditional Kodaly chants.
- The children singing on the CD are Hannah Siaw, Jonathan French Wilsons, Vincenzo Franco and Zoe Mackenzie from the Priory C. of E. Primary School, Wimbledon.
- The page numbers in square brackets refer to relevant text in the book.
- Tracks 1–24 are sung by Soo, Marjorie and the children.
- Tracks 25–47 are the instrumental versions of tracks 1–16 and 18–24 so that you and the children you care for can sing along. The relevant instrumental version is given in brackets next to the heading for each sung track. Track 17 has no instrumental version as it is spoken only.

Track 1 [page 25] (Instrumental version: Track 25.)
Pulse and rhythm in 'Polly put the kettle on'.

Track 2 [page 43] (Instrumental version: Track 26.)
A cold and frosty morning
See page 43 for words. Thanks to Louise Glatt for this song.

Track 3 [page 43] (Instrumental version: Track 27.)
Hello song
Hello! Hello! It's time to say, 'Hello!'
It's time to come to nursery, so we say, 'Hello!'

Track 4 [page 43] (Instrumental version: Track 28.)
Goodbye song
Goodbye, goodbye, It's time to say, 'Goodbye.'
It's time to go, so cheerio as we say, 'Goodbye.'

Track 5 [page 53] (Instrumental version: Track 29.)
Thank you song
Thank you, thank you, to everyone who helps us,
Builders, plumbers, glaziers too.
Life can be rough, the world can be tough,
But you help us all day through.

Thank you, thank you, to everyone who helps us,
Doctors, nurses, cleaners *too.*
Life can be rough, the world can be tough,
But you help us all day through.

(Note: line 3 is adapted according to the children's current interests.)

Track 6 [page 63] (Instrumental version: Track 30.)

The block song

One block, two blocks, three blocks in a tower…
Four blocks, five blocks, six blocks in a tower…
Seven blocks, eight blocks, nine blocks, ten,
Then knock them down and start again!

Track 7 [page 63] (Instrumental version: Track 31.)

The crate song

One crate, two crates, three crates in a line…
Four crates, five crates, six crates in a line…
Seven crates, eight crates, nine crates, ten,
Then we'll walk along the crates and start again!

Track 8 [page 63] (Instrumental version: Track 32.)

I'm off

I'm off, I'm off to dig up the ground,
Dig up the ground, dig up the ground.
I'm off, I'm off to dig up the ground.
Perhaps I'll find a little worm there.

I'm off, I'm off to dig up the ground,
Dig up the ground, dig up the ground.
I'm off, I'm off to dig up the ground.
Perhaps I'll find a little snail there.

(This song can continue with new verses for as many different mini-beasts as you and the children would like; perhaps a little ant, a wood louse and a slug.)

Track 9 [page 63] (Instrumental version: Track 33.)

Lots of jobs

I've got lots of jobs to do,
I can cook and clean things too.
With a work, work, work, till day
  is done,
Then I'll stop, stop, stop and have
  some fun.

I've got lots of jobs to do,
I can set the table too.
With a work, work, work, till day
  is done,
Then I'll stop, stop, stop and have
  some fun.

I've got lots of jobs to do,
I can feed my baby too.
With a work, work, work, till day
  is done,
Then I'll stop, stop, stop and
  have some fun.

I've got lots of jobs to do,
I can wash and iron too.
With a work, work, work, till day
  is done,
Then I'll stop, stop, stop and
  have some fun.

Track 10 [page 63] (Instrumental version: Track 34.]
This and that

A little bit of this and a little bit of that
Plus a little bit of something new.
I'm sorting out just what to use,
Then I'll stick them all with glue.

A little bit of this and a little bit of that
Plus a little bit of something blue.
I really don't know what it is,
But it's small (big, tall, square, round) *and stuck with glue.*

A little bit of this and a little bit of that
Plus a little bit of something blue.
I know exactly what it is,
And I made it just for you.

Track 11 [page 63] (Instrumental version: Track 35.)
Colours all around me

Colours all around me, which one shall I choose?
Colours all surround me, which one could I use?
Colours of the morning, colours of the night,
Colours for my painting, colours warm and bright.

Colours all around me, which one shall I choose?
Colours all surround me, which one could I use?
Colours for the autumn, which ones shall I choose?
Brown and green and yellow, that's what I will use.

(Whatever a child is painting could be added to a verse, for example:
Colours for an ice-cream, which ones shall I choose?
Pink and white and orange, that's what I will use.)

Track 12 [page 63] (Instrumental version: Track 36.)
Splish, splosh

To use anywhere:
Splish, splosh, splish, splosh,
I'm playing in the water.
Watch me, watch me while I pour.
What floats and what sinks, I'm
finding out,
And I've spilled some on the floor, Oh!

To use outside:
Splish, splosh, splish, splosh,
I'm playing with the water.
Watch me, watch me while I pour.
Down flows the water onto the ground,
So I'll run and get some more, Oh!

Track 13 [page 63] (Instrumental version: Track 37.)
The sand tray song

What shall I do in the sand today?
What shall I do in the big sand tray?
I'll go exploring that is what I'll do today
Oh yes, we'll all go exploring that is what we'll do today.

Track 14 [page 64] (Instrumental version: Track 38.)
I wonder where the skittles go?
See pages 64–5 for words.

Track 15 [page 66] (Instrumental version: Track 39.)
Henry's going shopping
See page 66 for words.

Track 16 [page 67] (Instrumental version: Track 40.)
Five chapatis in a baker's shop
See page 67 for words.

Track 17 [page 70] (No instrumental version)
See 'Rhythm' on page 70 for the words and instructions for this track.

Track 18 [page 71] (Instrumental version: Track 41.)
Hey! Hey! Look at me!
See page 71 for words.

Track 19 [page 71] (Instrumental version: Track 42.)
What's in my magic box?
See pages 71 and 72 for words.

Track 20 [page 72] (Instrumental version: Track 43.)
Doggy, doggy where's your bone?
See page 72 for words.

Track 21 [page 73] (Instrumental version: Track 44.]
Apple tree, apple tree
See page 73 for words.

Track 22 [page 73] (Instrumental version: Track 45.)
Touch your shoulders
See page 74 for words.

Track 23 [page 74] (Instrumental version: Track 46.)
Where is Michael playing today?
See page 74 for words.

Track 24 [page 95] (Instrumental version: Track 47.)
Bubbles songs

Bubbles, bubbles everywhere
Way up high and in the air.
When they fall and touch the ground
They will pop without a sound.

I will chase them everywhere,
Floating downwards in the air.
If I touch them they will burst,
Who will, who will touch one first?